Learning to Read and Write

A Cross-Linguistic Perspective

For many years, the development of theories about the way children learn to read and write was dominated by studies of English-speaking populations. As we have learned more about the way that children learn to read and write other scripts – whether they have more regularity in their grapheme–phoneme correspondences or do not make use of alphabetic symbols at all – it has become clear that many of the difficulties that confront children learning to read and write English specifically are less evident, or even non-existent, in other populations. At the same time, some aspects of learning to read and write are very similar across scripts. The unique cross-linguistic perspective offered in this book, including chapters on Japanese, Greek and the Scandinavian languages as well as English, shows how the processes of learning to read and spell are affected by the characteristics of the writing system that children are learning to master.

MARGARET HARRIS is Reader in Developmental Psychology at Royal Holloway, University of London. She has published widely on many aspects of language development, including *Language Experience and Early Language Development* (1992) and, with Max Coltheart, *Language Processing in Children and Adults* (1986). She is also the co-author with George Butterworth of *Principles of Developmental Psychology* (1994).

GIYOO HATANO is Professor of Educational Psychology at Keio University, Tokyo and an internationally known scholar in educational, cognitive and developmental psychology. He is a series editor of Cambridge Studies in Cognitive and Perceptual Development.

Cambridge Studies in Cognitive and Perceptual Development

Series Editors
George Butterworth (General Editor), University of Sussex, UK
Giyoo Hatano, Keio University, Japan
Kurt W. Fischer, Harvard University, USA.

Advisory Board
Patricia M. Greenfield, University of California, Los Angeles, USA
Paul Harris, University of Oxford, UK
Daniel Stern, University of Geneva, Switzerland
Esther Thelen, Indiana University, USA.

The aim of this series is to provide a scholarly forum for current
theoretical and empirical issues in cognitive and perceptual
development. As the twentieth century draws to a close, the field is
no longer dominated by monolithic theories. Contemporary
explanations build on the combined influences of biological,
cultural, contextual and ecological factors in well-defined research
domains. In the field of cognitive development, cultural and
situational factors are widely recognised as influencing the
emergence and forms of reasoning in children. In perceptual
development, the field has moved beyond the opposition of 'innate'
and 'acquired' to suggest a continuous role for perception in the
acquisition of knowledge. These approaches and issues will all be
reflected in the series which will also address such important
research themes as the indissociable link between perception and
action in the developing motor system, the relationship between
perceptual and cognitive development to modern ideas on the
development of the brain, the significance of developmental
processes themselves, dynamic systems theory and contemporary
work in the psychodynamic tradition, especially as it relates to the
foundations of self-knowledge.

Forthcoming titles include

Jacqueline Nadel and George Butterworth (eds.)
Imitation in Infancy

Paul Light and Karen Littleton
Social Processes in Children's Learning

Michael Siegal and Candida Peterson (eds.)
Children's Understanding of Biology and Health

Nobuo Masataka
The Onset of Language

Nira Granott and Jim Parziale
Microdevelopment

Learning to Read and Write

A Cross-Linguistic Perspective

Edited by

Margaret Harris and
Giyoo Hatano

CAMBRIDGE UNIVERSITY PRESS
Cambridge, New York, Melbourne, Madrid, Cape Town, Singapore, São Paulo

Cambridge University Press
The Edinburgh Building, Cambridge CB2 2RU, UK

Published in the United States of America by Cambridge University Press, New York

www.cambridge.org
Information on this title: www.cambridge.org/9780521621847

First published 1999
This digitally printed first paperback version 2006

A catalogue record for this publication is available from the British Library

Library of Congress Cataloguing in Publication data

Learning to Read and Write: A Cross-Linguistic Perspective / edited
by Margaret Harris and Giyoo Hatano.
    p.   cm.
ISBN 0 521 62184 4 (hardbound)
1. Language acquisition. 2. Literacy. 3. Language awareness in
children. I. Harris, Margaret, 1951– . II. Hatano, Giyoo, 1935– .
P118.L3899   1999 98-36594   CIP
401´.93–dc21

ISBN-13 978-0-521-62184-7 hardback
ISBN-10 0-521-62184-4 hardback

ISBN-13 978-0-521-02718-2 paperback
ISBN-10 0-521-02718-7 paperback

Contents

Contributors

ATHANASIOS AIDINIS, Institute of Education, University of London

KIYOMI AKITA, University of St Paul, Tokyo

PETER BRYANT, University of Oxford

GIUSEPPE COSSU, University of Parma, Italy

UTA FRITH, University College, London

VICKY GIANNOULI, Royal Holloway, University of London

USHA GOSWAMI, Institute of Child Health, University of London

J. RICHARD HANLEY, University of Liverpool

MARGARET HARRIS, Royal Holloway, University of London

GIYOO HATANO, Keio University, Tokyo

H.-S. HUANG, National Tainan Teachers' College, Tainan, Taiwan

KARIN LANDERL, University of Salzburg, Austria

IRIS LEVIN, Tel Aviv University, Israel

INGVAR LUNDBERG, Gothenburg University, Sweden

TEREZINHA NUNES, Institute of Education, University of London

LUCIA LINS BROWNE REGO, Universidade Federal de Pernambuco, Brazil

SUSAN RICKARD LIOW, National University of Singapore

DAVID SHARE, Haifa University, Israel

OVID TZENG, National Chung Cheng University, Taiwan

HEINZ WIMMER, University of Salzburg, Austria

1 Introduction: a cross-linguistic perspective on learning to read and write

Margaret Harris and Giyoo Hatano

For many years the development of theories about the way children learn to read and write was dominated by studies of English-speaking populations. As we have always been aware, English has an exceptionally irregular orthography both for reading and spelling, in that the relationship between graphemes and phonemes is highly inconsistent. As we have learned more about the way that children learn to read and write other scripts – which have less irregularity in their grapheme–phoneme correspondences or do not even make use of alphabetical letters at all – it has become clear that many of the difficulties that confront children who are learning to read and write English are less evident, or even non-existent, in other populations. At the same time it has also become clear that some aspects of learning to read and write are very similar across scripts. A cross-linguistic perspective thus provides a unique opportunity to discover how the processes of learning to read and spell are affected by the characteristics of the writing system that children are learning to master.

When we invited contributions to this volume we hoped that the authors would raise issues in common about the processes involved in learning to read and write different scripts. We were delighted to find that they had done so, but such was the commonality of themes across chapters that we were presented with a problem in organising the book. Our original plan had been to divide the book into sections but, in the light of the many inter-related issues that are discussed, we decided that sub-dividing the chapters would be misleading. Instead, what we have tried to do is to arrange them so that scripts that are most similar to each other occur in close proximity.

The first five chapters are all concerned with learning to read and spell alphabetic scripts where there are highly consistent letter–sound correspondences. Chapter 2 deals with Italian which the author, Giuseppe Cossu, describes as the equivalent in studies of reading to the *Drosophila* in the study of genetics because of its simplicity. Italian has fewer vowels than English, fewer syllable types and a predominantly open syllable structure (where the majority of syllables end with vowels). These features, together with an almost completely regular pairing of phonemes and graphemes, make Italian a highly transparent orthography.

Cossu reports that Italian children (who start school at the age of six) learn to read very rapidly and, only six months after the start of formal reading instruction, they are highly accurate at reading both words and non-words. The main change that occurs across the first grade is in reading speed which gradually increases towards the end of the school year. Spelling is not nearly so accurate, however, even though the correspondence between phonemes and graphemes is equally regular for reading and spelling. This evidence about discrepancies between reading and spelling in a transparent orthography is interesting because it suggests that, even where there are biunivocal correspondences between graphemes and phonemes, children are not initially able to spell every word that they can read. Cossu also discusses evidence from children who experience severe difficulties with reading and/or spelling following brain injury. He concludes that there are developmental dissociations between reading and spelling even in a transparent orthography.

Chapter 3, by Heinz Wimmer, Karin Landerl and Uta Frith, also considers evidence from children who have difficulties in reading. Their chapter focuses on German which, although less transparent than Italian, has very consistent grapheme–phoneme correspondences. The teaching of reading in German schools uses an explicit phonics programme in which the main grapheme–phoneme correspondences are taught and children are given explicit training in how to read words using grapheme–phoneme translation and blending. The orthographic regularity of German means that use of grapheme–phoneme correspondences yields a reasonably accurate pronunciation for most words. Contrast this with English where the same 'sounding out' strategy often does not produce an approximate pronunciation. This is a particular problem for beginning readers because many of the highly frequent words that young English children encounter in their first reading books cannot easily be sounded out.

A comparison between the non-word reading of young German and English readers showed that German-speaking children were very much better at applying letter–sound correspondences to read non-words than English children of the same age, even though the latter had had one additional year of reading instruction. German children thus seem to find the mastery of phonological coding for reading much easier than their English-speaking peers. This difference was also reflected in the performance of dyslexic children in the two populations. German-speaking dyslexics showed much greater accuracy in their use of grapheme–phoneme correspondences to read non-words and rare words than English dyslexics. Wimmer, Landerl and Frith argue that the demands placed on working memory in successfully applying grapheme–phoneme correspondences to reading are much lower for a regular orthography than an irregular orthography like English. Thus two dyslexic children, who have identically impoverished working memories, will have greater or lesser success in learning to apply grapheme–phoneme correspondences, depending on the transparency of the orthography.

The chapter by Margaret Harris and Vicky Giannouli examines learning to read and spell in Greek. Greek is unusual is having an orthography that is possibly even more transparent than Italian for reading but much less transparent for spelling. Like Italian, it has a small number of vowels and a predominantly open syllable structure. As in Italian and German schools, an explicitly phonics approach is used to teach reading and children make rapid progress. However, progress in spelling is much slower and, at the end of first grade, while children are highly accurate at reading words and non-words, they make many mistakes in spelling real words.

The main difficulty presented by Greek spelling lies in the ambiguity of vowels. Much of this ambiguity is resolved once children have a grasp of the extensive system of morphologically based spelling rules that appear in Greek. These rules govern the spelling of morphological word endings which vary according to the grammatical status of a word. Grasp of these rules is best predicted by children's pre-school syllabic awareness but the application of the rules appears to be a rather gradual process. Other Greek words, which reflect aspects of ancient Greek that are not present in the modern form, are exceptions to these morphological rules and the mastery of their spelling continues well past the end of third grade at school.

The chapter by Lucia Lins Browne Rego describes the acquisition of two different kinds of spelling rules in Brazilian Portuguese. Portuguese has a regular orthography but the level of regularity does not lie at the level of grapheme–phoneme correspondences alone: indeed there are only nine cases of unique mapping between letters and phonemes. However, for many other letters and phonemes, the ambiguity of mapping can be resolved by conditional rules, based on sound or letter position or on stress patterns. Portuguese also has morphological spelling rules that are somewhat similar to those found in Greek. Rego shows that, as in the case of Italian, Greek and German, mastering phoneme–grapheme correspondences is relatively easy for children. However, the acquisition of conditional and morphologically based spelling rules is a much more complex task in which learning is gradual rather than sudden. Application of morphological rules to spelling was better in children who had good morpho-syntactic awareness, echoing what Harris and Giannouli found for Greek. Rego also reports that children were usually able to acquire a rule for reading before they were able to use it in spelling, echoing Cossu's arguments about dissociations between reading and spelling.

Morphological structure plays a key role in the Hebrew script which is described by David Share and Iris Levin. Hebrew has a complex derivational morphology in which most content words consist of a tri-consonantal root together with infixes and/or affixes. For example, among many other words, the root KLT gives rise to KALAT (he grasped), HIKLIT (he recorded), KLITA (absorption) and MIKLAT (shelter). The additions to the semantic root give information about the grammatical status of a word such as person, number and gender. Written Hebrew represents consonants directly but vowels are indicated by diacritical marks in the 'pointed' script used to teach reading. Even pre-schoolers, who have not yet learned to read, reflect this primacy of consonants in their spontaneous writing. Pointed Hebrew has almost perfect grapheme–phoneme correspondence and so learning to read it is easy (although it takes much longer to be able to read unpointed Hebrew where the reader has to interpolate the vowels between the consonants). By contrast, phoneme–grapheme relationships are more variable and the vast majority of Hebrew words could, in theory, be spelled in more than one way. Indeed, such is the degree of potential ambiguity in Hebrew spelling, that the development of spelling in Hebrew appears to lag behind even that of English.

Share and Levin also discuss the relationship of phonemic awareness to learning to read Hebrew. They conclude that phonemic awareness is a much weaker predictor of early reading success than it is for English. They argue that this is because the unambiguous pronunciation that is provided by the pointed script read by young readers demands less skill and flexibility in phoneme manipulation than is required for English orthography. Share and Levin also argue that sub-syllabic consonant–vowel (CV) units as well as phonemes are important in reading Hebrew. This points to an important cross-linguistic issue because the units that will be important for the reading and spelling of a particular alphabetic script will depend, not only on the regularity of letter–sound correspondences, but also on the regularity of the syllabic and morphological structure.

The issue of morphological structure in spelling is addressed by Peter Bryant, Terezinha Nunes and Athanasios Aidinis. Their chapter is the first of three that compare reading and spelling in alphabetic scripts of varying transparency. Bryant, Nunes and Aidinis focus on children's developing understanding of morphologically based spelling rules in English, French and Greek. These three scripts provide a very interesting comparison because they vary considerably in their regularity for reading and spelling. Nevertheless they present children with common problems.

Multiple correspondences between graphemes and phonemes are generally more problematic for writing than reading. When there are alternative ways of pronouncing a word, children do not have to rely on morphological strategies for reading. This is because alternative pronunciations are constrained by the need for a word or sentence to make sense. For example, although [ea] could be pronounced as either /e/ or /i:/, children are likely to choose the correct pronunciation of [sweated /swetid/] in a sentence like 'I would like to take a shower because I sweated' since otherwise the sentence will not make sense. However, in writing, such constraints do not work unless children are highly familiar with written forms of sentences. For this reason, morphological knowledge plays a more significant role in writing than in reading. Indeed, the main problem that children face in learning about aspects of both derivational morphology (such as that evident in the relationship between 'know' and 'knowledge' or 'music' and 'musician') and inflectional morphology (such as 'burn – burned') is that the spelling system represents distinctions that are not apparent in the spoken form.

Bryant, Nunes and Aidinis argue that, over a period of about two years, children gradually learn to decide between two or more acceptable spelling patterns, to spell silent morphemes, and adopt the correct (conventional) spellings that violate modal grapheme–phoneme correspondence rules. They show that, in spite of differences between scripts, the course of development in the mastery of morphological principles in spelling is remarkably consistent. For example, where there are alternative spellings, children go through a stage where they have a marked preference for one particular spelling of a sound; and children begin to use morphological distinctions that are respected in spelling before they fully understand the 'logic' of the writing system. They also show that children's use of morphological knowledge in spelling can be predicted from their morpho-syntactic awareness assessed by the word and sentence analogy tasks. This highlights the fact that understanding morphological spelling rules draws on children's more general understanding of the way that morphology functions in the spoken language.

Usha Goswami's chapter offers an excellent summary of the findings on the relationships between varieties of phonological awareness and the ability to read words or pseudo-words for various European languages. According to her, phonological development seems to show the same

sequence across languages – from an awareness of syllable to an awareness of phoneme, through an awareness of sub-syllabic units (e.g., onsets
and rimes). However, the level of phonological awareness that is most
predictive of reading development may vary with the orthographic transparency in general and with the spelling units at which the regularity is
maximal. For example, the strong connection between rhyming and
early reading, well known in English, may not be observed in languages
in which script–sound correspondence is more or less regular. Only
those children who are learning non-transparent scripts develop a larger
phonological-orthographic unit at which the correspondence is fairly
consistent. That differences in grapheme–phoneme consistency influence reading development in a profound way is supported, as we have
seen, by the initial group of chapters. However, as Goswami repeatedly
emphasises, these summaries must be taken as tentative. We need more
cross-linguistic studies, including non-European languages and non-
alphabetic scripts, before we can reach firm conclusions. For example,
even though the sequence of phonological development is similar across
languages, the sub-syllabic units of which children become aware are
likely to vary from language to language.

Ingvar Lundberg's chapter discusses learning to read in Scandinavian
countries. These languages provide important points of comparison
because they vary in orthographic transparency. Lundberg begins by
discussing the role of phonological awareness in learning to read but he
then goes on to explain why it is important to remember that reading is
a cultural practice. He believes that socio-cultural variables, particularly
the status of reading and writing in a society, are at least as important
as orthographic–linguistic factors in reading achievement. It is certainly
true that informal literacy socialisation, exposure to print, and values
attached to literacy – to mention just a few socio-cultural factors –
influence children's learning of reading and spelling. Children learn to
read because it allows them to better participate in significant or interesting activities. Ease of participation in literacy practice may vary according to orthographic transparency, but without participation in these
activities, children will not learn to read even when the orthography is
completely regular. Likewise, teaching at school for phonemic awareness
may have some effect, but the contribution of schooling *per se* may not,
as Lundberg claims, be very large.

In the final set of chapters we move away from alphabetic writing
systems, in which the sounds of a word are represented by combinations
of letters, to consider how children learn to read Chinese characters.
Many of the same issues that were discussed in earlier chapters remain
relevant. These include the speed with which children learn to read, the

strategies that they adopt at the initial and later stages of reading, the relationship between learning to read and learning to spell and prerequisites for learning to read. Other issues – notably visual characteristics – are unique to the reading of scripts using Chinese characters.

Chinese characters are used in a number of Asian countries and they are not only visually complex but also large in number because each of them represents a morpheme rather than a phoneme. This suggests that the process of learning to read and write these characters, the phonological and visual readiness for learning, and the nature of informal and formal reading instruction must be different from those for alphabetic scripts. To make the learning of Chinese characters easier, auxiliary phonetic scripts (e.g. Pinyin) are sometime attached to them. These phonetic scripts enable readers to rely on an alphabetic strategy to read unfamiliar characters. The last chapter also deals with Japanese kana syllabaries, which originated as phonetic symbols attached to Chinese characters. Japanese children learn to read a text initially only in kana, and gradually learn to read a text involving Chinese characters with the help of kana. Kana characters each represent a syllable or mora and so their acquisition also poses problems similar to but different from those of alphabet scripts.

The chapter by Rick Hanley, Ovid Tzeng and H.-S. Huang starts with a description of the Chinese writing system and how it is taught in China, Taiwan and Hong Kong. As aptly pointed out by the authors, it is not accurate to refer to Chinese as a logographic writing system. Chinese characters represent morphemes, that is, the characters indicate unique pronunciations as well as meanings. The authors also argue that the underlying cognitive skills and strategies involved in learning Chinese and English are not as different as was once imagined. For example, recent studies they refer to have shown that phonological awareness is an important factor in learning to read Chinese. It is true that visual analytic and memory skills are also important in learning to read Chinese, probably more so than in learning to read alphabetical scripts but this does not reduce the importance of phonological processing skills. This can be seen in the comparison of learning to read in China, Taiwan and Hong Kong. Auxiliary phonetic scripts are used in China and Taiwan, but not in Hong Kong, before children are introduced to Chinese characters. This seems to exert an enormous effect on subsequent reading development: Hong Kong children are not only behind on tests of phonological awareness but also poorer at using the phonetic components in compound characters.

Susan Rickard Liow's chapter, after describing the oral and written languages used in Singapore, compares the development of reading skills in English between bilingual Mandarin-English- and Malay-English-speaking children. Her basic assumption is that Mandarin-English-speaking children have difficulty in learning to read and write in English because Singapore Chinese children are exposed to a logographic or morphemic script without the support of the auxiliary Pinyin script or phonics teaching. They thus have limited phonological awareness although enhanced visual analytic skills may compensate to some extent. In contrast, because Malay has a shallow alphabetic orthography and the grapheme–phoneme correspondences are explicitly taught in their reading lessons, she assumes that Malay-English-speaking children can acquire English literacy more easily. By reviewing her own, as well as other studies, she examines these assumptions regarding L1 to L2 strategy transfer and generally confirms them. It will be fascinating to examine in further studies whether such transfer will occur when English is a child's first language.

Kyomi Akita and Giyoo Hatano focus on Japanese children's acquisition of hiragana – one of the two kinds of kana syllabaries used with kanji (Chinese characters) in the Japanese writing system. Syllabaries, in which a different character represents a syllable or mora (sub-syllabic rhythmic unit), are extensively used in Japan. The use of syllabaries is appropriate for Japanese because there are fewer kinds of syllable than in European languages. However, the use of a small number of syllabary characters in Japanese (seventy-one) produces many homonyms, and thus educated Japanese use Chinese characters to distinguish them.

Learning to read hiragana is easy and is almost always completed in the lower grades of elementary school at the latest, the authors claim, because it does not presuppose advanced phonological awareness at the phonemic level, and also because the Japanese language has a limited phonological inventory. However, the learning process involves three stages that are highly similar to those proposed by Frith (1985) for English. Moreover, although the script–sound correspondence is generally regular for hiragana, children seem to rely on morphological knowledge to cope with some irregular patterns. Thus we again see more similarities than differences in the acquisition of literacy in different types of script.

It should be noted, though not emphasised in their chapter, that Japanese children have to learn, in addition to hiragana, at least 2,000 kanji that are used daily in Japanese. These are needed to compensate for the shallow hiragana orthography and the language's limited phonological inventory. In fact, there are many homophones in Japanese that can be differentiated only by writing them in kanji. In sharp contrast to the Chinese writing system that, as Akita and Hatano put it, 'may make life hard for the novices but has clear advantages for the skilled adult readers', the Japanese kana orthography, best suited to children and beginners, may have serious limitations for adult readers.

One of the themes to emerge very clearly from these chapters is that the speed with which children learn to read and spell – and the strategies that they adopt – is a product of many factors. Undoubtedly some scripts – those that are more regular in their representation of sounds – are easier to master. But there are important interactions between the characteristics of a script at the phonological, syllabic and morphological level and many other variables. These include children's pre-reading experience at home and in nursery school, the method of instruction used in school to teach reading and spelling and societal attitudes towards these activities. Cross-cultural comparisons are allowing us to draw a clearer picture of how these factors interact. Ultimately they also present us with an opportunity to discover which – if any – aspects of learning to be literate can really be considered universal.

REFERENCE

Firth, U. (1985). Beneath the surface of developmental dyslexia. In K. Patterson, M. Coltheart and J. Marshall (eds.), *Surface Dyslexia*. London: Lawrence Erlbaum.

2   The acquisition of Italian orthography

Giuseppe Cossu

Introduction

On a hypothetical 'transparency scale' of writing systems, Italian orthography should be placed close to one extreme. The reasons for this eccentric location are to be found in the convergence of a shallow phonology and a highly regular mapping between the visual and the oral language. Indeed, one might suggest that the 'simplicity' of Italian orthography is to reading research what the *Drosophila* has been for genetics: a simplified model to explore the neuro-psychological intricacies of literacy acquisition.

This chapter investigates the idiosyncrasies of a regular orthography of this kind and seeks to highlight the cognitive requirements that have to be met by a child acquiring a transparent orthography. To this end, I will draw on data from normal school children as well as from clinical cases which show developmental dissociations between reading (or writing) and other neuro-psychological functions. From this double perspective, of normality and pathology, I will concentrate on the word level and the cognitive processes of transcoding single words (and non-words). This is not to deny the relevance of other components and levels of the reading processes, such as syntax, or text comprehension and production; rather, the choice is determined by the logical and chronological primacy of single-word decoding for setting up the orthographic system. Furthermore, the tasks of reading and writing at the word/non-word level circumscribe the range of the requisite cognitive resources by selecting those skills specifically involved in the transcoding process and in the access to the orthographic lexicon.

Before exploring the details of this perspective, it is necessary to survey the main features of Italian phonology and, subsequently, the orthographic rules that transcribe phonology into print and vice versa.

Italian phonology

Paradoxical as it might appear, the origins of the Italian language were nourished by the selection of a particular orthography. As Laura and Giulio Lepschy put it, 'the Italian language is based upon the literary Florentine of the fourteenth century, spread through Italy as a written language, and recognized as a literary national language in the sixteenth century' (Lepschy and Lepschy, 1981; p. 81). However, several more centuries had to elapse before the Italian language came to be accepted as a spoken national language. Morphological discrepancies between the dialects and the 'standard' language have gradually vanished, along with syntactical and lexical idiosyncrasies, whereas the phonology of the pre-existing dialects has to some extent been retained. As a consequence, different regions of the country host peculiar phonological versions of the Italian language. This diversity notwithstanding, I will limit my attention to a description of 'standard' phonology, as it allows a full grasp of the relation between the spoken and the written Italian language.

Spoken Italian comprises seven vowels (i, e, ɛ, a, o, ɔ, u) in a stressed position and only five (i, e, a, o, u) in an unstressed position (Ferrero, Magno-Caldognetto, Vagges and Lavagnoli, 1978). With regard to their acoustic spectra, Italian vowels are highly distinct and non-overlapping in formant frequencies, whereas spoken English, for instance, has a dozen or more vowels since the seven basic vowel nuclei are significantly modified by the presence of an off glide (Agard and Di Pietro, 1965).

The Italian language contains relatively little morpho-phonological alternation (as compared with English) and the constituent consonants have a clear-cut distribution (Vagges, Ferrero, Magno-Caldognetto and Lavagnoli, 1978). In addition, although Italian has a mixed stock of syllable types, it has fewer than half the number present in English. Moreover, unlike English, which has a predominantly closed syllable structure (e.g. CVC, CVCC, CCVC, etc.), Italian's most frequent syllable form by far is the open syllable (e.g. CVCV, CVCVCV, CCVCV, etc.) with relatively few variations (Carlson, Elenius, Granstrom and Hunnicut, 1985).

In Italian, the stress assignment for a syllable in a particular word is not fully predictable, although it is usually the penultimate syllable that is stressed. In many cases, the displacement of the stress modifies the meaning of the word as in *fini* (aims) and *finì* (he/she ended up); *còmpito* (task) and *compìto* (courteous); *sùbito* (immediately) and *subìto* (underwent). For the printed forms of such words, there are usually no diacritical signs to mark the stress positions; hence, the selection of the correct pronunciation is context-dependent and the reader must rely upon knowledge of the lexical items.

Italian orthography

Historically, then, Italian orthography emerged from the acceptance of a common linguistic model, based upon the 'dialect' spoken in Florence in the fourteenth century. Paradoxically (again), Dante Alighieri, in his Latin treatise *De Vulgari Eloquentia* criticised the pretended superiority of the Florentine dialect over the other dialects of Italy as a standard model for literary language. However, the linguistic excellence of his *Commedia* and, a few decades later, the sophisticated idiom of Petrarch's *Canzoniere* and Boccaccio's *Decameron* gave the Florentine dialect a pre-eminent literary position. The consequent debate was focused upon the alternative choices for the optimal orthography of the Florentine 'dialect'. There were two contrasting approaches: one favouring a detailed 'phonetic' transcription of the Florentine lexicon, the other one invoking an etymological view that preserved the Latin tradition. The phonetic approach gained acceptance, as it yielded reasonable solutions to most of the problems of orthographic transcription. As a result of this debate, the key features of Italian orthography were in place by the sixteenth century and became formally attested in the eminent *Vocabolario degli Accademici della Crusca* in 1612. This provided a large lexicon of the Italian literary language and an authoritative prescription for the orthography. Furthermore, since the first edition of the *Vocabolario*, many refinements have been introduced across the centuries aimed at removing the ambiguities of pre-existing orthographic transcriptions (Maraschio, 1993). The outcome of this chisel work was a highly transparent orthography, characterised by an almost biunivocal grapheme–phoneme correspondence.

Regardless of the context in which they occur, each of the five vowels has only one orthographic rendition in Italian. Consonants have only one graphemic rendition and vice versa, except for a few stop consonants and affricates (i.e. /k/ and /g/; /tʃ/ and /dʒ/). In these cases, the same grapheme followed by different vowels has different phonological renditions. For instance, the letters (g) + (a) are rendered as /ga/, but (g) + (i) as /dʒi/; in order to obtain the voiced velar /gi/, we need to insert the letter h (ghi). A similar pattern applies to the voiceless velar /k/ as well.

In a few cases, the orthographic rendition of the word is phonologically unpredictable: the voiceless velar /k/ followed by the vowel /u/ which appear in /kuadro/ (picture) are written as 'quadro', in /kuore/ (heart) as 'cuore' and in /akua/ (water) as 'acqua'. Similarly unpredictable, on

Table 2.1 *Correspondences between graphemes and phonemes in Italian orthography.*

Phones ⇒	**Letters**	⇒ Phones	Phones ⇒	**Letters**	⇒ Phones
a	**a**	a	λ	**gl** (+ i)	λ
e	**e**	e	ŋ	**gn**	ŋ
i	**i**	i	—	**h**	—
o	**o**	o	l	**l**	l
u	**u**	u	m	**m**	m
b	**b**	b	n	**n**	n
k	**c** (+ a, o, u)	k	p	**p**	p
k	**ch** (+ i, e)	k	k	**q** (+ u)	k
ʧ	**c** (+ i, e)	ʧ	r	**r**	r
d	**d**	d	s, z	**s**	s, z
f	**f**	f	ʃ	**sc** (+ i, e)	ʃ
g	**g** (+ a, o, u)	g	t	**t**	t
ʤ	**g** (+ i, e)	ʤ	v	**v**	v
g	**gh** (+ i, e)	g	ts, dz	**z**	ts, dz

rare occasions, is the spelling of the voiceless palatal /ʧ/, the voiced affricate /dz/ and the fricative /ʃ/ before the vowel /e/. The word /ʧeleste/ (light blue) and /ʧelo/ (sky), /ʤelo/ (frost) and /ʧilieʤe/ (cherries) are rendered in orthography as 'celeste' and 'cielo', 'gelo' and 'ciliegie', respectively. In similar vein, /ʧero/ (candle) and /ʧeco/ (blind), /ʃena/ (scene) and /ʃentsa/ (science) are rendered as 'cero' and 'cieco', 'scena' and 'scienza', respectively. Apart from these few exceptions, Italian orthography is rendered by a fairly biunivocal correspondence between phoneme and grapheme (see table 2.1).

Developmental trajectories

What sort of developmental trajectories are likely to emerge in a child acquiring Italian literacy? Maria Montessori, at the dawn of the twentieth century, outlined two unconventional suggestions, which she drew from the results of her teaching method to four- and five-year-old children in Rome. The first suggestion claimed that the acquisition of writing skills is complete within a very short period of time (she dubbed it the 'explosion of writing') (Montessori, 1909; p. 241). The second suggestion maintained that 'writing precedes reading' (*ibid.*; p. 251). Montessori explicitly pointed out that: 'The experience led [her] to introduce a sharp distinction between *reading* and *writing* as it demonstrated that the *synchronism* between the two events was *far from perfect*' (italics in the original text; p. 251).

One can see the reasons why a transparent orthography minimises the difficulties of learning to read and write, yet there is a reluctance to concede that children achieve almost instant mastery of literacy skills. Unlike language, which is a biological object (Pinker, 1994), literacy is not recognised as an outcome of evolutionary adaptation and current views claim that the acquisition of literacy implies no more than dedicated teaching and laborious learning.

Likewise, it is hard to explain how a transparent orthography, particularly one with (almost) biunivocal grapheme–phoneme correspondences, could generate asymmetrical trajectories of reading and writing, without admitting the developmental independence of the two functions.

The questions implicitly raised by Montessori's work were too far in advance of the scientific interests of the times. In fact, an overview of the studies on the acquisition of Italian orthography indicates that the analysis of reading and writing was mostly confined within the boundaries of pedagogical concern. Particular attention was devoted to the selection of the 'appropriate' teaching method (Deva, 1972) and when attempts were made to specify the cognitive mechanisms of literacy acquisition, the Piagetian model of intelligence was used as the theoretical frame of reference (Deva, 1982).

Growing attention to the problems of learning disabilities, however, stimulated new areas of research in Italian studies of reading and writing acquisition. Two approaches gained pre-eminence: (a) the assessment of reading proficiency in different grades and (b) studies of the emergence of literacy skills in pre-school children.

The first line of research attempts to provide reliable tools to evaluate the development of reading skills, with particular attention to the comprehension of the written text. The MT test (Cornoldi and Colpo, 1981) was developed for school children ranging from the end of first grade (seven years old) in elementary school up to the third grade of the 'middle' school (fourteen years old). Each child was individually presented with a printed text (selected for increasing length and conceptual complexity for each grade). Reading speed and accuracy were evaluated, as well as comprehension of the written story. The results provide normative data for decoding skills and text comprehension at different grade levels, thus yielding a guideline for educational evaluation in the classroom.

As a complement to the MT test, a new test was recently standardised which investigates reading and writing accuracy for words and nonwords (Sartori, Job and Tressoldi, 1995). Again, however, children from the first grade level were excluded from the sample which comprised school children from the second elementary grade (seven years) to the third grade of middle school (fourteen years).

A second line of research is mostly concerned with the cultural and emotional dimensions of early learning, as well as with the related cognitive variables of reading acquisition (Pontecorvo and Pontecorvo, 1986). A recent development of this approach, influenced by the work of Emilia Ferreiro (Ferreiro and Teberosky, 1985), focused upon the emergence of writing as a conceptual object for pre-school children. In one of these studies, the writing strategies of seventeen pre-school children (mean age 4.4) were investigated and their written production was accordingly analysed (Zucchermaglio, 1991). It was found that, in their early attempts, the pre-school children 'write' each word by arbitrarily combining a cluster of alphabetic letters unrelated to the target. The author observes that the 'children remain in [this] mode for a long time [. . .] from a minimum of six months to a maximum of fourteen months' (*ibid.*, p. 169). This is a very different picture from the 'explosion of writing' described by Montessori (for children of a similar age) and one worth investigating.

The emergence of literacy skills in normal children

Our main interest has focused on the analysis of the cognitive mechanisms that set up the orthographic architecture *sensu strictu*, i.e. the mechanisms of word (and non-word) decoding and the assembly of an orthographic lexicon. We approached the problem from a double perspective: (1) by focusing our attention upon the early stages of literacy acquisition in normal children and (2) by investigating the nature of the dissociation between orthographic skills and other aspects of cognition.

In a recent study (Cossu, Gugliotta and Marshall, 1995), we examined the reading and writing skills of seventy normal school children attending the first and second grade in Parma. All children were individually tested between the end of January and late March and the same list of words and non-words was presented for both reading and writing. In their classes, a 'synthetic-analytic' method (Deva, 1982) was adopted which gave equal emphasis to both orthographic functions.

In children from the first grade ($n = 35$), length had a significant effect on performance in the writing, but not on the reading task. Reading accuracy for short words and non-words was 95.2 per cent and 85.1 per cent correct, respectively, whereas writing accuracy was 90.6 per cent and 82.1 per cent correct, respectively. Correct responses in reading long words and non-words were 92.7 per cent and 78.5 per cent, respectively, whereas in writing the same list of words and non-words, correct responses were 55.2 per cent and 44.1 per cent correct, respectively (see figure 2.1). These data confirm: (1) the achievement of

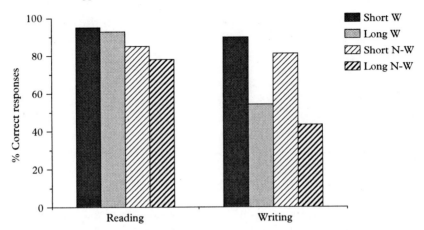

Figure 2.1   Reading and writing performance in Italian first graders.

a high degree of orthographic accuracy after a brief period of teaching; (2) the (partially) asynchronous trajectories for reading and writing.

Further support for these findings is provided by a recent research project, aimed at providing normative data for the neuro-psychological assessment of reading and writing skills. The study (not yet published) involved 1,436 Italian children from different regions of the country, attending the first ($n = 478$), second ($n = 482$) and third grade ($n = 476$), respectively. All children were tested between the middle of March and early May and both reaction times and accuracy scores were recorded. Inspection of the data from one of the reading (and writing) tests with twenty words and twenty non-words (see table 2.2) confirms that children at first-grade level achieve excellent orthographic accuracy just six to seven months after teaching has been started. Consequently, the discrepancy in accuracy levels between the three grades is reduced to a few percentage points (or fractions thereof). The early mastery of orthographic skills and the low standard deviation (a sample of 478 children in the first grade has an SD of 1.56), indicate that reading accuracy may not be the best (or the only) variable tailored to detect subtle individual differences in reading and writing Italian except, perhaps, in the case of severe reading disorders.

The insufficiency of reading accuracy as a discriminative paradigm, though, is not peculiar to Italian orthography, as revealed by the data from other transparent orthographies. Heinz Wimmer, for instance, has convincingly shown that reading time and not accuracy alone is required to detect finer orthographic discrepancies between good and poor readers acquiring literacy in German (Wimmer, 1993).

Table 2.2 *Mean correct responses (and SD) in reading and writing words and non-words in a sample of 1,436 school children.*

	Reading		Writing	
	Words ($n = 20$)	Non-words ($n = 20$)	Words ($n = 20$)	Non-words ($n = 20$)
First Grade	19.56	18.55	18.08	16.5
($n = 478$)	(1.56)	(3.01)	3.01	3.25
Second Grade	19.88	18.04	19.24	18.01
($n = 482$)	(1.18)	(2.21)	2.21	2.24
Third Grade	19.91	18.56	19.61	18.59
($n = 476$)	(0.39)	(2.05)	2.05	2.15

Inspection of our normative data on the acquisition of Italian literacy shows that the reaction times can capture fine-grained individual differences in reading skills. In the first graders, for instance, the mean reaction time for reading twenty words was 69 seconds (SD 23.6), whereas it dropped to 41 seconds (SD 16.2) in the third graders. Reading time likewise decreased for non-words, where the total time required for the twenty stimuli was 106 seconds (SD = 58.3) in first grade and 65 seconds (SD = 31) in the third grade.

A longitudinal track

These data show that around the middle, or close to the end of, the first grade Italian children achieve a near-perfect mastery of transcoding skills; a short time indeed and yet of crucial relevance for setting up orthographic skills. Thus the investigation of this endeavour may shed light upon the neuro-psychological mechanisms underlying the acquisition of literacy. Accordingly, in a series of longitudinal studies not yet published, we have investigated the evolution of transcoding skills for both reading and writing in normal first graders.

In one of these studies we analysed the development of literacy skills in ninety-five normal children attending the first grade in a school district in Parma. All children were tested for reading and writing at four different times (October, January, March and May) and both reading and writing skills were analysed. The data (as reported in figure 2.2) show that both functions are characterised by a steep decline in error rate between October and January. However, the developmental profiles of reading and writing differ quantitatively: reading performance is

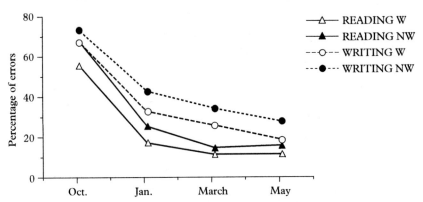

Figure 2.2   Development of reading and writing skills at Italian first grade level.

overall far better than spelling and the discrepancy between the two tasks widens between the second and the third testing sessions. The sharp decrease in error rate (between Time 1 and Time 2) involves words and non-words, in both the reading and spelling tasks. An orthographic input lexicon seems to be established earlier and more efficiently than an orthographic output lexicon.

The orthographic lexicon

According to the standard 'dual route' model, the computational distinction between lexical and non-lexical procedures is a key feature of the architecture of reading in adult subjects (Marshall and Newcombe, 1973; Patterson and Morton, 1985). Developmentally, however, it remains an entirely open question as to how these two sub-systems are constructed: whether the emergence of a visual lexicon implies a preliminary activation of the sub-lexical routine (aimed at 'stabilizing' the orthographic gestalt) or whether it is rather governed by an independent processing component. Furthermore, the existence of a unitary phonological route has been questioned on several grounds (Goswami and Bryant, 1990).

The question is of particular relevance in a regular orthography, where any sequence of alphabetic letters could be, at least in principle, efficiently parsed by mastery of the grapheme–phoneme correspondences. Within these constraints, the detection of developmental surface dyslexia in the early stages of reading acquisition should be, if not impossible, at least extremely unlikely. Not surprisingly, the few cases

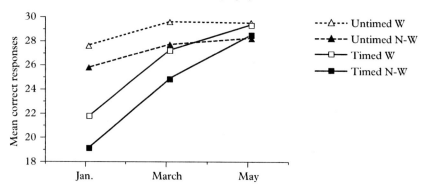

Figure 2.3 Development of reading accuracy under time constraints and free presentation.

reported of developmental surface dyslexia in Italian (Job, Sartori, Masterson and Coltheart, 1984; Morchio, 1989) are all adolescents.

In order to explore how an input orthographic lexicon is constructed in a transparent orthography, we planned a longitudinal study in which we tested forty first graders under two experimental conditions: (1) a 'timed condition', where the children had to read a balanced list of words and non-words under a time-constrained exposure (two seconds were allowed for inspection); (2) an 'untimed condition' in which no time limit was imposed to the inspection of the printed stimuli. The logic of the experimental design was to force the access to the ortho-graphic input lexicon in the task of timed reading words. We reasoned that if an orthographic lexicon was being set up under the control of independent mechanisms, the time-constrained condition would amplify the discrepancy across time between accuracy in word and non-word reading.

All children were individually tested at three consecutive times: in January, March and May 1997. Unsurprisingly, the 'timed' condition exacts a high fee in terms of accuracy at the early stages of reading acquisition (see figure 2.3). However, by the end of the school year, a limited exposure of two seconds has no detrimental effect on reading accuracy. The interesting aspect is that in both experimental conditions the progression in non-word accuracy appears to parallel the trajectory of word reading across time testing. Furthermore, the few longitudinal data we have collected show that a similar picture holds for writing as well.

These data suggest that, in a transparent orthography, the early devel-opment of a visual route requires an equivalent degree of efficiency in the phonological route. However, since the data from normal children are correlational, the issues can best be faced by inspecting developmental pathological conditions. One might speculate that the early detection of a surface dyslexia in a transparent orthography would be an unlikely event. Unfortunately, the available evidence neither confirms nor rules out this hypothesis; very few studies of surface (and phonological) dyslexia in Italian are reported (Job *et al.*, 1984; Sartori and Job, 1982) and none of them provides longitudinal data. The discrepancy between the visual and the phonological route may indeed become evident after several years of schooling, when a partial orthographic lexicon can be slowly established (Morchio, 1989).

One might reason that different orthographies foster different strategies in setting up the orthographic architecture. For a deep orthography, some evidence has been acquired showing that normal accuracy in the sub-lexical route is not sufficient to promote a standard efficiency in the direct route (Castles and Coltheart, 1996). However, children with this type of reading disorder show a slowed response pattern which extends to their non-word as well as their word reading (Seymour and Evans, 1993). This finding casts doubts upon the developmental independence of a direct route since, although deep orthographies are likely to enhance the assembling of the orthographic lexicon, an efficient grapheme–phoneme transcoding process may indeed represent a necessary condition for stabilising the process, as exemplified by the strategy of 'reading by analogy' (Baron, 1977; Goswami, 1986).

In a transparent orthography, on the other hand, the primacy of the transcoding processes should become more salient, being reflected in a developmental correspondence between the improvement of efficiency in the phonological route and the emergence of an orthographic lexicon. In sum, although at present no definite option can be supported uncontroversially, the few available data for a transparent orthography suggest some correspondence between the efficiency of the phonological route and the development of an input (and output) orthographic lexicon. Whether such a correlation implies a primacy of the transcoding processes in setting up the orthographic systems, though, requires further evidence.

Phonemic awareness

Phonemic awareness (PA) should be considered in the analysis of literacy acquisition, though not a component intrinsically involved in the orthographic computation. This is for two reasons: (1) the ability of a school child to recognise (and to explicitly manipulate) the phonological units of a word has been a central topic in the literature on reading acquisition for two decades now (Liberman, 1973); (2) phonemic awareness is currently credited with a major role in the acquisition of orthographic skills (Morais and Kolinsky, 1995). However, notwithstanding the many studies devoted to the topic, the causal connections between metalinguistic skills and learning to read remain problematic (Marshall and Cossu, 1987; Cossu, Rossini and Marshall, 1993a).

Leaving aside the issues of whether segmental analysis is predictive of later reading achievement, or whether improvement in PA skills has direct implications on orthographic accuracy, I will focus on the relevance of phonology in the development of metalinguistic skills. To this end, it is worth examining a comparative study of American and Italian pre-school children on a phoneme and syllable segmentation task (Cossu, Shankweiler, Liberman, Tola and Katz, 1988). American and Italian children showed a similar *qualitative* pattern of performance, since both samples fared much better in the latter than in former task. The two samples, however, revealed remarkable *quantitative* discrepancies in both tasks: 67 per cent and 80 per cent of the Italian children at the kindergarten and nursery level, respectively, reached the criterion of six successive correct responses on the syllable segmentation task. By contrast, 46 per cent and 48 per cent of the American pre-school children (at corresponding grade level) reached the criterion. Likewise, in the phoneme segmentation task 13 per cent of the Italian nursery children reached the criterion, whereas no American child of corresponding grade level did so.

The quantitative discrepancy between the two samples was replicated when we compared a sample of American first graders with a group of eighty Italian school children from an identical grade level. No comparison could be made for the syllable task, since the Italian children were at ceiling (100 per cent reached criterion), whereas the American ones were not (90 per cent reached criterion). In the phoneme segmentation task, only 3 per cent of the Italian children failed to reach criterion, whereas 30 per cent of their American counterparts still did not master the task. Thus, the data suggest that the combinatorial phonology of different languages has a contrasting effect on pre-school children's accuracy in both syllable and phoneme segmentation tasks – a quantitative discrepancy in correct performance which extends to school age as well.

A second aspect worth looking at concerns the correlation between different metaphonological tasks and the performance in reading and writing in Italian orthography. In agreement with the findings of the current literature, a number of longitudinal studies on Italian first graders have documented the symmetrical increase of orthographic and metaphonologic skills (Tressoldi, 1989; Cossu, Gugliotta, Cristante, Emiliani and Villani, 1990).

In sum, it appears that studies of phonemic awareness in normal children are unlikely to go beyond the detection of simple correlations between metalinguistic skills and reading (or writing) accuracy. It is for this reason that we turned our attention to the study of pathological cases, namely the developmental dissociations between literacy and phonemic awareness.

Comparison of reading and writing acquisition

Reading has been the primary focus of concern in studies on literacy acquisition (and developmental dyslexia), whereas the function of writing has received only marginal attention or has been totally neglected. This position could be accepted only on the assumption that writing a word merely implies the reverse of reading it. However, the classical neuro-psychological literature has documented cases where adult patients are sometimes unable to read what they themselves have correctly written (Dejerine, 1892; Benson and Geschwind, 1964).

The importance of a parallel study of both functions is further motivated by some evidence (for a deep orthography, at least) that writing sometimes exceeds reading. It has been shown that children as young as 3.6 and 4 years of age can write messages in a phonologically plausible way, although they are unable to read back the messages they have just printed (Read, 1971; Read, 1986). These young children represented English words with the standard alphabet, though employing an orthography of their own invention. To give an example, the 'word' RUDF ('Are you deaf?') was the first printed message sent by a 5.1-year-old boy to capture the attention of a busy mother (Bissex, 1980). At this early age, the dominant option to orthography appears to sound like 'Write first, read later' (Chomsky, 1971). This discrepancy, though, has been reported for older children as well (Bryant and Bradley, 1980; Bradley, 1985). Furthermore, a reverse pattern has been documented in English school children who were 'good readers and atrocious spellers' (Frith, 1980; p. 496). The implications for the architecture of orthographic processes are relevant, since the dissociations 'suggest that the two skills must be to some extent independent' (Bradley 1985, p. 67). Other accounts, though, point out that 'the ease of spelling a particular word is determined by the number of possible spellings for a given pronunciation, while ease of reading is determined by the number of possible pronunciations for a given spelling pattern' (Waters, Bruck and Seidenberg, 1985); hence, children may be using similar processes for reading and spelling. This latter (and elegant) hypothesis can explain the reading/spelling discrepancy in English orthography. Implicitly, however, it also makes strong predictions for a transparent orthography, where a biunivocal grapheme–phoneme correspondence would make the discrepancies almost impossible.

Reading/spelling dissociations in a transparent orthography

As we have already noted, the Italian language is rendered by a transparent orthography and yet developmental discrepancies between reading and spelling can be observed in clinical practice. I encountered for the first time one such case in 1978 in the outpatient service for Paediatric Neurology at the University of Sassari (Sardinia). MC was a nine-year-old girl, with no history of brain damage, mild mental retardation (WISC full-scale IQ was 79) and learning disabilities. Her parents' (and teacher's) main concern was a severe inability to read even single disyllabic words. However, on the first task of written naming, MC correctly named all of the twenty pictures and made only two errors in writing: she misspelled *pcere* for 'bicchiere' (glass) and *tevsisona* for 'televisione' (television). A few days later, MC was presented with the same list of printed words, but not one single item she read bore the least resemblance to the target: for example, the misspelled words 'bicchiere' and 'televisione', were read as *cena* (dinner) and *mano* (hand), respectively. The discrepancy between reading and writing was too striking not to alert even the most absent-minded neurologist: the data strongly suggested that reading and writing were *developmentally* dissociable functions. The following week, a new list of thirty disyllabic words was presented for writing to dictation and MC's performance was 100 per cent correct. As we can see from figure 2.4, MC had neat handwriting, and so I asked her to read back each word she had just written. Her responses are reported in figure 2.4 and need no further comment. Since I was struck by the distance between the target and the responses provided by MC, I asked her to explain her strategy in reading. 'How do you come to read "mare" [sea]?' I asked her, while pointing to the target stimulus 'mela' (apple). She replied that 'The letter *m* is for the word "mare".' On my further enquiries, she explained to me that *r* was the letter for the word 'ruota' (wheel); likewise, she read 'ape' (bee) for 'pane' (bread) 'because the letter *a* is the letter for "ape"'. When I asked her how she had produced the word 'foglia' (leaf) (when the target was 'ieri' (yesterday)), MC pointed to the diphthong 'ie' and replied that '*ia* is a sound in the word foglia'. In sum, when facing a printed word, MC arbitrarily selected one letter from within the graphemic sequence, turning the corresponding syllable into a root morpheme, thus gaining access to her phonological lexicon.

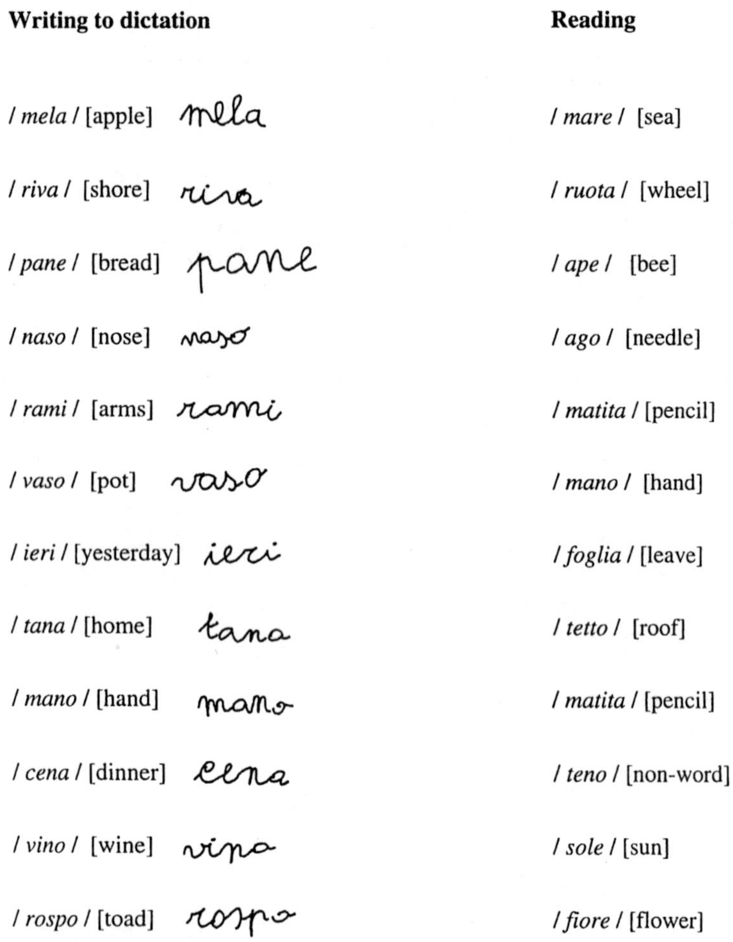

Writing to dictation		Reading
/ *mela* / [apple]	mela	/ *mare* / [sea]
/ *riva* / [shore]	riva	/ *ruota* / [wheel]
/ *pane* / [bread]	pane	/ *ape* / [bee]
/ *naso* / [nose]	naso	/ *ago* / [needle]
/ *rami* / [arms]	rami	/ *matita* / [pencil]
/ *vaso* / [pot]	vaso	/ *mano* / [hand]
/ *ieri* / [yesterday]	ieri	/ *foglia* / [leave]
/ *tana* / [home]	tana	/ *tetto* / [roof]
/ *mano* / [hand]	mano	/ *matita* / [pencil]
/ *cena* / [dinner]	cena	/ *teno* / [non-word]
/ *vino* / [wine]	vino	/ *sole* / [sun]
/ *rospo* / [toad]	rospo	/ *fiore* / [flower]

Figure 2.4   MC's writing to dictation and reading the same words she had just written.

A few months later, a new case of orthographic dissociation came to my attention, but this time the strategy for reading was different. RC was an 8.2-year-old boy, with a past clinical history of partial epilepsy and a mild mental retardation. On neurological examination, no abnormality was revealed; RC was still under anti-convulsant therapy, although he had been free from seizures for several years. His writing was fairly accurate (he only occasionally omitted some double consonants, as in 'bottiglia' (bottle), which he wrote as *botiglia*). On writing a list of twenty disyllabic words, RC scored 100 per cent correct, whereas he failed to read correctly nineteen out of the twenty words. This time, however, RC's attempts to read revealed a letter-by-letter reading strategy, a constraint that (almost) never allowed him to 'blend' correctly the sequence of phonemes. Thus, two contrasting strategies for reading appear to be at work in these children, and yet the discrepancy between reading and writing is of a similar magnitude, with a persistent predominance of writing accuracy over reading.

Cossu and Marshall (1985) describe two children who had developed adequate phoneme–grapheme conversion rules, even though they had a grossly impaired 'phonic' reading route. For instance, in one test of sixty-four non-words, one of these children, CA, could write correctly to dictation thirty items and read correctly only two items. The other child, CF, wrote fifteen non-words correctly and read two of them. Similar results were obtained with a corresponding number of words: CA wrote thirty-two words out of sixty-four and read four of them correctly, whereas CF was able to write twenty-three words and read nine words correctly. These two children, though, relied upon contrasting strategies in their attempts to read both words and non-words: CA adopted a letter-by-letter reading strategy, displaying no ability to extract the corresponding phonemes from the letter he named correctly. CF, on the other hand, made every effort to turn the sequence of letters directly into a real word.

These observations further support the hypothesis that reading and writing are non-parallel functions which can be selectively impaired even in a transparent orthography, where one would expect a symmetrical improvement (or delay) of both orthographic skills.

The question then arises as to whether reading and writing are independent functions, governed by distinct computational components, or whether the dissociation merely arises as an odd outcome of early brain damage. In order to answer this question we need to monitor the trajectories of literacy acquisition in normal children. To this end, I will present the main findings from a longitudinal study which involved 155 normal Italian school children from the beginning of the first grade up to the end of the second grade (Cavalli, 1996). All children were individually tested four times at six-monthly intervals: in November and in May each child was presented with thirty words and a corresponding number of non-words for reading and writing to dictation. The results are summarised in table 2.3 and show that reading accuracy exceeds writing accuracy. An extraordinary improvement in reading skills bounces first graders from an error rate of 62.8 per cent at Time 1 to 7.63 per cent at Time 2, after six months of teaching. Writing skills show a similarly striking improvement in accuracy: the total error rate moves from 72.6 per cent at Time 1 to 16.5 per cent at Time 2. This is a

Table 2.3 *Longitudinal perspective on reading and writing acquisition from a sample of 155 Italian school children through first and second grade (mean errors and SD).*

Age	First grade		Second grade	
	6;4	6;10	7;4	7;10
Reading words	**17.2**	**0.987**	**0.929**	**0.948**
($n = 30$)	(10.6)	(3.34)	(2.98)	(1.08)
Reading non-words	**20.49**	**3.59**	**2.54**	**2.58**
($n = 30$)	(9.32)	(4.56)	(3.49)	(2.86)
Writing words	**21.17**	**3.42**	**2.99**	**2.63**
($n = 30$)	(7.84)	(4.55)	(3.43)	(2.23)
Writing non-words	**22.39**	**6.48**	**4.76**	**3.96**
($n = 30$)	(7.26)	(5.55)	(3.72)	(2.7)

remarkable improvement; yet a highly significant discrepancy between the two functions persists across the first and the second grade. Clearly, during the early stages of literacy acquisition, reading and writing skills appear to move along discrepant trajectories, even in a highly transparent orthography. In (some) pathological conditions the discrepancy can be amplified, but the phenomenon is very evident during the course of normal development.

The analysis of reading/writing discrepancy in a transparent orthography, though, reveals a further paradox: reading is easier than writing in normal graders, whereas writing is better than reading in (some) pathological children. We must acknowledge that the fine-grained dynamic of literacy acquisition is still too poorly understood even to provide a reliable explanation for the discrepancy between reading and writing, let alone the reversed direction of discrepancy in (some) pathological cases and normal children. It remains inexplicable that a complex task can be easy for a mentally retarded child and becomes a more difficult task for a normal child. From our longitudinal studies, however, it appears that the relation between reading and writing changes over time, with a rapid improvement of reading accuracy at some point, which is not paralleled by writing. Furthermore, in some poor readers of normal intelligence writing is equal to, or slightly more accurate than reading.

Whatever the outcome of future studies, Montessori's two suggestions seem to receive some support: the acquisition of Italian orthography is accomplished within a very short time and (in the early stage of acquisition) there is a significant discrepancy between reading and writing.

The nature of reading and writing errors

The analysis of reading and writing errors may help to illuminate the developmental discrepancy between the two functions. In a previous study (Cossu *et al.*, 1995) we attempted to explore the role of phonological, orthographic and lexical variables in determining the quality of reading and writing errors during the early stages of literacy acquisition. To this aim, the performance of seventy normal children attending the first and second grade of an elementary school in Parma was analysed.

At the molecular level of the orthographic architecture, inspection of errors from first graders ($n = 35$) reveals that the asymmetrical frequency of errors for consonants and vowels is proportionally similar in both tasks. In reading, the rate of consonant and vowel errors corresponds to 72 per cent and 28 per cent of the total, respectively. In writing, the discrepancy was replicated: 75 per cent and 25 per cent of the total for consonant and vowel errors, respectively. A similar symmetry was evident in the sensitivity to the syllable-position effect for both reading and writing tasks. The final syllable induced 71 per cent and 76 per cent of the total errors in reading and writing, respectively, whereas the initial syllable gave rise to only 29 per cent and 24 per cent of the total errors in reading and writing, respectively.

By analysing the role of the orthographic structure of words and non-words we obtained a different picture. The effect of length in regular words and non-words was paradigmatic: the task of writing the long regular words provoked thirty-two deletion errors (50 per cent of the total in that category), whereas reading the same words elicited deletion errors, corresponding to 15 per cent of the total (in the same category). Likewise, in writing words containing a consonant geminate cluster, the first graders made 126 deletion errors (76 per cent of the total), but they made only twelve deletion errors (38 per cent of the total) in reading the same words. In presenting the corresponding number of non-words for reading and writing we confirmed a highly significant discrepancy between the two modalities.

From these preliminary data it appears that the (early) orthographic system displays a qualitatively similar sensitivity to the consonant/vowel and syllable position paradigms for both reading and writing. At the lexical level, on the other hand, reading and writing appear to be unequally affected by an identical type of orthographic complexity. The quantitative (and qualitative) discrepancies between the two tasks thus suggest that a structural asymmetry between reading and writing is a feature of a transparent orthography with regular bi-directional links between grapheme and phoneme.

Developmental dissociations

Brain damage may sometimes spare (or impair) a particular processing component, thus determining an asymmetrical construction of the child's cognitive system. Therefore, excellence of orthographic skills, in the face of concomitant neuro-psychological disorders, denies relevance to those impaired functions in the construction of an orthographic competence. At the same time, the asymmetries within the child's cognitive system implicitly delineate some neuro-psychological properties of reading and writing and their developmental trajectories. For these reasons, the study of reading acquisition in children with 'exceptional' cognitive architectures can illuminate the role of processing components inaccessible to standard scrutiny during normal acquisition.

A first example comes from the study of those children who are mentally retarded and yet acquire excellent mastery of reading and writing *qua* transcoding. We have reported the case of TA (Cossu and Marshall, 1990), an 8.6-year-old boy, with a full-scale IQ of 47 (and a verbal memory span of 2) who was the best reader in his class. He had acquired excellent decoding skills after a few weeks of school and in the absence of any special tutoring. TA could write non-words of nine letters effortlessly, read prose passages with correct prosody and yet be unable to grasp the slightest idea of the story he had just read. But the most disturbing feature in TA's orthographic skills was his complete failure in the different types of metalinguistic tasks he was presented with. Although we had been investigating him for some eighteen months, and the same types of tasks had been repeatedly presented, he could never deal either with the rhyming recognition task or the phonemic blending task. In this regard, his strategy in phonemic blending is illuminating. TA was able to 'blend' the names of a letter string (and thus pronounce the correct name) when the letters were displayed in front of him in an orderly array, but was unable to repeat the task when the letters were removed. Clearly, his reduced resources in verbal memory might explain his failure, but this point deserves further comment. When a phoneme segmentation task was presented, TA showed he understood the task; he tapped carefully, but the sequence he performed always contained a wrong number of strokes. He gave five correct responses out of forty-five, whereas an age-matched control group scored forty-three correct. In a deletion task he obtained eighteen correct responses out of forty-two, whereas the control group scored thirty-seven correct. TA's efficiency in this difficult task might be surprising, but we cannot rule out the possibility that in this case he was using a strategy of 'reading' (i.e. representing visually the word pronounced by the examiner), thus

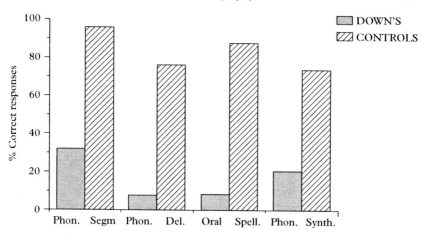

Figure 2.5   Correct responses on phonemic awareness tasks of Down's syndrome and normal (younger) children matched for reading age.

computing the deletion task upon letters, rather than phonemes. This is a plausible strategy in a transparent orthography like Italian and one which TA may put to use in the 'blending task'. Therefore, the paradox might be that TA is (partially) successful in some phonemic awareness tasks *because* he can use his reading skills efficiently.

Further evidence for the dissociation between reading and phonemic awareness was provided by a study (Cossu *et al.*, 1993a) of a group of ten Down's syndrome children (mean age 11.4) compared with a corresponding number of chronologically younger normal children, matched for reading age. The Down's syndrome children, who had a mean IQ of 44 (range 40–56), read correctly 93.8 per cent of the words and 88 per cent of the non-words: a degree of accuracy slightly higher than in the control group. Their reading skills notwithstanding, the Down's children performed very poorly on all of the metalinguistic tasks (see figure 2.5).

It has been argued (Bertelson, 1993; Morais and Kolinsky, 1995) that the failure of these hyperlexic children to perform the metalinguistic tasks reflects their inability to understand the task instructions, rather than task failure *per se*. However, our Down's syndrome children did understand the task, since they tapped during the segmentation task, they deleted a segment in the deletion task and they attempted to blend in the phoneme synthesis task; rather, they appeared to lack 'intellectual access to the concept of phones' (Cossu, Rossini and Marshall, 1993b; p. 299).

The failure of our Down's syndrome children may thus derive from limitations in cognitive resources that are necessary to compute the metalinguistic tasks, but not crucial for the acquisition of orthographic skills *per se*. This contrasts with a case where the availability of general cognitive resources allowed a very bright dyslexic child (with a verbal IQ of 144) to solve the metalinguistic tasks correctly, although his reading skills remained persistently inefficient (Cossu, Maggetti and Marshall, 1998).

From the reading/IQ dissociations it appears that, just as good general intelligence is not sufficient for mastering a 'simple' orthography like Italian, low intelligence does not prevent some mentally retarded children from acquiring orthographic skills.

Conclusions

The (relatively) simple architecture of Italian orthography provides a reliable model for the investigation of the early processes of literacy acquisition. The results thus far show that normal children achieve orthographic accuracy within a few months of teaching. By mid-school year, children at first-grade level are over 97 per cent and 94 per cent correct in reading words and non-words, respectively. However, in spite of the biunivocal correspondence between grapheme and phoneme, the development of reading and writing skills appears not to follow the same trajectory: reading accuracy significantly exceeds writing accuracy for both words and non-words. Improvement of orthographic skills removes the discrepancy (due to a ceiling effect), though it can still be detected at second grade in writing long non-words. A marked discrepancy between reading and writing skills is documented in (some) brain disordered children as well, but in the reverse direction: it is writing accuracy that exceeds reading. This condition, though, appears to be a transitory stage, and it decreases over time.

As expected, words are easier to read (and write) than non-words. However, we have documented that an increase in word-reading accuracy is systematically paralleled by a corresponding improvement in non-word reading. It is as if, in a transparent orthography, the construction of an orthographic lexicon implies a corresponding mastery of the phonological route.

Since a transparent orthography is mastered with no special effort by normal children, it is not surprising that even (some) mentally retarded children can easily grasp the orthographic principles and become efficient readers and writers (*qua* decoders). This particular condition shows that general intelligence, verbal memory or psycho-motor skills are largely irrelevant factors for the acquisition of literacy. It also shows that some of these mentally retarded subjects can be excellent readers and yet fail in a number of metalinguistic tasks. Under these constraints it becomes more puzzling that some very bright children can deal successfully with a number of metalinguistic tasks and yet make little progress over the years in reading accuracy and speed.

From an overall consideration of the data from the normal and pathological acquisition of Italian orthography, one gains the impression that the process of literacy acquisition can hardly be accounted for by unconstrained learning. Rather, it appears to be governed by highly selective, domain-specific, computational mechanisms, which have the functional properties of a modular system – a controversial hypothesis, I agree, but one which might reconcile a number of recalcitrant facts from the fields of both the normal and the pathological acquisition of literacy.

NOTE

I thank John C. Marshall for insightful comments on an earlier version of this chapter.

REFERENCES

Agard, F. B. and Di Pietro, R. J. (1965). *The Sounds of English and Italian.* Chicago: University of Chicago Press.

Baron, J. (1977). Mechanisms for pronouncing printed words: use and acquisition. In D. LaBerge and S. J. Samuels (eds.), *Basic Processes in Reading: Perception and Comprehension* (pp. 175–216). Hillsdale, NJ: Lawrence Erlbaum Associates Inc.

Benson, F. and Geschwind, N. (1964). The Alexias. In P. J. Vinken and G. W. Bruyn (eds.), *Handbook of Clinical Neurology. Disorders of Speech, Perception and Symbolic Behaviour* (vol. IV, pp. 112–40). Amsterdam: Elsevier.

Bertelson, P. (1993). Reading acquisition and phonemic awareness testing: how conclusive are data from Down's syndrome? Remarks on Cossu, Rossini and Marshall (1993). *Cognition*, 48, 297–303.

Bissex, G. L. (1980). *GNYS AT WRK.* Cambridge, MA: Harvard University Press.

Bradley, L. (1985). Dissociation of reading and spelling behaviour. In D. D. Duane and C. K. Leong (eds.), *Understanding Learning Disabilities* (pp. 65–85). New York: Plenum Press.

Bryant, P. E. and Bradley, L. (1980). Why children sometimes write words which they do not read. In U. Frith (ed.), *Cognitive Processes in Spelling* (pp. 355–70). London: Academic Press.

Carlson, F., Elenius, K., Granstrom, B. and Hunnicut, S. (1985). Phonetic and orthographic properties of the basic vocabulary of five European languages. *KTH Speech Transmission Laboratory* (pp. 63–94).

Castles, A. and Coltheart, M. (1996). Cognitive correlates of developmental surface dyslexia: a single case study. *Cognitive Neuropsychology*, 13, 25–50.

Cavalli, L. (1996). Indici predittivi dell'acquisizione della lettura e scrittura. Unpublished dissertation, Psychology Department, University of Padua.

Chomsky, C. (1971). Write first; read later. *Childhood Education*, 47, 296–9.

Cornoldi, C. and Colpo, M. (1981). *La verifica della lettura*. Florence: Organizzazioni Speciali.

Cossu, G., Gugliotta, M., Cristante, F., Emiliani, M. and Villani. D. (1990). Consapevolezza fonemica e acquisizione della lettura. *Saggi*, 16, 47–60.

Cossu, G., Gugliotta, M. and Marshall, J. C. (1995). Acquisition of reading and written spelling in a transparent orthography: two non parallel processes? *Reading and Writing*, 7, 9–22.

Cossu, G., Maggetti, S. and Marshall, J. C. (1998). A highly specific dyslexia in a child with superior cognitive abilities. (*Submitted*)

Cossu, G. and Marshall, J. C. (1985). Dissociation between reading and written spelling in two Italian children: dyslexia without dysgraphia? *Neuropsychologia*, 23, 697–700.

(1990). Are cognitive skills a prerequisite for learning to read and write? *Cognitive Neuropsychology*, 7, 21–40.

Cossu, G., Rossini, F. and Marshall, J. C. (1993a). When reading is acquired but phonemic awareness is not: a study of literacy in Down's Syndrome. *Cognition*, 46, 129–38.

(1993b). Reading is reading is reading. *Cognition*, 48, 297–303.

Cossu, G., Shankweiler, D. P., Liberman, I. Y., Tola, G. and Katz, L. (1988). Awareness of phonological segments and reading ability in Italian children. *Applied Psycholinguistics*, 9, 1–16.

Dejerine, J. (1892). Contribution à l'étude anatomopathologique et clinique des différentes variétés de cécité verbale. *Mémoires de la Société de Biologie*, 4, 61–90.

Deva, F. (1972). *L'apprendimento della lettura e della scrittura*. Turin: Loescher Editore.

Deva, F. (1982). *I processi di apprendimento della lettura e della scrittura*. Florence: La Nuova Italia Editrice.

Ferreiro, A. and Teberosky, A. (1985). *La costruzione della lingua scritta nel bambino*. Florence: Giunti Editore.

Ferrero, F. E., Magno-Caldognetto, E., Vagges, K. and Lavagnoli, C. (1978). Some acoustic characteristics of the Italian vowels. *Journal of Italian Linguistics*, 3, 87–96.

Frith, U. (1980). Unexpected spelling problems. In U. Frith (ed.), *Cognitive Processes in Spelling* (pp. 495–515). London: Academic Press.

Goswami, U. (1986). Children's use of analogy in learning to read: a developmental study. *Journal of Experimental Child Psychology*, 42, 73–83.

Goswami, U. and Bryant, P. (1990). *Phonological Skills and Learning to Read*. Hove: Lawrence Erlbaum Associates Ltd.

Job, R., Sartori, G., Masterson, J. and Coltheart, M. (1984). Developmental surface dyslexia in Italian. In R. N. Malatesha and H. A. Whitaker (eds.), *Dyslexia: A Global Issue*. The Hague: Martinus Nijhoff.

Lepschy, A. L. and Lepschy, G. (1981). *La lingua italiana*. Milan: Bompiani.

Liberman, I. Y. (1973). Segmentation of the spoken word and reading acquisition. *Bulletin of the Orton Society*, 23, 65–77.

Maraschio, N. (1993). Grafia e ortografia: evoluzione e codificazione. In L. Serianni and P. Trifone (eds.), *Storia della lingua italiana* (vol. I, pp. 139–227). Turin: Giulio Einaudi Editore.

Marshall, J. C. and Cossu, G. (1987). Segmental analysis: modular representations and processes. *Cahiers de Psychologie Cognitive*, 7, 482–7.

Marshall, J. C. and Newcombe, F. (1973). Patterns of paralexia: a psycholinguistic approach. *Journal of Psycholinguistic Research*, 2, 175–99.

Montessori, M. (1909). *Il metodo della pedagogia scientifica applicato all'educazione infantile nelle case dei bambini*. Rome: Bretschneider.

Morais, J. and Kolinsky, R. (1995). The consequences of phonemic awareness. In B. de Gelder and J. Morais (eds.), *Speech and Reading. A Comparative Approach* (pp. 317–33). Hove: Erlbaum.

Morchio, B. (1989). Esistono disgrafie correlate a dislessia in età evolutiva? *Età evolutiva*, 32, 16–28.

Patterson, K. E. and Morton, J. (1985). From orthography to phonology: an attempt at an old interpretation. In K. E. Patterson, J. C. Marshall and M. Coltheart (eds.), *Surface Dyslexia* (pp. 335–59). London: Lawrence Erlbaum Associates.

Pinker, S. (1994). *The Language Instinct*. London: Allen Lane.

Pontecorvo, C. and Pontecorvo, M. (1986). *Psicologia dell'educazione*. Bologna: Il Mulino.

Read, C. (1971). Pre-school children's knowledge of English phonology. *Harvard Educational Review*, 41, 1–34.

Read, C. (1986). *Children's Creative Spelling*. London: Routledge and Kegan Paul.

Sartori, G. and Job, R. (1982). Phonological impairment in Italian: acquired and developmental dyslexia. In D. R. Rogers and J. A. Sloboda (eds.), *The Acquisition of Symbolic Skills* (pp. 123–30). New York: Plenum Press.

Sartori, G., Job, R. and Tressoldi, P. E. (1995). *Batteria per la valutazione della dislessia e della disortografia evolutiva*. Florence: Organizzazioni Speciali.

Seymour, P. H. K. and Evans, H. M. (1993). The visual (orthographic) processor and developmental dyslexia. In D. M. Willows, R. S. Kruk and E. Corcos (eds.), *Visual Processes in Reading and Reading Disabilities* (pp. 347–76). Hillsdale: Lawrence Erlbaum Associates.

Tressoldi, P. E. (1989). Lo sviluppo della lettura e della scrittura: segmentazione e fusione fonemica. *Età evolutiva*, 33, 53–8.

Vagges, K., Ferrero, E. F., Magno-Caldognetto, E. and Lavagnoli, C. (1978). Some acoustic characteristics of Italian consonants. *Journal of Italian Linguistics*, 3, 69–85.

Waters, G. S., Bruck, M. and Seidenberg, M. (1985). Do children use similar processes to read and spell words? *Journal of Experimental Child Psychology*, 39, 511–30.

Wimmer, H. (1993). Characteristics of developmental dyslexia in a regular writing system. *Applied Psycholinguistics*, 14, 1–33.

Zucchermaglio, C. (1991). *Gli apprendisti della lingua scritta*. Bologna: Il Mulino.

3   Learning to read German: normal and impaired acquisition

Heinz Wimmer, Karin Landerl and Uta Frith

Phonological coding, that is, the systematic translation of graphemes and grapheme strings into a phonological code, is one of the central processes in reading. Because of its importance it was called the bottle-neck (Stanovich, 1986) and the *sine qua non* (Share, 1995) of reading acquisition. This process was postulated as a major step in developmental models of reading acquisition (Frith, 1985; Jorm and Share, 1983). The acquisition of phonological coding in word recognition – termed the 'alphabetic stage' in Frith's model – allows the child to use grapheme–phoneme correspondences in a systematic way to read the many words which are encountered for the first time in print by the child. The ability to tackle new words is critical for further reading development, because it functions as a self-teaching device for building up memory representations (i.e. word recognition units) for word spellings. The assumption here is that words which are successfully decoded by the young reader will eventually be stored in the orthographic lexicon. Thus, this remarkable cognitive ability is a vital prerequisite for becoming a skilled reader or, in Frith's (1985) terminology, one who uses an orthographic strategy for reading.

Empirical research has provided convincing evidence that it is precisely this process of phonological coding which is deficient in dyslexic readers. One of the main diagnostic indicators of the impaired phonological coding component of word recognition in dyslexic individuals is a specific difficulty with the reading of non-words. They often fail to pronounce them accurately. Clearly, non-word reading depends on phonological coding to a greater extent than word reading. A review by Rack, Snowling and Olson (1992) brings together the surprisingly consistent research in this field and underlines the importance of non-word reading as a diagnostic tool.

The main limitation of psychological research on reading development and dyslexia is its focus on English orthography. This is a serious limitation, since English differs from other alphabetic orthographies in terms of its atypically low grapheme–phoneme consistency (Venezky, 1970). It seems obvious that acquisition and execution of phonological coding is much more demanding for an orthography with exceptionally low grapheme–phoneme consistency than for more typical orthographies with consistent grapheme–phoneme correspondences. To illustrate, any phonological coding mechanism must run into difficulties when confronted with inconsistencies such as *hear, bear, heard* and *beard*. One could then further hypothesise that children with a phonological language impairment may have relatively less difficulty in acquiring phonological coding for a transparent orthography. It therefore needs to be established whether the phonological deficit account of dyslexia is specific to English and whether it applies to children who have difficulties in learning to read and spell in a language with a consistent orthography, i.e. German. Clearly, the different phonological structures inherent in German and English may also influence the nature of the phonological impairment, but this is a matter for future research. In the following we will examine some of these issues by first presenting evidence on how German children acquire phonological coding in reading development. We will then address the question of whether German and English dyslexic children exhibit a similar phonological coding impairment.

Orthography and reading instruction

German orthography, like English orthography, tends to represent the morpho-phonemic level of language, but does so more consistently than English. To illustrate, in the German words Hand, Ball, Garten, and Katze the grapheme *a* is always pronounced the same way, while in the corresponding English words hand, ball, garden and cat the pronunciations differ. The umlaut signs of German contribute to consistency. Besides broadening the orthographic means for vowel representation, they allow the preservation of morpheme identity and mark changes in the vowel associated with morphological processes such as pluralisation (e.g. *Hand – Hände*). The main complexity of vowel representation in German has to do with length. For example, there is more than one orthographic device for explicitly marking that a vowel is long: the doubling of the vowel grapheme (e.g. *Boot, Aal*), the silent h after the vowel grapheme (e.g. *Bohne, Bahn*) and the long i (e.g. *Biene, viel*). It should be noted that such complexities have more effect on spelling than on reading. For example, there are usually several ways of spelling long vowels, e.g., *Lied* (English: song) vs. *Lid* (English: lid), both pronounced /li:d/. But although the phoneme–grapheme correspondence for /i:/ is inconsistent, the grapheme–phoneme correspondences of both spellings are entirely consistent. Even if orthographic markings of vowel length are neglected in phonological coding, there is still enough information for correct word recognition. A description of German orthography is provided by Eisenberg (1988). English orthography has been analysed by, amongst others, Albrow (1972).

Initial reading instruction for the German children who participated in our studies makes use of the consistency of German orthography by relying on a slowly advancing phonics programme in the first year of school. In kindergarten there is no reading preparation at all. Critical features of the phonics programme are as follows: the main grapheme–phoneme correspondences – including all multi-letter graphemes (e.g. *sch, ch, ck, au, eu, ei, ie*) – are directly presented and immediately used for word recognition. There is also direct modelling and training on how to recognise words via grapheme–phoneme translation and blending. This training starts with words like *Mimi* and *Mama*, for which blending is easy to demonstrate and to practise, and uses graphical devices to mark syllable boundaries. In the beginning, the blending ritual results in word preforms, which characteristically have artificially lengthened phonemes and incorrect stress assignments. However, due to the consistency of German orthography, these preforms are usually close enough to the target pronunciation to allow recognition. A reasonable expectation is that this combination of an 'easy' orthography and a systematic phonics teaching approach makes the acquisition of phonological coding in word recognition relatively easy for German children. In contrast, English children are exposed to more eclectic methods, combining memory for stories and whole-word recognition as well as basic letter-sound instruction. This approach may well have evolved as an adaptation to the vagaries of English orthography. In everyday life young children are frequently exposed to irregular and/or inconsistent words (e.g. *laugh, bread, shoes*). Thus, practising regular letter-sound patterns will not always reinforce children's attempts to decode and to learn unfamiliar words encountered in their reading books.

The acquisition of phonological coding in young German and English readers

Here we will report the main results of two studies which compared word and non-word reading in young German and English readers. A first study by Wimmer and Goswami (1994) examined how seven-, eight-, and nine-year-old English and Austrian children read number words and analogous non-words. (As the Austrian children were learning

Table 3.1 *Mean percentages read correctly by English and German children (normal readers).*

		English		German	
		7 years	9 years	7 years	9 years
Wimmer and Goswami 1994					
Number words	'ten'	96	100	99	100
Non-words	'sen'	66	76	87	91
Frith, Wimmer and Landerl 1998					
Words	'hand'	69	94	92	100
Non-words	'nand'	47	79	85	96

to read in German, they are referred to as German children throughout this chapter for ease of exposition.) Number words between two and twelve were used because these words have similar pronunciation and spelling in the two orthographies (e.g. *two – zwei, nine – neun*). Non-words were derived from the number words by exchanging the graphemes that denote the consonantal onsets (e.g. *sen* was created from *seven* and *ten*). For this reason, *one, eight* and *eleven* had to be omitted. Therefore, the non-words in both orthographies consisted of the very same letters and letter clusters (for word onsets and word rhymes) as the words. Because of the latter feature (preservation of onset and rhyme clusters), reading these non-words could be based on analogies to the number words and gives a conservative estimate of any difficulties of phonological coding. The reading task was simply to read aloud lists of number words or non-words, each list consisting of thirty-six items. Reading time and accuracy were measured.

A further German–English reading comparison study (Frith, Wimmer and Landerl, 1998) extended the first study by using a different and enlarged list of words and non-words. The task format (reading aloud a list of items) was the same as in the Wimmer and Goswami study. Again, only words with identical meaning and similar pronunciation and spelling in the two languages were chosen (e.g. *hand – Hand, word – Wort, green – grün*). Again the non-words were derived from the word stimuli by exchanging the consonantal word-onset graphemes. The results of these studies are presented in table 3.1 which shows the mean percentage correct for word and non-word reading. For each study, only the results for the youngest and the oldest age groups are shown in order to illustrate the developmental trend.

German–English differences in word and non-word reading

The main finding evident from table 3.1 is that young German readers had little difficulty with phonological coding compared to their English counterparts who had begun school one year earlier and thus had had about one year more reading instruction. After only one year of reading instruction they read non-words – the relevant measure for phonological coding – with relatively high accuracy. In contrast, the young English readers experienced a certain amount of difficulty with phonological coding. This difficulty was observed for the non-words derived from the number words, where about a third of the readings were incorrect, and even more so for the non-words derived from the words, where slightly more than half of the readings were unacceptable. The first finding is particularly astonishing. Clearly, the English children had little difficulty in reading the number words from which the non-words were derived, and, since only nine different word and non-word items were used, it should have been easy to base non-word reading on analogies with the number words.

A striking observation from table 3.1 is that the youngest group of German readers, with about one year of schooling, tended to commit fewer errors on non-words derived from words than the oldest group of English readers, with about four years of schooling. English children showed not only impaired reading accuracy for non-words, but also enormously impaired reading speed on the lists of non-words. An important further observation was that English children differed markedly from each other (and to a much greater extent than German children) in their ability to read non-words. Quite a number of the youngest English readers had no difficulty in producing acceptable non-word readings at fast speed, while some children in this group were hardly able to produce any correct response at all.

When interpreting the poor non-word reading of the English children it is important to note that reading refusals occurred very rarely and that the scoring of their reading was very liberal. In fact, any pronunciation was accepted as long as existing grapheme–phoneme correspondences were observed. For example, in the case of *theart* (analogous to *heart*), four different readings were obtained. Taking into account only the pronunciation of the vowel: the *ea* corresponded to *heard* eight times, to *heart* four times and to *hear* and *bear* twice each. All four pronunciations were counted as correct. Of course, no such liberal scoring was used for children's reading of real words. For example, the eight readings of *heart* as 'hurt' were counted as incorrect. Inspection of errors showed that the errors of the German children tended to be closer to the grapheme sequence than the errors of the English children. For example, erroneous responses of the German children to the non-word *glinken* were 'blinken', 'lingen', 'gliken' and 'glink'. In all these errors the grapheme sequence was preserved, and the main problem was that graphemes were omitted (e.g. in 'glink'), or that wrong grapheme–phoneme rules were applied or that a grapheme was visually misidentified (e.g. b for g). Among the errors of the English children more instances occurred where the grapheme sequence was not observed and where phonemes were added. Examples for sequence deviations in the case of the non-word *glink* were 'gelk', 'gilk' and 'garlic', where the /l/ of the onset cluster /gl-/ was moved towards the end of the syllable. Examples of additions were 'grink', 'groos' and 'grikin' where a wrong phoneme appeared in the initial cluster.

Some conclusions about normal acquisition

The main conclusion from these findings for young German readers is that phonological coding in word recognition poses little difficulty. Apparently the combination of an easy, consistent orthography and a phonics approach to initial reading instruction means that, after only a relatively short time, children are able to assemble quite reliably pronunciations for any pronounceable letter pattern. The ease with which the German children mastered phonological coding stands in marked contrast to the difficulty posed by phonological coding for many of the English children. These orthography-related differences in the acquisition of phonological coding skills were found for children who were not selected for exhibiting specific reading difficulties. The next section will examine whether similar differences in the ease or difficulty of phonological coding exist between German and English dyslexic children.

Phonological coding in German and English dyslexic children

Here, some findings of a study (Landerl, Wimmer and Frith, 1997) will be presented which compared the reading and phonological processing abilities of eighteen German and eighteen English dyslexic children (mostly boys) with a mean age of twelve years (English: $M = 12;3$, range: 10;9–13;11; German: $M = 11;7$, range: 10;7–12;7). Most of the English dyslexic children were recruited from a special school for dyslexic children. The German dyslexic children came from two

Table 3.2   *Mean error percentage read correctly by English and German dyslexic children (aged twelve years).*

		English children	German children
Number words	'ten'	99	100
Non-words	'sen'	55	82
Frequent short words	'milk'	81	97
Non-words	'bilk'	42	92
Infrequent long words	'paradise'	48	89
Non-words	'posidise'	27	77

longitudinal studies and were diagnosed at least twice as showing specific reading and spelling difficulties before participating in our study. Both the English and the German dyslexic subjects read at the level of eight- to nine-year-old children. Their mean percentiles on a standardised test of word recognition (English: BAS word recognition test, Elliot, Murray and Pearson, 1983; German: Salzburger Lese- und Rechtschreibtest, Landerl, Wimmer and Moser, 1997)[1] were eight for the English and twelve for the German children while their non-verbal intelligence (measured by Raven's Standard Progressive Matrices – Raven, 1987) was average.

One of the tasks used was the number word–non-word reading task of Wimmer and Goswami (1994). Furthermore, a word–non-word single-item reading task was constructed, where item length (one, two and three syllables) and frequency (within the one- and two-syllable words) varied. In this latter task, again, words with identical meaning and similar spelling and pronunciation in the two orthographies were used. Again, for the one- and two-syllable words analogous non-words were derived by exchanging the consonantal onset graphemes. Examples of the word items were *milk – Milch, butter – Butter*; examples of analogous non-word items were *bilk – Bilch, sutter – Sutter*. The three-syllable non-words were created by reassembling the syllables of the three-syllable words with the constraint that the position of the syllable in the word was preserved in the non-word. Examples of three-syllable words were *radio – Radio, paradise – Paradies*; examples of non-words are *inlio – Inlio* and *posidise – posidies*. The scoring of the non-word readings of the English children was again done liberally.

Table 3.2 shows the mean percentages of correct readings for the number word–non-word task and for the word–non-word task (i.e. one- or two-syllable words and corresponding non-words, and three-syllable words as well as their corresponding non-words).

One interesting observation from table 3.2 is that, on the number word–non-word task, the dyslexic children from both orthography groups performed at a similar level to the normally learning children at the age of about seven years (as shown in table 3.1). That is, the number words were read nearly perfectly by both the English and the German dyslexic children, while the analogous non-words were read quite accurately by the German, but not by the English dyslexic children. The difficulty of non-word reading for the English dyslexic children was also confirmed by a mean reading time of 2.6 seconds per item for the non-word list compared to 1.6 seconds per item for the German dyslexic children.

The word–non-word task offered additional observations. One is that the non-word reading difficulty reached dramatic dimensions for the English dyslexic children in the case of the three-syllable non-words where the large majority of the items were read incorrectly and where the mean reading time for the correctly read items was 5.6 seconds. Another finding was that the reading accuracy of the English dyslexic children was strongly influenced by word frequency: accuracy dropped from the number words to the frequent one- and two-syllable words and decreased further for the long and rather infrequent words. In contrast, German dyslexic children tended to read even the infrequent three-syllable words quite accurately. They also mastered the vast majority of corresponding non-words.

The comparison of reading errors between German and English dyslexic children shows that the few errors of the German dyslexic children tended to follow the grapheme sequence, while a substantial number of the errors of the English dyslexic children did not do so. For the simple German non-word *bilch* (analogous to *Milch*) the only error was 'bich' with one grapheme omitted, while for the corresponding English non-word *bilk* (milk) readings were 'blink' (eight times), 'blank' and 'brink'. In each of these errors at least two deviations from the grapheme sequence occurred in that the initial simple consonantal onset /b/ was always replaced by a cluster with one phoneme added and the final cluster '-lk' was always replaced by '-nk'. For the three-syllable non-word *posidise* the English children produced twelve errors, typical examples being 'posdens', 'posdis', 'proisid' and 'prodisise', while the two German errors to the corresponding non-word *posidies* were 'positivs' and 'prosidies'. For *paradise*, English children also were often far off the target with readings such as 'pardon', 'proudest', 'president', 'paper-disc', 'pard', 'pepikel', 'predi' and 'partees'. In contrast, the only error of the German children to *Paradies* was /par'adi:s/ with all phonemes correct, but with wrong stress assignment on the second syllable.

Different organisation of phonological recoding in English and German

The most striking difference between the German and the English dyslexic children – and also between the young German and English children – emerged in the error rates for rare words and for non-words, which require phonological coding. The high error rates in English and also the kind of errors made suggest not just a quantitative but a qualitative difference in phonological coding processes: the process of phonological coding itself may be organised differently for German and English children. This different organisation of phonological coding may be triggered by the key orthographic feature distinguishing German and English orthography, namely the difference in the consistency of grapheme–phoneme relations for vowels. Treiman, Mullennix, Bijeljac-Babic and Richmond-Welty (1995) have demonstrated that, in English monosyllabic CVC words which share the same vowel grapheme, the vowel pronunciation will be consistent in only about 60 per cent of cases. We hypothesise that the high consistency of the German grapheme–phoneme relations for single vowels allows for the immediate on-line assembly of syllables. Therefore, problems of working memory for unconnected phonemes as well as misleading intrusion from the phonological word lexicon are less likely. For example, for the low-frequency word *Biber*, the reader might produce "/bi/-/bib/-/bi-be/-/bi-ber/". Notice that this on-line phonological recoding process involves a re-syllabification from incorrect /bib/ to the correct syllable /bi/. However, the transcoded phonemes are always included in syllables, and no sequence of isolated phonemes has to be retained in working memory. Furthermore, the number of syllables is usually small, again reducing working memory load. No such immediate on-line assembly of syllables can be assumed for English.

In a study with skilled English readers, Berent and Perfetti (1995) provided evidence for a two-cycles model of phonology assembly, where in a first, fast and automatic cycle a consonant grid is obtained, while in a second, slower and resource-demanding cycle the vowels are inserted. Thus, for the word *beaver*, the first cycle would provide the consonant grid /b?v?r/, and the second cycle would include the vowels. Specification of the first vowel may pose a problem because *ea* is related to more than one vowel sound. One possibility is to go through all possible grapheme–phoneme relations for *ea*. An alternative would be to search the phonological word lexicon with the phoneme sequence /b?ver/. Both of these options are prone to error, for which we propose three major sources. First, an inappropriate grapheme–phoneme relation for the vowel may be selected. For example, the majority of the English dyslexic children read *sweat* as 'sweet'. Overall, in 19 per cent of the readings of the English word stimuli, that is in 61 per cent of the incorrect responses, the vowel sound was wrong. Second, Berent and Perfetti's (1995) two-cycles model requires unconnected consonants to be retained in the correct order in working memory, while a correct vowel is selected. The reading speed of the English dyslexic children (four seconds for the three-syllable words and about six seconds for the three-syllable non-words) provides a striking demonstration of the memory demands involved. Loss of phoneme or order information from working memory may be the main reason why the responses of the English dyslexic children frequently deviated from the given grapheme sequence. Working memory overload may also explain why the three-syllable non-words appeared to cause a complete breakdown in performance for most of the English dyslexic children. A third error source is that search of the phonological word lexicon for specification of the vowel may cause the consonant information in working memory to be overwritten. For example, if the word *flesh* is presented, the first cycle may correctly translate the consonant grid /fl?ʃ/. Instead of processing through the second, slower and more resource demanding vowel cycle, the mental lexicon could be searched for words containing this consonant grid. This lexical search could also result in the wrongly activated word 'fresh' whose consonant grid is similar, but not identical. In this case, the consonantal onset cluster resulting from the first cycle of phonological coding would be overwritten by the information of the lexical search. This would go some way towards explaining why a high number of errors contained consonant intrusions, such as 'brush' or 'blush' for *bush*.

Obviously, these error sources will operate for both the normal and the dyslexic English readers. However, there are additional and plausible reasons why the difficulties inherent in the two-cycle process may be even greater for English dyslexic children than for normal readers. There is ample evidence for a working memory limitation in dyslexic children (reviews by Brady, 1991; Pennington, Van Orden, Kirson and Haith, 1991). One interpretation of the working memory deficit in dyslexic children is that the rate at which phonological items in working memory can be refreshed is slower (McDougall and Hulme, 1994). Consistent with the idea of a slower refreshment rate is the further assumption that grapheme–phoneme coding processes are slower for dyslexic than for normal readers. Findings from the letter name matching paradigm (Ellis, 1981) and the letter naming paradigm (Denckla and Rudel, 1976) support this assumption. We note that working memory limitations and slower grapheme coding processes may also hold for the German dyslexic children. However, for them – in contrast to the English children – the effect on reading accuracy is less marked, because the orthographic system serves as a protective factor. Thus, on-line assembly of syllables, made possible by the consistent grapheme–phoneme relations for vowels, prevents the loss of phonemic information from working memory and simultaneously ensures that phonology assembly is less dependent on the phonological lexicon. Thus, the opportunities to overwrite material in working memory with wrongly activated words or parts of words are minimised.

Phonological impairment in dyslexia: general or language specific?

The comparison of German and English dyslexic children gives rise to a conclusion that is similar to that emerging from the comparison of young German and English normal readers. Again, the difficulty of phonological coding was confirmed for English children. The German dyslexic children showed much less evidence of such a difficulty. Indeed we found that the groups contrasted quite markedly on the reading tests we used. This finding is certainly in line with the initially raised doubts on the generality of the phonological deficit conception of dyslexia, which is based on findings from English dyslexic children. However, it would be wrong to conclude that the phonological impairment account does not apply to German dyslexic children.

This conclusion would be based on the erroneous assumption that poor reading, or rather, poor non-word reading, is the only possible manifestation of a phonological coding impairment. Phonological coding impairments will manifest themselves in speech-related tasks too, and there is evidence that in such tasks the contrast between German and English dyslexics is less marked. Landerl *et al.* (1997) presented German and English dyslexic children with a Spoonerism task consisting of ten items for which the consonantal onsets of two orally presented words had to be exchanged (e.g. *man – hat → han – mat*). The performance of the two dyslexia groups was compared with that of children of a similar age (English: mean age = 12;7, range: 11;6–14;0; German: mean age = 11;7, range = 10;4–13;2) as well as with groups of children of similar reading levels (English: mean age = 8;3, range: 7;4–9;1; German: mean age = 8;8, range: 7;4–9;5). Table 3.3 shows the mean error percentages for the two dyslexia groups and the control groups.

It is evident that the two dyslexia groups do not differ from each other, while they both show a reliably worse performance than the

Table 3.3 *Percentage of correct responses on the Spoonerism task for German and English dyslexic, age-level control and reading-level control children (standard deviations in parentheses).*

German children			English children		
Dyslexics	Reading-level controls	Age-level controls	Dyslexics	Reading-level controls	Age-level controls
63.3	42.9	31.7	72.9	64.5	39.5
(23.3)	(23.4)	(22.6)	(22.0)	(21.9)	(20.9)

corresponding age-level controls. The German dyslexics' performance is even reliably worse than that of the German reading-level control children. Thus, it is obvious that German as well as English dyslexic children suffer from a deficit in phonological processing. However, this deficit does not manifest itself in erroneous non-word reading since grapheme–phoneme coding is comparably simple in German. The manifestation of a phonological deficit may be different. Indeed, there are now several converging findings suggesting that German dyslexic children exhibit a specific speed deficit in phonological coding.

Evidence for a specific speed deficit of phonological coding among German dyslexic children

There were indications for such a speed deficit in the Landerl *et al.* (1997) study. For example, the twelve-year-old German dyslexic children were found to read the non-words derived from the number words more slowly than the nine-year-olds of the reading-level-matched control group, and a similar – but not always reliable – tendency was found for several non-word categories of the word–non-word task. In a study of reading impairments and cognitive deficits among German dyslexic children at grade levels 2, 3 and 4, Wimmer (1993) found that these children suffered from a pervasive speed deficit for all types of reading tasks, including text, high-frequency words and non-words. This speed deficit – particularly the one for non-words – points to an impairment in phonological coding. Another main finding, also suggesting a deficit in speed of access to phonological codes, was that the dyslexic children scored lower than reading-level control children on rapid naming tasks and that numeral-naming speed turned out to be the most important predictor of reading speed differences. In contrast, the performance of the dyslexic children on a phoneme substitution task (e.g. 'Hans' →

Table 3.4   *Mean reading time per item and mean error percentages of German dyslexic and reading-level-matched control children.*

Reading measures	Dyslexic children	Reading-level controls
Time/word (in seconds)		
Frequent words *M* (SD)	0.98 (0.20)	0.98 (0.21)
Analogous non-words *M* (SD)	1.99 (0.56)	1.7 (0.41)
'Japanese' non-words *M* (SD)	2.84 (0.68)	2.4 (0.58)
Errors		
Frequent words	4	3
Analogous non-words	9	5
'Japanese' non-words	16	9

'Hins') was high in absolute terms and they had hardly any problems in spelling words phonologically correct, that is to represent all the sounds of a spoken word by an acceptable grapheme (e.g. the incorrect spelling *schwimt* for *schwimmt* represents all sounds of the spoken word).

A follow-up study by Wimmer (1996b) tried to establish that the speed deficit of German dyslexic children for non-word reading systematically exceeds their speed deficit for word reading. This is important for theoretical reasons, since non-word reading involves phonological coding to a greater extent than word reading. In this study the grade 4 dyslexic children were carefully matched on a one-to-one basis with grade 2 normal readers on reading speed for frequent short words. Then reading speed was assessed for analogous non-words derived from the frequent short words by the usual procedure of changing consonantal onsets between the words. In addition, the 'Japanese' non-words of Wimmer (1993) were also used. These non-words have little similarity to German words and consist of two or three simple syllables without any consonant cluster. Examples are *toki, filuno,* and *torukim.* Table 3.4 shows the mean reading time per item and mean error percentages for the two types of non-words.

From table 3.4 it is evident that dyslexic grade 4 children – although reading the frequent words at exactly the same speed as the grade 2 normal children – were slower at reading analogous non-words and the 'Japanese' non-words than the control group. The difference in reading time between the two groups was reliable for both types of non-words. In addition, it is evident that the slower reading time of the dyslexic children was also accompanied by more errors. A further interesting finding was that on a visual matching task – instances of a given Chinese target logogram had to be detected in a long series of similar logograms – the dyslexic children performed as fast and accurately as age-matched control children. This rules out the possibility that the dyslexic children may have suffered from a general processing speed deficit.

Preliminary conclusions from German–English comparisons

One main conclusion from the German–English reading comparison studies is that differences in grapheme–phoneme consistency (and/or differences in language phonology) influence reading development in a profound way. We found that the acquisition of phonological coding in word recognition was much easier for German than for English children. This conclusion is based on the findings which showed that German children in the early phase of learning to read have much less difficulty in reading than their English counterparts. We also found that phonological coding in word recognition was much less of a hurdle for the German dyslexic children. Given the importance of phonological coding for further reading development, it follows that the risk of serious arrest in reading development is smaller for children who are learning to read a consistent orthography. The different levels of consistency in German and English apparently also affect the organisation of phonological coding. The differences in reading errors both between young German and English readers and between dyslexic German and English readers, suggested that German children rely on simple on-line phonological coding while English children have to acquire a complex process of phonological coding which is possibly organised in two cycles.

The second conclusion from the findings presented has to do with the manifestation and causation of dyslexia in German and English children. The main difference in manifestation was that German dyslexic children showed accurate, if slow, non-word reading. In contrast, the English dyslexic children, in agreement with several other studies (review by Rack *et al.*, 1992), were found to exhibit high percentages of non-word reading errors (as well as being slow). Accurate non-word reading was documented previously by Wimmer (1993) for dyslexic German children from the end of grade 2 onwards. However, we cannot conclude that German dyslexics never have more than a problem in the speed of decoding. Wimmer (1996a) found that in the very early phases of learning to read, German children who later exhibited persistent reading difficulties did have problems with accurate phonological coding in word recognition. Thus, the difference seems to be that most German dyslexic children can quickly overcome their difficulties with accurate phonological coding, while most English dyslexic children show their difficulties more glaringly and for much longer.

German dyslexic children appear not to be able to overcome their reading speed deficit. Their slowness in reading is such that they are very considerably handicapped, especially with longer texts. Given that this slowness was specific to non-word reading and was not shown in a visual matching task, we concluded that the reason for the slowness is a persistent impairment in the efficiency of phonological coding in word recognition. This finding is highly important for theories of dyslexia; it shows that the very same reading mechanism – namely phonological coding in word recognition – is affected in both English and German dyslexic children. We therefore suggest that the cause of dyslexia is the same – but that the manifestation is different. In English dyslexic children the faulty mechanism manifests itself most strikingly in lower accuracy, whereas for German dyslexic children the faulty mechanism manifests itself most strikingly in slow speed. The excruciating slowness of the phonological coding mechanism among the German dyslexic children in fact constitutes strong evidence for the phonological deficit account of dyslexia. It is complemented by anecdotal findings with adult English dyslexics who (with remedial education) have learned to read non-words with high accuracy, but continue to do so very slowly.

The German children we studied were learning to read an easy (i.e. consistent) orthography and experienced a strict phonics teaching approach, which directly introduced them to phonological coding in word recognition. The expectation was that such a combination of orthography and instruction would give even phonologically impaired children a good chance of acquiring phonological coding skills successfully. With respect to a basic coding competence this actually seems to be the case. Nevertheless, despite this advantage, speed of phonological coding in word recognition remained persistently impaired. This persistent speed impairment is consistent with findings suggesting a biological hardware problem in the language areas of the brain as the ultimate cause of developmental dyslexia. Of course, finding such a biologically based impairment should not discourage investigators from searching for educational means of alleviating and circumventing the problem, whatever the language and whatever the orthography.

NOTES

The research reported in this paper was supported by a grant from the Austrian Science Foundation to Heinz Wimmer and a grant from the Austrian Ministry of Science to Karin Landerl.

1 It should be noted that the English word reading test is a test of reading accuracy while the German test mainly assesses reading speed, since reading accuracy is usually high, even among poor readers.

REFERENCES

Albrow, K. H. (1972). *The English Writing System: Notes Toward a Description.* London: Longman.
Berent, I. and Perfetti, C. A. (1995). A rose is a REEZ: the two-cycles model of phonology assembly in reading English. *Psychological Review*, 102, 146–84.
Brady, S. A. (1991). The role of working memory in reading disability. In S. A. Brady and D. P. Shankweiler (eds.), *Phonological Processes in Literacy* (pp. 129–52). Hillsdale, NJ: Erlbaum.
Denckla, M. B. and Rudel, R. (1976). Rapid automatized naming (RAN): dyslexia differentiated from other learning disabilities. *Neuropsychologia*, 14, 471–9.
Eisenberg, P. (1988). Die Grapheme des Deutschen und ihre Beziehung zu den Phonemen [The German graphemes and their relationship to the phonemes]. *Germanistische Linguistik*, 93/94, 139–54.
Elliot, C. D., Murray, D. J. and Pearson, L. S. (1983). *British Ability Scales: Word Reading.* Windsor: NFER-Nelson.
Ellis, N. (1981). Visual and name coding in dyslexic children. *Psychological Research*, 43, 201–18.
Frith, U. (1985). Beneath the surface of developmental dyslexia. In K. Patterson, J. Marshall and M. Coltheart (eds.), *Surface Dyslexia* (pp. 301–30). Hillsdale, NJ: Erlbaum.
Frith, U., Wimmer, H. and Landerl, K. (1998). Differences in phonological recoding in German- and English-speaking children. *Scientific Studies of Reading*, 2, 31–54.
Jorm, A. F. and Share, D. L. (1983). Phonological recoding and reading acquisition. *Applied Psycholinguistics*, 4, 103–47.
Landerl, K., Wimmer, H. and Frith, U. (1997). The impact of orthographic consistency on dyslexia: a German–English comparison. *Cognition*, 63, 315–34.
Landerl, K., Wimmer, H. and Moser, E. (1997). *Salzburger Lese- und Rechtschreibtest* [Salzburg reading and spelling test]. Bern: Huber.
McDougall, S. and Hulme, C. (1994). Short-term memory, speech rate and phonological awareness as predictors of learning to read. In C. Hulme and M. Snowling (eds.), *Reading Development and Dyslexia* (pp. 31–44). London: Whurr Publishers.
Pennington, B. F., Van Orden, G., Kirson, D. and Haith, M. (1991). What is the causal relation between verbal STM problems and dyslexia? In S. A. Brady and D. P. Shankweiler (eds.), *Phonological Processes in Literacy* (pp. 173–86). Hillsdale, NJ: Erlbaum.
Rack, J. P., Snowling, M. J. and Olson R. (1992). The nonword reading deficit in developmental dyslexia: a review. *Reading Research Quarterly*, 27, 29–53.
Raven, J. C. (1987). *Manual for Raven's Progressive Matrices and Vocabulary Scales, Section 3. Standard Progressive Matrices.* London: H. K. Lewis.

Share, D. L. (1995). Phonological recoding and self-teaching: sine qua non of reading acquisition. *Cognition*, 55, 151–218.

Stanovich, K. E. (1986). Matthew effects in reading: some consequences of individual differences in the acquisition of literacy. *Reading Research Quarterly*, 19, 278–301.

Treiman, R., Mullennix, J., Bijeljac-Babic, R. and Richmond-Welty, E. D. (1995). The special role of rimes in the description, use, and acquisition of English orthography. *Journal of Experimental Psychology: General*, 124, 107–36.

Venezky, R. L. (1970). *The Structure of English Orthography.* The Hague: Mouton.

Wimmer, H. (1993). Characteristics of developmental dyslexia in a regular writing system. *Applied Psycholinguistics*, 14, 1–33.

(1996a). The early manifestation of developmental dyslexia: evidence from German children. *Reading and Writing.* 8, 171–88.

(1996b). The nonword reading deficit in developmental dyslexia: evidence from German children. *Journal of Experimental Child Psychology*, 61, 80–90.

Wimmer, H. and Goswami, U. (1994). The influence of orthographic consistency on reading development: word recognition in English and German children. *Cognition*, 51, 51–103.

4 Learning to read and spell in Greek: the importance of letter knowledge and morphological awareness

Margaret Harris and Vicky Giannouli

Introduction

The last two decades of research in learning to read have firmly established that phonological awareness plays an important role. Many researchers (e.g. Bradley and Bryant, 1983; Fox and Routh, 1984; Marcel, 1980; Snowling, 1981; Montgomery, 1981; Read, 1985; Liberman, Rubin, Duques and Carlisle, 1985; Morais, Bertelson, Cary and Alegria, 1986; Snowling, Goulandris, Bowlby and Howell, 1986) have argued that phonological awareness is a precursor of reading achievement. At the same time, other authors (e.g. Ehri and Wilce, 1987; Mann and Liberman, 1984; Stanovich, Cunningham and Cramer, 1984; Bradley and Bryant, 1985; Wagner and Torgesen, 1987) have argued that phonological awareness develops as a direct consequence of learning to read.

Although these two views may appear contradictory, more recent research has suggested that both claims are compatible with the view that the strength – and direction – of the relationship between phonological awareness and reading success is dependent on the level of phonological awareness under consideration. One important distinction can be drawn between *implicit phonological awareness,* which is the ability to analyse words into their constituent sounds at the level of the syllable or sub-syllabic unit, and *explicit phonological awareness* or *phonemic awareness* which is the ability to detect and manipulate phonemes within words. Implicit phonological awareness develops before children start school and does not require any knowledge of reading or, indeed, any exposure to print. Phonemic awareness, by contrast, develops as children learn to read.

The relationship between these two kinds of phonological awareness has now been studied for several European languages as well as English (including German, Italian, Spanish and Scandinavian languages). Many of these studies are described elsewhere in this volume (see the chapters

51

by Cossu, Lundberg, Rego, and Wimmer, Landerl and Frith). The common finding has been that phonemic awareness is not only positively correlated with children's subsequent reading and spelling achievement but it also plays a central role in learning to read. Despite qualitative differences in learning to read alphabetic scripts with differing levels of orthographic regularity, after IQ, phonemic awareness tends to be a strong – if not the strongest – predictor of children's reading age. In other words, developing phonemic awareness goes hand in hand with developing expertise in reading an alphabetic script. This is because the ability to segment and manipulate phonemes is one essential component in the development of good grapheme–phoneme correspondence skills which are required when children read using an alphabetic strategy and convert letters to sounds.

In contrast to phonemic awareness, the relationship of implicit phonological awareness to reading progress varies with the degree of orthographic regularity. For orthographically irregular languages, implicit phonological awareness predicts early reading success, as pioneering studies in England and Sweden have revealed (Bradley and Bryant, 1983; Lundberg, Frost and Petersen, 1988; Hoien and Lundberg, 1988; Stuart and Coltheart, 1988). However, a different picture emerges with more regular languages. Wimmer, Landerl and Schneider (1994) found that, in the case of German, performance on a rhyme judgement task predicted only later success in reading and spelling rather than early success. Wimmer *et al.* argue that implicit phonological awareness is not predictive of early success in learning to read a regular orthography because children are able to develop an alphabetic reading strategy very rapidly; and this reading strategy is related to the development of phonemic awareness rather than to rhyme awareness. They argue that this contrasts with irregular orthographies where early reading makes greater use of units larger than the phoneme in the initial stages of reading (see chapter 3 in this volume for a discussion of this issue).

In addition to implicit and explicit phonological awareness, another component of early reading success is letter knowledge. Ehri (1987) has argued that being able to recognise letters, and the sounds that they represent, directly paves the way for the development of an alphabetic strategy in which individual graphemes are recognised and their corresponding phonemes sounded out. This appears to be the case both for an irregular orthography like English, as demonstrated in studies by Stuart and Coltheart (1988) and Johnston, Anderson and Holligan (1996), and for a more regular script like German (Wimmer *et al.*, 1991). All three studies found that children's knowledge of letters was a significant predictor of reading success.

The orthography of modern Greek

This chapter is concerned with the relationship between phonological awareness, letter knowledge and learning to read and spell Greek. From this perspective, Greek is a particularly interesting language because the level of orthographic regularity is substantially different for reading and spelling. In the case of reading, Greek has a degree of regularity that is akin to German, Italian or Spanish in that each grapheme is realised by a single phoneme. This regularity in reading is emphasised by the explicitly phonological approach that is used to teach reading in Greek schools. One major feature of spoken Greek that accounts for this regularity is that there are only five vowels (compared to the dozen or more that occur in spoken English). There are no vowel distinctions and vowels sound the same whether stressed or unstressed. Greek also has fewer than half the syllable types of English and these most commonly have an open structure (i.e. end with a vowel).

In contrast to the high orthographic regularity for reading, Greek has considerable irregularity for spelling. One reason for this is that the written form of Greek has remained unchanged from antiquity even though the spoken form has changed significantly. Modern Greek spelling thus tends to reflect the phonetic etymology of words rather than their present spoken form. One major difference between reading and spelling lies in the representation of vowels. While consonants have only one graphemic rendition, regardless of the context in which they occur, three of the five Greek vowels have two or more possible spellings (although, in each case, one of these is more common than the others). The vowel sound /e/ can be represented either by ε or αι and /o/ can appear as either o or ω; and the vowel sound /i/ has six different graphemic renditions (ι, η, υ, ει, οι, υι). These alternatives often present difficulty in choosing the correct spelling for a word, particularly since the great majority of Greek words are multi-syllabic and so contain several vowels. However, in many cases, vowel spelling is not arbitrary since there are morphological rules that determine the correct spelling of vowels occurring in morphological endings. For example, in the case of the two spellings of the phoneme /o/, the letter o is used for all adjectives and both masculine and neutral gender nouns with that ending while the letter ω is used for verbs ending in /o/. This can be seen in the contrasting spellings of the noun νερο /nero/ which means water and the verb 'I write' which is γραφω /grafo/.

Although morphological rules resolve much of the ambiguity in Greek spelling, there remains a small number of words (some of them borrowed from foreign languages and other compound words that have survived from ancient Greek) that have an orthographically exceptional spelling pattern. These words have to be learned by rote. Becoming a competent speller in Greek thus requires knowledge of grapheme-to-phoneme relationships, the assimilation of morphological spelling rules and the rote learning of exceptional words.

These asymmetries in the orthographic regularity of reading and spelling suggest that Greek children's progress in learning to read and spell will be rather different. Previous studies of learning to read and spell in regular and irregular orthographies suggest that children will make very rapid progress in learning to read Greek through the early development of an alphabetic strategy – comparable to that in Italian (Cossu *et al.*, 1988; Thorstad, 1991) – but that progress in spelling will be slow and more comparable to that in English or Swedish. This pattern was evident in the first published study of Greek by Porpodas (1991). He compared first and second graders' performance in reading and spelling the same words and found that spelling was considerably less accurate than reading.

Porpodas also compared the reading and spelling ability of children who were good and poor segmenters (assessed on the basis of both phoneme and syllable segmentation). Reading and spelling achievement was assessed by word and non-word reading and spelling tests at the end of first and second grade. The good segmenters were better than the poor segmenters at word reading at the end of grade 1 but there was no difference between the groups one year later, at the end of the second grade. Porpodas argued that there is a rapidly diminishing association between phonemic awareness and reading ability for Greek because the high level of regularity allows children to become fluent readers very rapidly. However, there was a different pattern for spelling where good segmenters were more accurate than poor segmenters in both the first and second grades. As expected, all subjects spelled regular words much more accurately than exception words and both good and poor segmenters performed very poorly with the latter, misspelling the great majority even in the second grade. This suggests that facility with letter-sound rules (as evidenced by reading performance) was not of any benefit in spelling exceptional words since it can be assumed that such knowledge was better in the good segmenters than in the poor segmenters and also better at the end of grade 2 than at the end of grade 1.

The next section of this chapter describes a series of studies that further investigate the development of Greek reading and spelling skills in the first years of school and the various factors that are associated with reading and spelling success.

Early knowledge of Greek and Roman orthography

When Greek children first enter grade 1 at the age of six they receive their first formal reading instruction. However, as with children in other countries where there is mass literacy, the beginning of learning to read at school is unlikely to provide the first experience of print. Unlike many of their peers in other European countries, however, Greek children encounter two different alphabets – the Greek alphabet that they will use for reading and the Roman alphabet that is widely used in Greece for brand names, advertising and in the translation of place names provided for foreign visitors. The first study that we describe compared children's knowledge of Greek and Roman orthography early in grade 1.

Giannouli (1998) tested fifty-seven children soon after entry into grade 1 (mean age 6;9) on their reading of words in the two alphabets. By this time the children had already received six weeks of formal reading instruction for Greek but no instruction for Roman script. The aim of testing was to see whether there would be differences in the reading of the two scripts after this short period of instruction.

Reading was assessed using materials based on both the Greek and Roman alphabets. In the case of the Greek alphabet, thirty-two logo and sight vocabulary words were presented in upper and lower case forms. The logo and sight words were chosen as ones that were frequently encountered by the children. The difference between the two types of word was that logo words always appeared in identical upper case format whereas sight vocabulary words occurred in both upper and lower case forms although upper case forms were much more common.

The Greek sight words included the name of a football team (ΠΑΟΚ) and a type of sweet (ΙΟΝ) while the logo words included the sign for Taxi (ΤΑΞΙ) and the name of a type of cheese (ΦΕΤΑ). All the words were initially presented in upper case (which in the case of logo words contained all the unique characteristics of the logo) and then in lower case. Following Wimmer *et al.* (1991), children's responses were counted as correct either when the child responded with the exact word or with a partial recoding of the graphemic sequence of the word into a legal non-word.

The children were also presented with logo and sight vocabulary words written in Roman script. Whereas the Greek words most often appeared in upper case, the foreign stimuli typically occurred in lower case. These words were therefore initially presented in lower case (reproducing the exact format in the case of logo words) and then in upper case. The Roman script logo words included the brand names of a toothpaste (Colgate), a drink (Coca-Cola) and a make of car (Ford)

Table 4.1   *Comparison of reading words in Greek and Roman script seven weeks after school entry: mean percentage correct (and standard deviation).*

	Logo words		Sight words	
	Typical format	Atypical format	Typical format	Atypical format
Greek	54.8 (14.7)	53.2 (15.0)	25.8 (8.1)	23.5 (8.1)
Roman	13.5 (9.3)	0.3 (1.6)	12.9 (5.0)	9.4 (9.3)

while the sight words included 'kiss' and 'stop'. The scoring of correct answers was carried out in the same way as for the Greek reading task.

The rationale for presenting words in both upper and lower case was to compare children's reading strategies in the two orthographies. If the children were recognising words logographically, that is, they were attending to overall word shape, then they should perform less well when words were presented in an atypical case, that is, in lower case for the Greek words and upper case for the Roman script words. However, if the children were reading alphabetically, then their reading performance should be relatively unimpaired by presentation in an atypical case. Accordingly, it was predicted that the reading of words in the Roman alphabet (which was expected to be logographic) would be more accurate when they were presented in their typical (lower case) format than when presented in atypical (upper case) format, whereas the reading of Greek words (which was expected to be alphabetic) would not be significantly affected by case.

The results showed a strikingly different pattern for words in the two different alphabets (see table 4.1). As would be expected, the reading of Greek words was better than the reading of Roman script words. More interestingly, for Greek words, there was no significant difference between the reading of typical (upper case) format and atypical (lower case) format. Furthermore, reading scores in the two formats were highly correlated (even when the effects of IQ were accounted for). For words in Roman script, reading words in typical (lower case) format was significantly better than reading these same words in atypical (upper case) format and performance in the two reading conditions was not significantly correlated.

The clearest evidence that the children were reading words in Roman script logographically can be seen in their almost complete failure to read the Roman logo words when they were presented in atypical (upper case) format. They fared rather better with the atypical (upper case) format sight words, presumably because, in the Roman alphabet, upper and lower case letter are often similar in appearance so that some words like stop/STOP, kiss/KISS or pizza/PIZZA looked very similar in both versions.

The difference between the reading of words in Greek and Roman scripts showed that, even after a few weeks of formal reading instruction, the Greek children were beginning to read Greek words alphabetically, while their reading of words in Roman script remained logographic. Given this evidence of precocious alphabetic reading so soon after the beginning of grade 1, it is relevant to look at the reading ability of Greek children during the year before they enter the first grade and to ask how well they can read and how well their letter knowledge and phonological awareness have developed.

During their year at nursery school, Greek children do not receive any formal reading instruction. However, they are given a lot of exposure to print, which should encourage the learning of sight vocabulary and the development of letter knowledge, and they learn many rhyming songs and games, which would be expected to develop implicit phonological awareness.

Giannouli and Harris (1997) tested a group of nursery children at the beginning and end of the school year. The children were aged 4;8 when they were first tested. They were given a number of tasks to assess letter knowledge, reading and phonological awareness. Letter knowledge was tested with a letter orientation task (adapted from Harris and Beech, 1995) which required the children to place Greek letters in their correct orientation. This task, which is suitable for young children who do not yet know letter names but are beginning to recognise letter shapes, uses letters on a magnetic board that are presented in an incorrect orientation. Sixteen lower case letters were used, taking care to exclude letters where the correct orientation was ambiguous. (For example ε and ω were not used as they could easily have been confused with each other.) Children were asked to name letters that they orientated correctly and they were also asked to read a simple word starting with the letter. Explicit phonological awareness was tested using vowel substitution and phoneme counting and implicit phonological awareness was assessed with syllable counting.

The pre-schoolers did well on the letter orientation task, correctly orientating an average of thirteen letters. However, although they were good at letter orientation – and were able to recognise letter shapes – most children were unable to name even one letter. On the syllable counting task – a measure of implicit phonological awareness – mean scores were high (10.25/12). However, as would be expected, the children

Table 4.2   *Comparison of performance from entry into nursery school to the end of grade 1 (percentage correct).*

Task	Start of nursery	End of nursery	Start of grade 1	End of grade 1
Letter knowledge	00.0	27.5	71.0	100.0
Syllable counting	85.4	97.5	98.0	100.0
Phoneme counting	00.0	20.8	49.6	100.0
Vowel substitution	00.0	17.0	54.5	100.0

were totally incapable of tackling either the phoneme counting task or vowel substitution. Interestingly, there was a highly significant correlation (when the effects of IQ were accounted for) between syllable counting and letter orientation.

At the end of the nursery year, the children were tested again on the three phonological awareness tasks. Letter knowledge was retested by presenting sixteen Greek letters for recognition and one highly frequent word beginning with each of the letters. Unfortunately it was only possible to retest ten of the original twenty children as an earthquake occurred just as the testing was about to resume. Retesting showed a significant improvement on all four measures (see table 4.2).

The increase in letter knowledge and implicit phonological awareness are not surprising given the kind of experience provided in the nursery school. Perhaps more surprising is the increase in the two measures of explicit phonological awareness. Neither task was managed by any child at the beginning of the nursery year, yet, by the end, some children were already beginning to develop their ability to segment phonemes and substitute vowels. In a later study, reported in the next section, we followed up these children to see how these abilities were related to reading and spelling two years later. However, before turning to the follow-up study, we want to consider the development of phonemic awareness in more detail.

In the introduction, we noted that phonemic awareness appears to develop in the course of learning to read an alphabetic script. Some of the nursery children were showing signs of emergent phonemic awareness by the end of their year at nursery school but they were not yet able to recognise the simple words that we presented. However, the children were very good at recognising letters and this seemed the most likely source of their dawning phonemic awareness. The relationship between the two skills was evident in the pattern of correlations that we found between letter knowledge and the measures of phonological awareness at the end of the nursery year. The correlation between letter knowledge and syllable counting was close to zero ($R = 0.08$) but the correlation between letter knowledge and each of the measures of phonemic awareness was just over 0.40. Although these correlations were not statistically significant in light of the small sample size (reduced by the occurrence of the earthquake) they point to the existence of a different relationship between letter knowledge and the two kinds of measure. Stronger evidence for the relationship between letter knowledge and phonemic awareness emerged from the next study which investigated progress in reading and spelling over the first grade.

Learning to read and write in the first year at school

Twenty first graders took part in a longitudinal study (Giannouli and Harris, 1997). They were initially tested within their first week of entering grade 1 when their mean age was 6;0. The same three phonological awareness tasks used with the nursery children – syllable counting, phoneme counting and vowel substitution – were presented along with the test of letter knowledge.

Six children from the sample of twenty first graders were able to read some of the words (starting with previously identified letters). Their scores ranged from one to nine. The other children were totally unable to read any words. Mean letter knowledge was ten letters out of a possible maximum of sixteen. Performance on implicit phonological awareness was found to be very close to ceiling but performance on both measures of explicit phonological awareness was considerably lower.

It is informative to compare these scores, from children on their entry into grade 1, with the scores from the group of nursery children tested at the end of their year. The comparison can be seen in table 4.2. Although these are different children in the nursery group and in grade 1, since they came from the same area of Greece and from very similar home backgrounds there is every reason to suppose that they are directly comparable. There were marked differences in letter knowledge and scores in both phonemic awareness tests, with the performance of the first graders being consistently higher. The suggestion that letter knowledge is closely related to the development of phonemic awareness is supported by the finding of highly significant correlations between letter knowledge and both phoneme counting and vowel substitution and, at the same time, by the failure to find any association between letter knowledge and syllable counting.

The striking growth in letter knowledge over the summer months, from the end of nursery in June to grade 1 entry in September, can be put down to the home teaching that took place. Parents typically saw it as their responsibility to prepare their children for the beginning of formal reading instruction by teaching them letter names and sounds. This home instruction appears to have both a direct effect on letter knowledge at school entry and also an indirect effect on the development of phonemic awareness.

At the end of grade 1 the children were retested with the three phonological awareness tasks. By this time all scores were at ceiling for all children, showing that phonemic awareness had developed considerably in the nine months of reading instruction that had taken place since the beginning of grade 1 (see table 4.2).

Word and non-word reading was assessed using a test adapted from Wimmer *et al.* (1991). This involved three groups of twenty words each. The first group contained familiar words that were selected from the classroom reading books. The second group contained unfamiliar words. These were phonetically similar to the familiar words but did not occur in the reading books and so were likely to be novel to most children. For example, if the familiar words were βολος /volos/ and γραμμα /gramma/ the unfamiliar words were θολος /tholos/ and δραμμα /dramma/. The third group consisted of non-words which were derived from familiar and unfamiliar words by exchanging the vowels within their middle syllabic boundaries (e.g. word = μαθητης /mathitis/, non-word = μηθατης /mithatis/). Each of the sixty stimulus items was presented twice for two different exposure durations. The first exposure was short (300 ms) and the second was twice as long (600 ms).

Children's spelling was assessed by two tests. In the first, which tested alphabetic spelling, they were asked to write ten non-words out of the group of twenty used for reading. Orthographic spelling was assessed by asking children to write down ten words selected from their classroom reading book. Correct spelling of words was not possible for a child who simply segmented and transcribed the spoken words using an alphabetic strategy. For example, had the word θαλασσινη been spelled as θαλασινη this spelling would have been considered alphabetically correct (since all the phonemes of the word were represented) but orthographically incorrect since the double consonant was omitted.

The reading scores for the three-word categories – familiar, unfamiliar and non-words – under long exposure were all at ceiling. Short exposure reduced performance on each word category but in the case of the two-word categories the reduction was minimal. Thus, by the end of the first grade, children were highly accurate at reading both familiar and unfamiliar words even when they saw them for only a short time. Reducing reading time had a much greater effect on non-words and so scores

Table 4.3 *Predictors of reading and spelling at the end of grade 1 (T values and significance levels).*

Predictors	Non-word reading	Word spelling
IQ	2.51*	1.23
	$p = 0.03$	$p = 0.24$
Letter knowledge	2.69*	−0.80
	$p = 0.02$	$p = 0.44$
Syllable counting	−0.74	2.24*
	$p = 0.48$	$p = 0.04$
Phoneme counting	0.01	−1.09
	$p = 0.99$	$p = 0.30$
Vowel substitution	−0.56	0.13
	$p = 0.58$	$p = 0.90$

Note: * indicates significant predictors ($p < 0.05$)

for non-word reading at short exposure were used as the most sensitive indicator of reading ability in subsequent analysis. This was also appropriate because non-word reading can also be considered the best measure of alphabetic reading (since non-words cannot be read by a direct lexical procedure).

The pattern for spelling was very different. Spelling of non-words was completely accurate. However, spelling of real words was poor, with children achieving a mean of only 36 per cent correct. There was a great deal of individual variation in ability, with the worst spellers being able to spell only two out of the ten words correctly while the best spellers could spell all ten words correctly.

Multiple regression was carried out on non-word reading (under short exposure) and word spelling to assess the significance of each of the measures taken on school entry. The results are summarised in table 4.3 where it can be seen that, for non-word reading, both IQ and letter knowledge were significant predictors whereas, for word spelling, the only significant predictor was syllable counting.

Before discussing these results it is worth noting that, although syllable counting scores were relatively high on school entry, nevertheless they were sufficiently variable to predict progress in spelling scores at the end of grade 1. Accordingly it seems appropriate to consider the non-significant relationship between syllable counting and non-word reading as a real one. This pattern confirms the findings of Cossu, Rossini and Marshall (1993) and Wimmer, Landerl and Schneider

(1994) that, in the case of highly regular orthography, implicit phonological awareness – measured in our study by syllable counting – does not predict reading success as it does with more irregular orthographies. Our study does show, however, that letter knowledge on school entry makes an important contribution to reading. This underlines the importance of letter knowledge in learning to read an alphabetic script and it suggests that being able to identify and name letters is an essential first step in the mastery of alphabetic reading.

The results also support Porpodas' finding that reading was very accurate by the end of grade 1. However, Porpodas found a difference between the reading skills of good and poor segmenters at the end of grade 1, whereas we found that reading at the end of grade 1 was not predicted by phonemic awareness on school entry. There are some problems in drawing a direct comparison between the two studies because of differences in the methodology. However, one possible explanation for the apparent difference in the results is that the children in our study were generally good segmenters. If this were the case, then we might not only expect their reading level to be high at the end of grade 1 (as it was) but we might also expect that the relationship between phonemic awareness and learning to read would disappear sooner than in the sample of children tested by Porpodas. Whereas, in our sample, there was no relationship at the end of grade 1, Porpodas found no relationship when he retested his children at the end of grade 2. Thus, our results support Porpodas' general conclusion that the association between phonemic awareness and reading ability for Greek diminishes rapidly.

Turning to spelling, it will be remembered that alphabetic spelling (as evidenced by performance with non-words) was at ceiling by the end of grade 1, so we can assume that the children were able to apply letter–sound correspondences equally successfully to spelling. However, their low level of success with word spelling confirms the view that the difference in the orthographic regularity for reading and spelling leads to a large discrepancy between the children's ability in these two areas. The regression analysis revealed that the only predictor of word spelling at the end of grade 1 was syllable counting. This is similar to the pattern found by Cataldo and Ellis (1988) for English, but it contrasts with the Wimmer *et al.* (1994) study of German where only later success in spelling (in grade 3) was predicted by rhyme awareness on school entry. Given that the irregularity of Greek spelling is arguably closer to English than to German, this is the pattern that might be expected. We return to this issue in the next section.

What emerges from the study of Greek reading and spelling during the pre-school year and in the first year of formal reading instruction is that there are distinct differences between the two. Children rapidly develop an alphabetic strategy for reading which is evident even after only a few weeks of reading instruction. This precocious development is possible because the children already have good letter knowledge when they begin formal reading instruction and this knowledge is exploited by the phonics approach that is used to teach reading. By the end of the school year, children are reading very accurately and only non-words pose any problems at all. Even non-words can be read accurately when there is plenty of time to inspect them and difficulties only arise with short exposure. Presumably the non-words require a longer exposure because, even though children are familiar with all letter–sound rules, it takes more time to apply these to generate the correct pronunciation when the letter sequence is unfamiliar. A similar finding also emerged from the Porpodas (1991) study where words with regular spelling patterns were read more accurately in grade 1 than those with an irregular spelling pattern (even though both classes of word were regular for reading).

In contrast to their reading, Greek children still have a lot to learn about spelling at the end of grade 1. Alphabetic spelling is well established (as indicated by the highly accurate non-word spelling) but the spelling of real words is poor since other principles – notably a grasp of morphological rules – is required. The regression analysis suggested that syllabic analysis skills are important in the early stages of learning to spell. We consider this possibility in the next study which looks over a longer time period to a point where spelling is becoming well established.

Becoming a competent speller

In our final study, we followed up the two groups of children who were initially tested on entry into nursery and grade 1 to see how well they were able to spell three years later. The nursery children were then coming to the end of grade 2 and the first graders to the end of grade 3.

In the introduction, we noted the importance of morphological rules in Greek spelling. We anticipated that the learning of these would be an important feature of children's learning of spelling over the second and third grades. Arguably one key to mastering morphological rules in spelling is to be able to recognise morphological boundaries within words. This skill allows a child both to recognise morphological components that are spelled in common (notably stem morphemes) and those that are the subject of morphological spelling rules (notably affixes). In other scripts, where morphological endings are distinguished in spelling but not in the spoken form, it has been shown that children's morphological awareness is an important component of spelling success. For example, Fayol, Thevenin, Jarousse and Totereau (in press) have shown that French children's accuracy in spelling morphological endings can be improved by specific training; and Bryant and Nunes (in press) report that English children are more accurate in aspects of spelling where there are important morphological constraints if they have good morpho-syntactic awareness (see also the chapter by Bryant, Nunes and Aidinis in this volume).

In the case of Greek, we predicted that syllable counting would predict spelling of morphologically regular words, since this ability would assist children in the segmentation of words into morphological units. We also predicted that children who had good morphological awareness would be good at spelling morphologically regular words. In order to assess morphological knowledge, the children were given a test in which they were asked to derive adjectives from verbs and vice versa. This test, which was adapted from the analogy task used by Nunes, Bryant and Bindman (1997), was presented at the same time as the spelling test.

In addition to gaining mastery of morphological spelling rules, children also have to learn to spell exceptional words where neither alphabetic principles nor morphological rules can generate a correct spelling. As we noted earlier in the chapter, many exceptional words have their origins in ancient Greek which made use of distinctions that are no longer represented in the pronunciation of modern Greek. One such example is the number eight which has the form οκτω /okto/. This ends with the morpheme ω normally used for verb endings. This use of the letter ω to represent the sound /o/ reflects the fact that, in ancient Greek, this ending was a long vowel. Such distinctions between long and short vowels do not occur in the pronunciation of modern Greek. We predicted that children would only gradually learn such exception words and that the learning of morphological rules would be well established before children could begin to make significant progress with the exception words.

In order to gain a clear picture of spelling at the end of the second and third grades, the children were required to spell to dictation six different categories of word (with twenty-four words in each category). First there were alphabetically regular words that could be spelled correctly purely on the basis of knowledge of sound-to-letter rules. The spelling of vowels in these words was considered to be regular because, in the case of the three vowels with several possible graphemic renditions (/e/, /o/ and /i/), only the most common spelling was used. The

Table 4.4 *Mean error scores on spelling tests at the end of grades 2 and 3 (maximum score = 24).*

	Regular HF	Regular LF	Ending HF	Ending LF	Exceptn HF	Exceptn LF
Grade 2	0.24	2.47	1.06	4.00	11.71	23.47
Grade 3	0.00	1.30	0.25	0.65	5.95	12.15

Note: Ending = spelling of morphological ending only
     Exceptn = exception words
     HF   = high frequency
     LF   = low frequency

regular words were sub-divided into two groups of high and low frequency words. As there are no word frequency norms for modern Greek, judgements about relative frequency were based on the children's written vocabulary in school. The high frequency words were all used in written vocabulary exercises in first and second grade. The low frequency words appeared in vocabulary lists for reading books used by children in the fifth and sixth grades.

In addition to regular words of high and low frequency, there were also morphologically regular words and exception words. Morphologically regular words conformed to morphological spelling rules while exception words did not. Each of these two categories was sub-divided into low and high frequency words following the criterion for regular words. Our expectation was that, by the end of grade 2, children would be close to ceiling on the spelling of both high and low frequency regular words, since our previous study had shown that non-word (i.e. alphabetic) spelling was highly accurate at the end of the first grade. We assumed that, in contrast to performance at the end of grade 1, spelling of morphologically regular words would be well established, although it seemed likely that spelling would be more accurate with the familiar high frequency words than with the lower frequency items. Finally, we expected that spelling of exceptional words would be poor, although frequency would have a marked effect so that, overall, low frequency exception words would be the most difficult of the six categories. At the end of grade 3 we expected to find that the spelling of morphologically regular and exception words would have improved, although we considered it unlikely that the latter category – especially low frequency items – would produce performance at ceiling.

Table 4.4 shows the mean error scores for spelling in the six categories. The score shown for the two morphologically regular categories is for spelling the morphological ending only. As predicted, the spelling of regular words was highly accurate for both grades. Spelling of morphological endings was also well established and the only notable errors occurred in the second graders' spelling of low frequency items, where the error rate was 17 per cent (4/24). There was a marked effect of frequency with the exception words and the second graders failed almost completely with the low frequency exception words while managing to spell half of the high frequency words correctly. By the end of the third grade, spelling of exception words had improved considerably, although there was still a marked frequency effect with the error rate for low frequency words falling to 50 per cent and for high frequency words to 25 per cent.

Turning to the factors associated with spelling performance, we found that accuracy with morphological endings was associated both with syllabic awareness (as measured by syllable counting on entry into the nursery year) and morphological awareness (as measured by the morphological analogy task). We found that, after entering IQ, syllable counting was a highly significant predictor of spelling of morphological endings in high frequency words at the end of grade 2. At the end of grade 3, spelling of morphological endings in low frequency words was also marginally predicted by syllable counting (measured on entry into grade 1). Performance on the morphological analogy task – which was completed very accurately by both second and third graders – was also significantly correlated ($R = 0.50$) with spelling of these same words at the end of second grade.[1]

The spelling of low frequency exception words at the end of grade 2 was predicted by letter knowledge at the end of nursery. At the end of grade 3, the spelling of these words was predicted by syllable counting measured at the beginning of grade 1.

Overall, the measures of phonemic awareness had little predictive power. They did not predict any of the spelling measures at the end of grade 3 and, at the end of grade 2, the only significant prediction occurred between vowel substitution and the spelling of the stem of morphologically regular words.

It is clear from these results that the best predictor of Greek spelling, from grade 1 right through to grade 3, is syllabic awareness. We suggest that this is because the major part of learning about Greek spelling over this period concerns the gradual mastery of morphological spelling rules. It seems likely that children who are good at dividing words into syllables are better at dividing the multi-syllabic words of Greek into their constituent morphemes, so that the appropriate spelling rules can then be learned and applied. There is some direct evidence for this hypothesis because we found a significant partial correlation between syllable counting (measured on entry into nursery) and performance on the morphological analogy task at the end of grade 2. Furthermore, in another study (Giannouli, 1998), we also found that rhyme judgement early in grade 1 was a highly significant predictor of word spelling, although in that study we did not sub-divide words according to their degree of regularity.

We suggest that familiarity with morphemic structure and the associated spelling rules then assists in learning the spelling of exception words. Such a relationship would explain why syllable counting marginally predicted the spelling of high frequency exception words at the end of grade 2 and strongly predicted the spelling of low frequency exception words at the end of grade 3.

Conclusion

We began this chapter by considering the role of implicit and explicit phonological awareness in learning to read alphabetic scripts with differing levels of orthographic regularity. We argued that implicit phonological awareness appeared to be a predictor of early reading success for irregular but not regular orthographies, whereas phonemic awareness was a consistently strong marker of reading progress in both regular and irregular orthographies. The pattern that we found for learning to read the highly regular Greek orthography fits in with this general picture but with some important provisos.

Reading progress was rapid and six weeks into the first grade there was evidence that children had already developed an alphabetic strategy. As expected, implicit phonological awareness did not predict reading success. However, we also found that our measures of phonemic awareness did not predict reading progress by the end of the first grade either, whereas letter knowledge was a significant predictor. Our pattern of results suggests that, in the case of Greek, learning to identify letters is the key to the rapid development of both phonemic awareness and an alphabetic strategy because, by the start of grade 1, letter knowledge was high but phoneme counting and vowel substitution remained comparatively poor whereas by the end of the grade both measures were high.

For spelling there was a rather different picture. Most notably, progress in spelling was generally very much slower than for reading, underlining the marked discrepancy in the regularity of Greek orthography with respect to these two tasks. Given the rapid development of an alphabetic strategy for reading, it was not surprising to find that Greek children rapidly become good at spelling non-words and regular words (to which alphabetic principles can be applied). However, errors in spelling morphologically regular words were still evident in second grade and errors in spelling exception words persisted into third grade.

We found that both syllabic knowledge and morpho-syntactic awareness – as measured by the morphological analogy task – were important predictors for spelling words which contained a morphological ending, whereas measures of phonemic awareness had generally little predictive power for spelling. Throughout our spelling tests we also found a marked effect of frequency, with more common words being easier to spell than less common words. This effect was particularly marked for exception words which have to be learned on a case-by-case basis. However, high frequency morphologically regular words were also easier to spell than their low frequency counterparts, even though they contained identical morphological spelling patterns. This underlines the fact that children are not able to assimilate and then apply a morphological spelling rule to new cases but, rather, that considerable experience with the individual words is necessary.

One reason why Greek children seem to find it difficult to apply morphological spelling rules across the board is that school instruction does not make the link between morphology and spelling explicit. Morphology is taught in schools but this is not linked to spelling, which tends to be presented as a rote learning task. We would suggest that making an explicit link between morphology and spelling patterns could produce a marked improvement in the way that Greek children learn to spell.

NOTE

1 There was no correlation between performance on the analogy task and the spelling of morphologically regular words at the end of grade 3 because performance was close to ceiling on the analogy task and very close to ceiling for low-frequency morphologically regular words.

REFERENCES

Bradley, L. and Bryant, P. E. (1983). Categorising sounds and learning to read: a causal connection. *Nature*, 301, 419–21.
    (1985). *Rhyme and Reason in Reading and Spelling*. International Academy for Research in Learning Disabilities Monograph Series, vol. I. Ann Arbor: University of Michigan Press.
Bryant, P. E. and Nunes, T. (in press). The development of orthographic knowledge. In T. Nunes (ed.), *Learning to Read: An Integrated View from Research and Practice*. Dordrecht, Holland: Kluwer.

Cataldo, S. and Ellis, N. (1988). Interaction in the development of spelling, reading and phonological skills. *Journal of Research in Reading*, 11, 86–109.

Cossu, G., Shankweiler, D., Liberman, I. Y., Katz, L. and Tola, G. (1988). Awareness of phonological segments and reading ability in Italian children. *Applied Psycholinguistics*, 9, 1–16.

Cossu, G., Rossini, F. and Marshall, J. C. (1993). When reading is acquired but phonemic awareness is not: a study of literacy in Down's syndrome. *Cognition*, 46, 129–38.

Ehri, L. C. (1987). Learning to read and spell words. *Journal of Reading Behavior*, 19, 5–31.

Ehri, L. C. and Wilce, L. S. (1987). Does learning to spell help beginners to learn to read words? *Reading Research Quarterly*, 22, 47–65.

Fayol, M., Thevenin, M. G., Jarousse, J. P. and Totereau, C. (in press). On learning French written morphology. In T. Nunes (ed.), *Learning to Read: An Integrated View from Research and Practice*. Dordrecht, Holland: Kluwer.

Fox, B. and Routh, D. K. (1984). Phonemic analysis and synthesis as word attack skills. *Journal of Educational Psychology*, 68, 70–4.

Giannouli, V. I. (1998). The development of reading and spelling in Greek preschool and primary school children. Unpublished Ph.D. thesis, University of London.

Giannouli, V. I. and Harris, M. (1997). The relationship of phonemic awareness to reading and spelling acquisition in Greek. Paper presented to the Eighth European Developmental Psychology Conference: University of Rennes, France.

Harris, M. and Beech, J. (1995). Reading development in prelingually deaf children. In K. Nelson and Z. Reger (eds.), *Children's Language*, vol. VIII (pp. 181–202). Hillsdale, NJ: Lawrence Erlbaum Associates.

Hoien, T. and Lundberg, I. (1988). Stages of word recognition in early reading development. *Scandinavian Journal of Educational Research*, 32, 163–82.

Johnston, R. S., Anderson, M. and Holligan, C. (1996). Knowledge of the alphabet and explicit awareness of phonemes in pre-readers – the nature of the relationship. *Reading and Writing*, 8, 217–34.

Liberman, I. Y., Rubin, H., Duques, S. and Carlisle, J. (1985). Linguistic abilities and spelling proficiency in kindergarteners and adult poor spellers. In D. B. Gray and J. F. Kavanagh (eds.), *Biobehavioural Measures of Dyslexia*. Parkton, MD: York Press.

Lundberg, I., Frost, J. and Petersen, O. P. (1988). Effects of an extensive program for stimulating phonological awareness in preschool children. *Reading Research Quarterly*, 23, 263–84.

Mann, V. A. (1984). Longitudinal prediction and prevention of early reading difficulty. *Annals of Dyslexia*, 34, 117–36.

Mann, V. A. and Liberman, I. Y. (1984). Phonological awareness and verbal short-term memory. *Journal of Learning Disabilities*, 17, 592–9.

Marcel, T. (1980). Phonological awareness and phonological representation: investigation of a specific spelling problem. In U. Frith (ed.), *Cognitive Processes in Spelling* (pp. 373–404). London: Academic Press.

Montgomery, D. (1981). Do dyslexics have difficulty accessing articulation information? *Psychological Research*, 43, 243–53.

Morais, J., Bertelson, P., Cary, L. and Alegria, J. (1986). Literacy training and speech segmentation. *Cognition*, 24, 45–50.

Nunes, T., Bryant, P. E. and Bindman, M. (1997). Morphological spelling strategies: developmental stages and processes. *Developmental Psychology*, 33, 637–49.

Porpodas, C. (1991). The relation between phonemic awareness and reading and spelling of Greek words in the first school years. In M. Carretero, M. L. Pope, P. R. Simons and J. I. Pozo (eds.), *Learning and Instruction: European Research in an International context*, vol. III (pp. 203–17). Oxford: Pergamon Press.

Read, C. (1985). Effects of phonology on beginning spelling: some cross-linguistic evidence. In D. Olson, N. Torrance and A. Hildyard (eds.), *Literacy, Language and Learning*. New York: Cambridge University Press.

Snowling, M. (1981). Phonemic deficits in developmental dyslexia. *Psychological Research*, 43, 219–34.

Snowling, M., Goulandris, N., Bowlby, N. and Howell, P. (1986). Segmentation and speech perception in relation to reading skill: a developmental analysis. *Journal of Experimental Child Psychology*, 41, 489–507.

Stanovich, K. E., Cunningham, A. E. and Cramer, B. B. (1984). Assessing phonological awareness in kindergarten children: issues of task comparability. *Journal of Experimental Psychology*, 38, 155–90.

Stuart, M. and Coltheart, M. (1988). Does reading develop in a sequence of stages? *Cognition*, 30, 139–81.

Thorstad, G. (1991). The effects of orthography on the acquisition of literacy skills. *British Journal of Psychology*, 82, 527–37.

Wagner, R. K. and Torgesen, J. K. (1987). The nature of phonological processing and its causal role in the acquisition of reading skills. *Psychological Bulletin*, 101, 192–212.

Wimmer, H., Landerl, K., Linortner, R. and Hummer, P. (1991). The relationship of phonemic awareness to reading acquisition: more consequence than precondition but still important. *Cognition*, 40, 219–49.

Wimmer, H., Landerl, K. and Schneider, W. (1994). The role of rhyme awareness in learning to read a regular orthography. *British Journal of Developmental Psychology*, 12, 429–84.

5 Phonological awareness, syntactic awareness and learning to read and spell in Brazilian Portuguese

Lucia Lins Browne Rego

Introduction

The Portuguese language uses an alphabetic script. However, according to recent linguistic descriptions there are only nine cases in which there is a unique mapping between letters and phonemes. Lemle (1987) records seven of these cases. The phonemes /p/, /b/, /f/, /v/, /t/, /d/, /a/ are represented by the consonant letters P, B, F, V, T, D and the vowel A. In addition, Faraco (1992) included as cases of regularity the phonemes /ñ/ and /λ/ because they are consistently represented by the digraphs NH, LH and excluded the vowel A because in some contexts this letter also represents the nasal vowel /ã/. The descriptions provided by the work of these linguists also indicate other important sources of regularity in the Portuguese orthography. Although there are letters (e.g. M, N, L, R, E, O) that represent more than one phoneme and phonemes (e.g. /R/, /g/, /j/, /k/) that are represented by more than one letter, these different alternatives can be predicted by the position of the letter or the sound in the word and in a few cases by its stress pattern. Another source of regularity are the morphemes and the word class which can also be used as a criterion to define the connections between letters and sounds. According to Faraco (1992), cases where specific lexical knowledge is required for correct spelling are much less frequent and this renders Portuguese orthography quite predictable.

Learning to read and to spell in Portuguese is, thus, to a great extent, learning about the alphabetic principle and about conditional rules. Although most of these contextual restrictions involve grapho-phonic information, and so ultimately require phonemic analysis, there are also cases where morpho-syntactic information can be successfully applied in order to solve ambiguities in spelling. How children learn to generate correct spellings in Portuguese and what language skills account for their success in such an acquisition process is the theme of this chapter.

Discovering the alphabetic principle

Learning about conditional spelling rules in an alphabetic script is certainly preceded by the major discovery that letters in an alphabetic script represent the sounds in the words. This is a challenge shared by children with different language backgrounds, living in cultures which use alphabetic scripts. How children come to grips with the alphabetic scripts represents a milestone in theories of literacy development (Ferreiro, 1985; Frith, 1985; Marsh, Friedman, Welch and Desberg, 1980) and is a topic which has fascinated researchers, who in the past twenty years have looked at the metalinguistic factors that facilitate the mastering of such scripts (Bradley and Bryant, 1985; Lundberg, Oloffson and Wall, 1980; Tunmer and Nesdale, 1985).

The theory of literacy development which, in our view, provides the most relevant description of the developmental process which leads to the discovery of the alphabetic principle was proposed by Ferreiro (1985) based on two extensive studies, one conducted in Argentina and the other in Mexico (Ferreiro and Palacio, 1982; Ferreiro and Teberosky 1986). According to Ferreiro's theory there is no abrupt qualitative change between the stage at which children make no connections between letters and sounds and the alphabetic stage, as proposed in Marsh *et al.*'s model, and there is no extensive logographic period in which reading is disconnected from spelling, as proposed by Frith's six-step model of literacy development.

Using a Piagetian framework, Ferreiro and her collaborators were concerned with children's conceptions about the written language. One of the tasks used in their research consisted of asking children to spell and immediately read their spellings of words of different numbers of syllables as well as one sentence given by the experimenter. They found that the pre-alphabetic invented spellings of these children as well as their reading were quite systematic.

The spelling stages detected by Ferreiro and her collaborators have also been found with Brazilian children and their theoretical framework can be used to describe the literacy development of Portuguese-speaking children until they reach an understanding of the alphabetic principle (Carraher and Rego, 1983; Rego, 1985). In a first stage, there is no connection between children's spelling and the spoken words. The children conceptualise print as disconnected from the sound pattern of the language. Letters are just alternative forms of representing meaning.

When children begin to relate the letters to the sounds in the words, phonological units such as syllables play a major role. At a more primitive level this type of phonological analysis may not involve qualitative

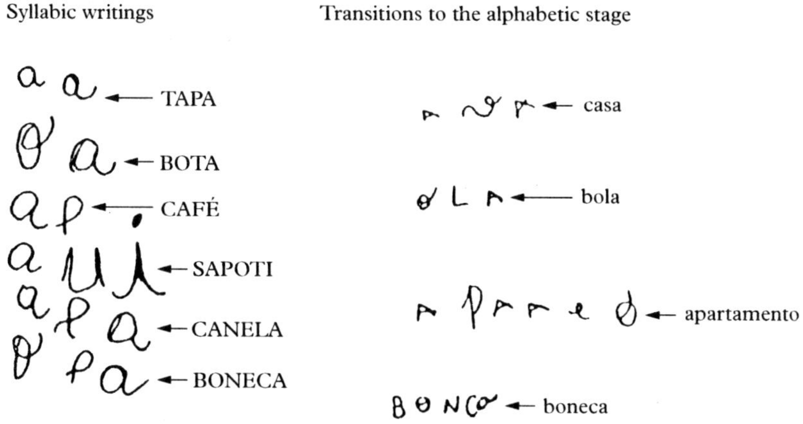

Syllabic writings   Transitions to the alphabetic stage

Figure 5.1

correspondences. A child may represent a word like *elefante* (elephant) as 'ICAO' in which each arbitrarily chosen letter stands for one of the four syllables in this word. In reading, the child segments the spoken word into four syllables, one corresponding to each letter. In a more advanced syllabic stage qualitative correspondences are added. These qualitative correspondences are mostly made by using the vowel sounds. These syllabic writings are followed by a period of transition to the alphabetic stage in which children's spellings become partially syllabic and partially alphabetic. Figure 5.1 shows examples of these types of spelling taken from Rego (1985).

However, Ferreiro's theory of literacy development does not account for what happens in reading and in spelling development when children reach the alphabetic stage.

The acquisition of conditional spelling rules

Violation of conditional spelling rules appeared as a main category of errors in many studies which have focused on the type of spelling errors made by children in Brazil who are using an alphabetic strategy for reading (Abaurre, 1988; Alvarenga, Nicolau, Soares, Oliveira and do Nascimento, 1989; Carraher, 1985). This early research showed that the spelling errors produced by children who were at the alphabetic stage of spelling were not random and revealed children who were attempting to generate spellings but who had not yet mastered the conventional rules of the Portuguese orthography. One of the interesting points raised by this early work based on the analysis of children's spelling errors was the inadequacy of stage models to describe spelling development after the alphabetic stage. Abaurre (1988) and later Nunes (1990) had claimed that the types of errors produced by children after they reached the alphabetic stage cannot be considered as evidence of a phonetic stage separated from an orthographic stage in spelling. They argued that, in children's written story texts, one can find errors of quite opposite origins. Children may produce phonetically motivated errors in words in which they apply the alphabetic principle without hesitation and, at the same time, they may write other words using overgeneralisations derived from the orthographic patterns of the language. This last pattern of errors shows that children's ideas about spelling, soon after they begin to read and to spell alphabetically, are also derived from an orthographic analysis, even though they have not yet mastered the conventional spelling rules of Portuguese orthography.

Another important piece of evidence, which also supports the inadequacy of stage models to account for orthographic development in Brazilian Portuguese, comes from cross-sectional studies in which children's acquisition of specific spelling rules was tested through specially devised spelling and reading tasks. The first of these studies was conducted by Nunes (1992). In this study Nunes investigated the acquisition of two quite similar contextual spelling rules of Brazilian Portuguese. According to the first of these conditional rules, the letter 'o' always represents the sound /u/ when this vowel sound is unstressed and appears at the end of a word. When the vowel sound is stressed it is always spelled with the letter 'u'. The word [pátu] which means 'duck' is written 'pato' while the word [perú] which means 'turkey' is written 'peru'. In a similar fashion, the letter 'e' always represent the vowel sound /i/ when this sound is unstressed and appears at the end of a word. However, when the vowel appears in the same position but is stressed, it is spelled with the letter 'i'. The word [báti] which means 'hit' is written 'bate' while the word [abacaxí] which means 'pineapple' ends with a stressed /i/ and is spelled 'abacaxi'. When children begin to read and write they tend to pronounce these words phonetically and to use phonetic spellings in words ending with these unstressed vowels. They write words like 'pato' as 'patu' and words like 'bate' as 'bati'.

Nunes asked children from seven to fourteen years old to write and read non-words ending in these unstressed vowels. She obtained a very interesting pattern of results. The correct spelling of non-words ending with the unstressed /u/ sound appeared earlier than the correct spelling of non-words ending with the unstressed /i/ sound. Therefore, although the spelling rules investigated by Nunes were quite similar, children did not master them in parallel. Moreover, Nunes also found that phonetic reading of non-words ending with the letter 'o' disappeared earlier than phonetic reading of non-words ending with the letter 'e', but that, on the whole, both rules were first acquired in reading before children could transfer them to spelling.

The second cross-sectional study was conducted by Monteiro (1995). In this study the acquisition of two other quite similar conditional spelling rules was also investigated, both in reading and in spelling. According to Brazilian Portuguese orthography, when the sound /g/ appears before an 'e' or an 'i' it is spelled with 'gu' as in the word 'guitarra' (guitar). In this same context, the consonant sound /k/ is spelled 'qu' as in the word 'quilo'. The letter 'g' before 'i' and 'e' sounds like /j/ and not like /g/ and the letter 'c' in this same context sounds like /s/ and not like /k/. Monteiro asked groups of children from kindergarten to fourth grade to read and write words and non-words containing the digraphs 'gu' and 'qu' and the letters 'g' and 'c' occurring before both 'i' and 'e'. The results obtained showed that the rules involving the use of those digraphs are not acquired simultaneously. The acquisition of the digraph 'qu' preceded that of 'gu'. Ninety per cent of the children who were in their first year at school correctly used the digraph 'qu' while only 60 per cent of these same children had acquired the digraph 'gu'. The acquisition of the digraph 'gu' only reached 90 per cent for children who were in their fourth year of school. Monteiro's cross-sectional data also showed that the conditional rules are acquired in reading before they can be transferred to spelling.

These two studies of conditional spelling rules support Frith's (1985) developmental model regarding the prediction that reading becomes orthographic before spelling. However, the acquisition of the conditional rules cannot be explained by a developmental model in which, at a particular stage, children become able to handle conditional rule patterns as proposed by Marsh, Friedman, Welch and Desberg (1981). As suggested by Nunes (1990), after the alphabetic stage, the assessment of children's progress in spelling as well as in reading can only be considered in terms of the number of spelling rules that they have mastered in reading and in spelling.

Monteiro's study also makes two other important contributions to the understanding of how children acquire conditional rules in reading and spelling. Her first contribution was a method of investigation in which children were tested not only on their reading and spelling of words containing the target spelling pattern (as, for example, the digraph 'gu') but on their spelling of other words in which the sound /g/ is spelled with a 'g' and words in which the letter 'g' is pronounced as /j/. These control words allowed Monteiro to detect the overgeneralisations that children made in reading and spelling when they find out about the ambiguities involved in some letter–sound correspondences. Monteiro's study suggests that there are possibly three main levels of performance in the acquisition of conditional spelling rules. The first level is characterised as a lack of knowledge regarding the spelling possibilities of particular letters. At the second level children make overgeneralisations. Although their errors may increase, this level reflects an advance in orthographic knowledge because children demonstrate that they have become acquainted with the spelling possibilities of Portuguese orthography. The third level is the correct use of the spelling pattern. Although Monteiro's cross-sectional data suggested a developmental sequence for these three stages, longitudinal studies were required to reach a better understanding of this acquisition process.

The second contribution of Monteiro's research was that she compared children's performance for words and non-words. She found that reading and spelling words were significantly easier than reading and spelling non-words; and that this pattern of result was more frequent with older children. The fact that older children perform more accurately when they use these spelling rules in words and do not transfer this knowledge to non-words shows that, for most children, the learning of orthographic rules does not become fully productive and reflects a lexical effect as children advance in reading and in spelling instruction. It is possible, as suggested by Monteiro, that what accounts for these results is the emphasis given in classroom practices to the memorising of correct spelling. Treating an orthography with so many generative possibilities as a matter of visual memory prevents children from gaining a full grasp of the conventional rules that govern Portuguese orthography. We shall return to this topic later.

The first longitudinal study focusing on the acquisition of conditional spelling rules in Portuguese was conducted by Rego and Buarque (1997a). The subjects in this study were seventy-nine children from public and private schools in Recife. These children were seen three times at intervals of six months, during a twelve-month period. A child was first asked to complete sentences, one at a time, by writing the word that was dictated by the experimenter. The experimenter read the complete sentence to the child and asked him to fill in the blank, writing the missing word that he had just mentioned. The experimenter pronounced the word naturally and he repeated it if the child wished. Afterwards the children were given a similar task, but this time they were told that the sentences should be completed with the strange word dictated by the experimenter. The words and non-words were carefully selected to assess how the children were dealing with two types of conditional spelling rules in Portuguese orthography. The first were rules whose application depended on the position of the phonological unit in the word or on the presence of a marker letter and the second were rules whose application require morpho-syntactic information. Some past tense morphemes and verb infinitives in Portuguese sound the same as some noun endings, although they are spelled differently. A total of eight rules were investigated, five of the first type and three of the second type.

The changes in performance with age identified by Rego and Buarque in each of the eight conditional rules could be described in terms of a three-phase process. In the first phase, children ignore the conditional rule and apply the alphabetic principle with no restrictions. In this phase, children tend to preserve the idea that a particular letter always represents a particular sound and to prefer phonetic transcriptions. They may write very frequent words correctly, but they fail to use the conventional rules in unfamiliar words and in non-words. In the second phase, children begin to find out that the same letter may represent more than one sound and that the same sound may be represented by more than one letter. The discovery of these inconsistencies, however, does not imply the acquisition of the conditional rule that determines the correct letter choice. In this phase, children begin to make use of overgeneralisations and start to make errors that were not present in phase 1, when they ignored the different ways of spelling the same sound. The third phase of this process is the mastering of the rule.

We shall illustrate this three-phase process by describing the pattern of performance found in two types of conditional rule, one which involved the sound position in the word and the other that implicated morpho-syntactic restrictions.

The phoneme /R/ in Portuguese which corresponds to the sound represented by the letter 'h' in English (e.g. 'hat') is always spelled with an 'r' in Portuguese, except when it occurs between vowels, as in the word 'terra' (earth). In these contexts it is spelled with double r (rr) because the letter 'r' in this same context represents the phoneme /r/. Children's acquisition of this orthographic principle involves a significant number of productive errors which can only be clearly detected if we ask children to write words containing the two sounds represented by the letter 'r' in different positions. Rego and Buarque (1997a) asked seventy-nine children from public and private schools in Recife to write words and non-words containing the /R/ sound at the beginning of the word and between a consonant and a vowel when it is always spelled with one 'r'. They also asked children to write words and non-words containing this same sound between vowels when it is always spelled with double r (rr). Finally they asked children to spell words and non-words which should be written with the letter 'r' between vowels but in these words this letter represented the phoneme /r/. Rego and Buarque found different patterns of performance which correspond to the three-phase process mentioned above.

At the least mature level, children tend to spell all the unfamiliar words and the non-words with a single 'r', ignoring the conditional rule involving the digraph 'rr'. At this level of performance children would write words like 'guita**rr**ista' as 'guitarista' but they would make no errors in the other contexts. Children in categories 2, 3 and 4 were in the second phase of this process. They used the digraph not only to represent the /R/ sound between vowels – the correct use – but they also used it to represent this sound in inappropriate contexts, producing overgeneralisations of different kinds. Children in category 2 used the digraph to represent the sound /R/ not only when it occurred between vowels as in 'guita**rr**ista' (correct use), but also when the /R/ sound occurred between consonant and vowels and when the /r/ sound occurred between vowels (incorrect uses). These children would spell a word like 'genro' as 'gen**rr**o' and a word like 'gorila' as 'go**rr**ila'. Children in category 3 made a sharp distinction between the sounds represented by the letter 'r' and used the digraph to represent the /R/ sound in every position including the beginning of words and the single 'r' to represent the sound /r/. These children would spell words like '**r**egime', 'guita**rr**ista', and 'genro' as '**rr**egime', 'guita**rr**ista' and 'gen**rr**o', preserving the single 'r' to words as go**r**ila. Children in category 4 restricted the digraph to the representation of the /R/ sound in the middle of the word including the context between a consonant and a vowel. These children differ from children in category 3 because they did not use the digraph at the beginning of words. Children in category 5 had nearly all the spellings correct and children in category 6 showed complete mastery of the rule, using the digraph only in the correct context.

Our second example is a type of conditional rule whose application requires morpho-syntactic information. In Portuguese there are nouns and verbs that end with the diphthong /iw/. When this diphthong occurs in the third person singular of the past tense form of particular verbs, it can only be written as 'iu' while it can to be written either as 'io' or 'il' when it occurs in a noun. Rego and Buarque found that younger writers tend to ignore the spelling alternatives and to write both verbs and nouns with 'iu', making a phonetic transcription. In the second phase children start to use all the possible spelling alternatives 'iu', 'io' and 'il' without considering the contextual restriction. Two categories of performance were identified at phase 2: some children use all the possible alternatives both in nouns and verbs while others use 'io' and 'il' for nouns and extend these spellings to verbs. The difference between categories 2 and 3 is that children in category 3 no longer use 'iu' for nouns. In phase 3 children begin to show mastery of the conditional rule using correct spellings in nouns and verbs.

The results which emerged from Rego and Buarque's longitudinal study can be summarised as follows. As in the Nunes, Bryant and Bindman (1997) longitudinal study of the acquisition of the past tense morpheme of English regular verbs, there were developmental progressions for each of the conditional rules studied by Rego and Buarque. Across time, children either tended to remain in the same category of performance or to progress to a more advanced one. Regression to less advanced hypotheses occurred in all cases but the frequency of this remained below 15 per cent. However, a more careful look at these regressions revealed further evidence concerning the dynamics of this developmental process. Take, for example, category 4, in the double r conditional rule. It is possible that a child who was classified in category 4 on one occasion because of using 'rr' between vowels and between consonants and vowels, might extend this 'rr' to words beginning with the /R/ sound on the next test session. This would be classed as category 3 performance. At first glance this looks like a case of regression based on the hierarchy of categories that we proposed. However, what the longitudinal analysis tells us is that this child was in a process of overgeneralisation which was completed in the second session. In other words most children in category 4 showed greater adherence to the double r conditional rule over time rather than regression towards category 3 performance. A few regressions were also observed even in children who had apparently acquired the rule on the first testing session. These were children who got all spellings correct including non-words. In the next session some of these children showed apparently lower levels of performance which showed that the overgeneralisation process was beginning to take place.

The second finding was that, as in previous studies (Monteiro, 1995; Nunes 1990), the rules were not acquired simultaneously. Moreover, the sequence in which the rules were being acquired in the private school setting was quite similar to the one found in the public school setting. At first sight this suggests that there may be a hierarchical complexity in the mastery of conditional rules which is derived from the orthography. Some rules are easier to acquire than others, independent of social class and teaching method.

However, a recent finding by de Melo (1997) suggested another interpretation. Her study demonstrated that the hierarchy emerging from Rego and Buarque's longitudinal data can be changed by instruction. She conducted a training study in which she demonstrated that one particularly difficult rule for young children, the one involving the use of the digraph 'rr', can be productively used by children even in their first year at school. In Rego and Buarque's data no children acquired this rule during their first year at school, although the digraph 'rr' is part of school programmes from an early age. This was also true at the time of the first test of de Melo's study. No children in the experimental and control groups matched by age, IQ, and phonological awareness were able to use the digraph 'rr' in non-words correctly. However, after a sequence of training sessions in which the children were encouraged to discuss their ideas about the use of the digraph 'rr' among themselves and in which they were provided with the necessary evidence to actively and explicitly construct this conditional spelling rule, all children in the experimental groups acquired the rule in a non-word task. Post-tests soon after the training and two months later showed a significantly superior performance in the experimental groups in relation to the groups that were given traditional instruction. Nevertheless, the superiority of the experimental groups in the use of the digraph 'rr' was not transferred to other conditional spelling rules that were also evaluated in the post-test but were not part of the training. These results are quite interesting because they indicate that the learning of conditional spelling rules can be enhanced if the teaching method provides children with opportunities to reflect upon and to find out about each of the spelling rules underlying the writing system. Therefore, the hierarchy of acquisition suggested by Rego and Buarque's result is probably the outcome of school practices in which there are no structured classroom activities to discuss spelling rules explicitly. As a result most children take a lifetime to discover the more intricate conventions of spelling in Brazilian Portuguese. One factor which seems to make the mastering of particular rules difficult seems to be the frequency of words which would naturally provide children with the necessary evidence to construct the rule.

The third important finding in Rego and Buarque's investigation was the striking differences between the children in terms of the number of rules that they were able to master after nearly two years of reading and spelling instruction. In both school settings (private and public) we were able to identify a group of children who distinguished themselves by the number of conditional spelling rules that they were able to handle successfully, despite the teaching approach. The individual cognitive skills that characterised this group of children were the main focus of Rego and Buarque's next longitudinal study.

Some of the conditional rules investigated clearly involved children's ability to deal with phonological information, while others required the use of morpho-syntactic information and implicated other levels of linguistic analysis. Consequently, a natural move in Rego and Buarque's investigation was to carry out a second longitudinal study which looked at the role played by phonological and syntactic awareness in the acquisition of different types of conditional spelling rules. There was already some evidence that the acquisition of certain orthographic patterns is related to children's sensitivity to morphology and syntax in a language such as English (Nunes, Bryant and Bindman, 1997), which has a quite irregular orthography in terms of letter–sound correspondences. Therefore, we needed a study of a more regular orthography which also included other measures of linguistic awareness (such as phonological awareness) and investigated other types of conditional spelling rules such as those requiring morpho-syntactic information.

Does phonological and syntactic awareness facilitate the acquisition of conditional spelling rules?

In the past twenty years a number of studies have shown that metalinguistic skills such as phonological and syntactic awareness are related to progress in reading and spelling. The connection between phonological awareness and learning to read and spell in alphabetic scripts is quite easy to explain, given the nature of such scripts, especially in more regular orthographies. The general principle underlying alphabetic scripts is that letters represent the sounds in the words. Even when this relationship is not a one-to-one correspondence, because it involves contextual restrictions, sophisticated phonemic analyses are clearly necessary (e.g. in Portuguese the phoneme /g/ is spelled as 'gu' when it appears before /e/ and /i/ but it is spelled as 'g' when it occurs before /a/, /o/ and /u/).

Recent findings suggest that measures of syntactic awareness are related not only to reading comprehension but also to the initial development of decoding skills (Bowey, 1986; Rego, 1991; Rego, 1993; Tunmer, Herriman and Nesdale, 1988; Willow and Ryan, 1986) as well as to the acquisition of conventional spelling (Rego, 1991). There are two possible explanations for these apparently puzzling results. One is that proposed by Tunmer *et al.* (1988). They claimed that one possible reason for the connection between performance in syntactic awareness tasks and initial progress in decoding is that children who are aware of the syntactic structure of the sentence use context more effectively to compensate for their initially insufficient word recognition skills and by this means they learn about the orthographic patterns of the language.

Rego and Bryant (1993) provided some direct evidence to support Tunmer *et al.*'s explanation. In a study with English-speaking children, measures of syntactic awareness were found to be specifically connected to children's performance in a contextual facilitation task in which they were required to read unfamiliar words with the support of a previously presented oral context.

More recently, Rego (1997) argued that the connection between syntactic awareness and children's decoding development might be the outcome of particular methods of instruction which emphasise the use of contextual strategies to read unfamiliar words. In a study with Brazilian children who were learning to read by the explicit teaching of letter–sound correspondences, Rego did not find a connection between syntactic awareness and performance in decoding tasks. However, in a previous study involving a group of Brazilian children who were taught by the whole language approach, this type of connection was found (Rego, 1993). Notwithstanding this possibility, Rego's (1997) results might have been different if she had looked at the connection between syntactic awareness and reading by using word and non-word reading tasks that involved the use of spelling rules that require morpho-syntactic information. In Rego's studies the decoding tasks did not contain words whose reading necessarily required this type of information.

Recently Nunes, Bryant and Bindman (1997) have proposed a second possible explanation for the relationship between syntactic awareness and children's progress in reading and spelling. They have argued that the connection between syntactic awareness and orthographic knowledge might be the outcome of orthographic regularities that involve morpho-syntactic information. They found that measures of morphological and syntactic awareness are good predictors of advances in spelling such as the past tense morpheme of the regular verbs in English. In Portuguese, as in other languages, there are many cases where morpho-syntactic information has to be applied in order to resolve ambiguities in spelling. In these cases grammatical analysis is clearly involved.

Rego and Buarque (1997b) decided to investigate the relationship between these two metalinguistic skills and children's mastery of two types of conditional spelling rules in the Portuguese orthography:

(a) rules whose application depended on the position of the phono-
    logical unit in the word or on the presence of a marker letter;
(b) rules whose application required a grammatical distinction between
    verbs and nouns.

Our hypothesis was that phonological awareness would mainly contribute to children's acquisition of conditional spelling rules based on the phonological context of the words, while syntactic awareness would only contribute to very specific types of conditional rules – those requiring the distinction of grammatical categories. Children who are sensitive to syntax should acquire these rules more easily.

The subjects in the study were forty-six Brazilian children who were taught to read by a strict phonic approach. We shall concentrate on the results of the first and last sessions of the study because the pattern of results was basically the same in the middle session.

The children were first seen in the first half of their first year at school when they were at the mean age of seven years two months. In the last session, which took place in the second half of their second year at school, the sample was reduced to forty children who were at the mean age of eight years and seven months. These children were in a private school where reading and spelling instruction started in kindergarten.

At the time of the first test, children were given a phonological aware-ness task and a syntactic awareness task. The phonological awareness task was a phoneme deletion task. Children were asked to pronounce words and non-words by deleting the first sounds. The syntactic aware-ness tasks were of two kinds. The first was a sentence anagram task. This was a version of the task devised by Pratt, Tunmer and Nesdale (1984) and used by Tunmer and by Rego (1991) in previous studies. In this task children are asked to transform a random string of words in a grammatical sentence by correcting the word order. The second was a word categorisation task specially devised for this study. In this task children had to categorise words, separating nouns from verbs and adjectives. This second task required an explicit knowledge of word class. The children were given a big card containing a noun, a verb and an adjective written at the top of each column and were given small cards with either nouns, verbs or adjectives written on them. They were asked to place the small cards in the appropriate column, according to word class. As control measures children were given two tasks: a prose reading task which assessed children's literacy development through their level of reading comprehension, since the prose passage involved words containing most of the orthographic difficulties that we were going to assess later in the study; and the WISC verbal sub-test involv-ing memory for digits. We chose this sub-test because the teaching of orthography in Brazil relies heavily on children's ability to memorise words and the order of the letters in the words.

In the last session of the study, the children were given a spelling task which aimed to test their acquisition of conditional rules. Five rules required the analysis of the phonological context of words and four rules involved morpho-syntactic aspects. We devised a dictation task, part of it involving forty words and part of it involving twenty-seven non-words. This task and the categorisation procedure of the children's performance in spelling was similar to the one used by Rego and Buarque (1997a) described earlier in the chapter.

Children who had acquired more than 50 per cent of the conditional rules requiring phonological analysis were assigned to group A spellers. There were sixteen children in this group. The remaining twenty-four were assigned to group B spellers. In relation to the conditional rules requiring morpho-syntactic information, children whose spellings demonstrated that they distinguished verbs from nouns in Portuguese orthography were classified in the acquisition category. Children who were classified in this category for more than 50 per cent of the rules investigated were assigned to group A spellers and the ones who did not reach this criterion were assigned to group B spellers.

The results of this longitudinal study indicated that, according to the Mann-Whitney U test, the children who were assigned to group A spellers in relation to the acquisition of rules involving morpho-syntactic information were significantly superior to children in group B in the phoneme deletion task ($Z = 2.21$, $p < 0.05$), in the sentence anagram task ($Z = 2.83$, $p < 0.01$) and in reading comprehension ($Z = 2.0$, $p < 0.05$). No significant differences were found between the two groups of children in relation to the word categorisation task and in the WISC verbal sub-test involving memory for digits. A fixed-order logistic regression showed that performance in the sentence anagram task predicted children's assignment to the groups even after controlling for children's performance in the phoneme deletion task and in reading comprehension. Therefore we found that implicit syntactic knowledge, as assessed by the sentence anagram task, facilitates the acquisition of conditional rules involving morpho-syntactic information. However, this same syntactic awareness task did not differentiate between the children who were assigned to group A spellers and those of group B in relation to conditional rules that just required grapho-phonic information. According to the Mann-Whitney U test, the children in group A spellers were just superior to group B spellers in the phoneme deletion task ($Z = 2.80$, $p < 0.01$) and in the reading comprehension task ($Z = 2.03$, $p < 0.05$). No other significant difference was found. Fixed-order logistic regression also indicated that after controlling for the effects of reading comprehension, the phonological awareness task showed a significant contribution to children's assignment to the spelling groups when the conditional rules just required phonological analysis.

The results of this study are quite interesting from several aspects. First of all, the results are consistent with those obtained by Nunes,

Bryant and Bindman (1997). They show that early measures of children's sensitivity to the syntax of the language predict the acquisition of orthographic patterns requiring syntactic information. Another interesting finding was that explicit syntactic knowledge is not a good predictor of this type of acquisition. This is probably because, at the beginning of the first school year, children are not explicitly taught about grammatical categories, and this is knowledge that requires explicit instruction. Children's performance in the word categorisation task was extremely poor. Finally, this study added an important control: the assessment of conditional rules that did not involve morpho-syntactic information and of children's phonological awareness. The addition of these variables allowed us to demonstrate how specific the contribution of syntactic awareness to spelling development is, at least in school settings in which contextual strategies are not encouraged when children are confronted with unfamiliar words. Future research will discover whether the results obtained by Rego and Buarque (1997b) could be replicated in a group of children who are exposed to the whole language approach from the outset of reading and spelling instruction. In these school settings it is expected that children learn about Portuguese orthography by interacting with texts both in reading and in spelling. This approach overloads children's working memory and places a strong emphasis on children's ability to find out about spelling rules through their experience with texts. Rego (1993) has already produced some evidence that, in such school settings, syntactic awareness predicts children's ability to read non-words which requires knowledge of conditional spelling rules that involve phonological information.

Conclusions

Learning to read and spell in a predictable orthography like Portuguese involves to a great extent the discovery of the underlying principles that govern such orthography. As was seen in this chapter, after Brazilian children reach the alphabetic stage, both in reading and spelling, a considerable amount of cognitive effort is involved in the mastering of conditional spelling rules. We have seen that learning about different spelling rules could be considered as a problem-solving task in which children's mastery of each rule can be described as a three-phase process, involving a period when children ignore the contextual rules although they may know the correct spellings by rote; a period in which overgeneralisation errors take place; and a period in which children reach an understanding of the correct context in which a sound or a letter is used in words. The same child can be in different phases for different spelling rules. These phases are also affected by the component skills of literacy. Children usually acquire a rule in reading before they are able to use the same contextual rule in spelling. Nunes (1992) and Monteiro (1995) found that this was true even for non-word reading, a task in which children have no contextual support from meaning. These results are consistent with recent findings by Cossu, Gugliotta and Marshall (1995). These authors reported a developmental asymmetry between the reading and spelling of words and non-words. Children learning to read and spell Italian, a language with a transparent orthography, performed significantly better in reading than in spelling non-words. Cossu *et al.* claimed that these unexpected discrepancies between reading and spelling cannot be explained in terms of the idiosyncratic nature of some orthographic systems. Their interpretation of these results is that the information-processing architecture that governs the development of reading has distinct functional properties from that of spelling.

Recently the idea that an explicit knowledge of orthographic rules is what differentiates good from poor spellers was empirically tested by de Morais and Teberosky (1994) through an interesting methodology. To test children's knowledge of orthographic rules they used a task in which children were asked to deliberately spell Portuguese words incorrectly. Their main hypothesis was that children who had a better performance in a dictation task would be able to misspell more effectively, preserving the sound pattern of the words. They found that the group of children who were more successful in the dictation task were also the ones with a superior performance in the misspelling task. These children not only misspelled more but they were also quite selective in terms of these misspellings: they substituted graphemes for other graphemes which also represented the same sound in other contexts.

Another important conclusion emerging from the evidence reported in this chapter, and which is also consistent with findings reported in Nunes *et al.*'s study, is that the acquisition of conditional spelling rules might be facilitated by an implicit awareness of the linguistic units directly involved in the type of contextual restrictions imposed by each rule. Children who are sensitive to grammatical units probably have an advantage in mastering morpho-syntactic restrictions. However, evidence from a training study is necessary to establish the direction of the links between syntactic awareness and the mastering of specific orthographic rules.

So far the generative power of Portuguese orthography and the relevance of metalinguistic awareness to the acquisition of conditional spelling rules have not been systematically considered in our classroom practices. In most school settings in Brazil, the emphasis has been on memorising the correct spellings of words or on the repetition of spelling rules by rote. Therefore children learn to write very frequent words and they may even repeat some well-known spelling rules, but they usually take a long time to generate correct new spellings based on those rules. However, the evidence brought out by de Melo (1997) suggests that a different approach in which children are engaged in organised reconstruction of the orthographic system would be beneficial to the teaching of orthography in Brazilian schools.

REFERENCES

Abaurre, B. (1988). The interplay between spontaneous writing and underlying linguistic representation. *European Journal of Psychology of Education*, 3 (4), 415–30.

Alvarenga, D., Nicolau, E., Soares, M. B., Oliveira, M. A. and do Nascimento, M. (1989). Da forma sonora da fala à forma gráfica da escrita. Uma análise lingüística do processo de alfabetização. *Cadernos de Estudos Lingüísticos*, 16, 5–30.

Bowey, J. (1986). Syntactic awareness in relation to reading skill and reading comprehension monitoring. *Journal of Experimental Child Psychology*, 41, 282–99.

Bradley, L. and Bryant, P. (1985). *Rhyme and Reason in Reading and Spelling*. Ann Arbor, MI: University of Michigan Press.

Carraher, T. N. (1985). Explorações sobre o desenvolvimento da ortografia no Português. *Psicologia, Teoria e Pesquisa*: Universidade de Brasília, 1, 269–85.

Carraher, T. and Rego, L. L. B. (1983). Understanding the alphabetic system. In D. Rogers and J. Sloboda (eds.), *The Acquisition of Symbolic Skills*. New York: Plenum Press.

Cossu, G., Gugliotta, M. and Marshall, J. (1995). Reading and spelling in a transparent orthography. *Reading and Writing; An Interdisciplinary Journal*, 7, 9–22.

de Melo, K. L. R. (1997). Uma proposta alternativa para o ensino da ortografia. Unpublished master's dissertation, Universidade Federal de Pernambuco.

de Morais, A. G. and Teberosky, A. (1994). Erros e transgressões infantis na ortografia do português. *Discursos*, 8, 15–51.

Faraco, C. A. (1992). *Escrita e alfabetização*. São Paulo: Contexto.

Ferreiro, E. (1985). *Reflexões sobre alfabetização*. São Paulo: Cortez.

Ferreiro, E. and Gomes Palácio, M. (1982). *Análisis de las perturbaciones en el proceso de aprendizaje escolar de la lectura*. México: Dirección General de Educación Especial.

Ferreiro, E. and Teberosky, A. (1986). *A psicogênese da língua escrita*. Porto Alegre: Artes Médicas.

Frith, U. (1985). Beneath the surface of developmental dyslexia. In K. Patterson, M. Courtheart and J. Marshall (eds.), *Surface Dyslexia*. London: Lawrence Erlbaum.

Lemle, M. (1987). *Guia teórico e prático do alfabetizador*. São Paulo: Editora Ática.

Lundberg, I., Olofsson, A. and Wall, S. (1980). Reading and spelling skills in the first school year predicted from phonemic awareness skills in kindergarten. *Scandinavian Journal of Psychology*, 21, 159–73.

Marsh, G., Friedman, M., Welch, V. and Desberg, P. (1980). A cognitive developmental theory of reading acquisition. In G. E. MacKinnon and T. G. Waller (eds.), *Reading Research: Advances in Theory and Practice*, vol. III. New York: Academic Press.

Monteiro, A. (1995). A aquisição de regras ortográficas de contexto na leitura e na escrita. Unpublished master's dissertation, Universidade Federal de Pernambuco.

Nunes, T. (1990). Construtivismo e alfabetização. Um balanço crítico. *Educação em Revista*, Belo Horizonte, 12, 33–43.

(1992). Leitura e escrita: processos e desenvolvimento. In E. Alencar (ed.), *Novas contribuições da psicologia aos processos de ensino aprendizagem*. São Paulo: Cortez.

Nunes, T. Bryant, P. and Bindman, M. (1997). E quem se preocupa com a ortografia? In Cardoso-Martins (ed.), *Consciência fonológica e alfabetização* (pp. 129–58). Petrópolis: Vozes.

Pratt, C., Tunmer, W. and Nesdale, A. (1984). Children's capacity to correct grammatical violations in sentences. *Journal of Child Language*, 2, 129–41.

Rego, L. L. B. (1985). Descobrindo a língua escrita antes de aprender a ler: algumas implicações pedagógicas. *Revista Brasileira de Estudos Pedagógicos*, 152, 66, 5–27.

(1991). The role of early linguistic awareness in children's reading and spelling. Unpublished doctoral dissertation, University of Oxford.

(1993). O papel da consciência sintática na aquisição da língua escrita. *Temas em Psicologia*, 1, 79–87.

(1997). The connection between syntactic awareness and reading: evidence from Portuguese speaking children taught by a phonic method. *International Journal of Behavioral Development*, 20 (2), 349–65.

Rego, L. L. B. and Bryant, P. E. (1993). The connection between phonological, syntactic and semantic skills and children's reading and spelling. *European Journal of Psychology of Education*, 7 (3), 235–46.

Rego, L. L. B. and Buarque, L. L. (1997a). O desenvolvimento da ortografia nas séries iniciais do primeiro grau e sua relação com a consciência fonológica e a consciência gramatical. Unpublished research report, Brasília.

(1997b). Consciência sintática, consciência fonológica e aquisição de regras ortográficas. *Psicologia: Reflexão e Crítica*, 10 (2), 199–217.

Tunmer, W. and Nesdale, A. (1985). Phonemic segmentation skills and beginning reading. *Journal of Educational Psychology*, 77 (4), 417–27.

Tunmer, W., Herriman, M. and Nesdale, A. (1988). Metalinguistic abilities and beginning reading. *Reading Research Quarterly*, 23 (2), 135–58.

Willows, D. M. and Ryan, E. B. (1986). The development of grammatical sensitivity and its relationship to early reading achievement. *Reading Research Quarterly*, 21, 253–65.

6   Learning to read and write in Hebrew

David Share and Iris Levin

This chapter reviews the available evidence on the development of reading and writing in the Hebrew language. In the first of four sections, we present a brief overview of the unique features of Hebrew language and orthography, with special emphasis on Semitic morphology (the 'root-plus-pattern' system) and the consonantal alphabet in both its pointed (fully vowelled) and unpointed (partly vowelled) forms. The next two sections review studies of pre-conventional reading and writing among pre-schoolers, followed by conventional in-school reading and spelling. A fourth section looks at research dealing with the cognitive and psycho-linguistic factors underlying individual differences in literacy acquisition. Our review concludes with a summary of both the language-specific and language-universal aspects of Hebrew literacy acquisition.

Aspects of Hebrew morphology and orthography

Morphology

The most characteristically Semitic feature of Hebrew is its derivational morphology (Berman, 1985). Most content words consist of a primarily consonantal 'root' and vocalic 'pattern'. The root is the semantic core of a word and usually consists of three consonants. Indeed, the entire Hebrew lexicon (some 50,000 to 100,000 words) is based on approximately 2,000 roots. Specific words are produced only when a root is embedded into a pattern consisting of vocalic infixes, and mostly CV prefixes and/or suffixes. For example, verb forms derived from the triconsonantal root קלט = KLT include: קָלַט = KALAT (he grasped), נִקְלַט = NIKLAT (was grasped/absorbed), הִקְלִיט = HIKLIT (he recorded). Most noun forms operate on the same root-plus-pattern principle. Nouns derived from the KLT root include: קְלִיטָה = KLITA (absorption), מִקְלָט = MIKLAT (shelter), הַקְלָטָה = HAKLATA (recording), מַקְלֵט = MAKLET (receiver). While some noun patterns represent semantic categories (for example, the form cAcAc is characteristic

89

of professions: KATAV – journalist, NAGAR – carpenter, SAPAR – barber), others are highly unpredictable.

As already noted, the semantic core of a word (the root) is usually consonantal, with vowels (and certain additional consonants) indicating mainly grammatical inflections such as person, number and gender. Possibly for this reason, Hebrew orthographies from the earliest times until the present day have been predominantly consonantal systems with either no vowels or vowels represented in a subsidiary manner. The major drawback of a consonantal system, however, is the abundance of homographic words (both homophonic and heterophonic), all deriving from the same consonantal root (Bentin, Bargai and Katz, 1984; Navon and Shimron, 1984). For example, כתב KTV could represent *journalist, orthography, he wrote*, and more. Shimron and Sivan (1994) estimate that almost one-quarter of the words appearing in regular text are homographic when presented out of context.

Two separate systems of vowelling exist today. The first, and oldest – called 'mothers of reading' – employs four of the consonantal letters (א ה ו י) to serve the dual function of signifying vowels as well as consonants. Apart from the ambiguity caused by using the same letter to represent both a vowel and a consonant (e.g. עול AVEL, 'injustice', עול OL 'burden'), this system is both inconsistent and incomplete (Levin, Ravid and Rapaport, in press; Shimron, 1993). Standard printed Hebrew appearing in today's books, newspapers and magazines is partly and inconsistently vowelled by means of the mothers of reading.

A second system of vowelisation employs diacritical marks or points (*nekudot*). So-called pointed Hebrew is restricted largely to poetry, sacred texts and children's books. In contrast to the mothers of reading, this diacritical system provides a complete and virtually unambiguous representation of the vowels by means of tiny dots and dashes appearing mostly under, but sometimes also above and between the letters. For example: ד = /di/, ד = /do/, ד = /du/, ד = /da/, ד = /de/. There is, however, considerable duplication in this system in that each sound has between one and four representations marking phonetic distinctions that no longer exist.

Children learn to read in pointed Hebrew, which has almost perfect grapheme-to-phoneme correspondence; both consonants and vowel diacritics have a single unambiguous pronunciation (Navon and Shimron, 1984). There are no phonologically irregular words in pointed Hebrew. Unlike grapheme-to-phoneme correspondence, however, phoneme-to-grapheme relationships are frequently variable, with a number of pairs of (once phonemically distinct) graphemes now representing the same phoneme. The vast majority of Hebrew words, therefore, contain consonants and vowels which could be spelled with alternative letters.

As the name *square alphabet* suggests, Hebrew letter architecture, relative to the Latin alphabet, is more uniformly block-like with more horizontal and vertical strokes and fewer curves and diagonals. Slower letter recognition times relative to English may be attributable to this uniformity (Shimron and Navon, 1981). Not only are letters less distinctive, but word length and word shape are also quite uniform: the former attributable to the ubiquitous three-letter root, and the latter to the paucity of ascenders and descenders.

Owing to its synthetic nature, Hebrew words are highly dense morphemically. Not only are tense, person, number, etc. usually indicated by inflecting roots, but many function words (*to, from, in, and, the,* etc.) and possessives (*my, your, our*) are frequently affixed to both nouns and pronouns. For example, the two-word sentence אכלנו בבוקר (AKHALNU BABOKER) translates into five English words 'We ate in the morning'. This demands considerable 'unpacking' on the part of the reader and creates an additional source of homography.

Although some influential scholars (e.g. Gelb, 1963) have claimed that early (unpointed) Semitic scripts were syllabaries, not alphabets, contemporary Israeli scholars are agreed that today's regular, unpointed Hebrew is a consonantal alphabet (Bentin and Frost, 1987; Frost and Bentin, 1992; Levin, Korat and Amsterdamer, 1996; Navon and Shimron, 1994; Shimron, 1993), with graphemes representing individual consonant phonemes. Owing to its distinctive morphology, full representation of vowels in Hebrew, at least for the skilled reader, may well be unnecessary in contrast to Indo-European languages such as English which use vowel distinctions to mark basic morphemic contrasts and for which the graphemic representation of vowels may be more critical (consider BUT, BET, BAT, BIT, BOAT, BEAT, etc.). Not only is vowel information less critical for the Hebrew speaker, but this information is far more easily inferred in printed Hebrew owing to simple and predictable syllable structures which consist almost exclusively of CV and CVC syllables.

Writing among pre-school children

In Israel, formal instruction in reading and writing begins on entry to first grade at six to seven years of age. However, from a very young age children are exposed to print, story books, video cassettes, educational games and lists of letters and numbers. Consequently, various aspects of literacy begin to develop well before the onset of formal schooling. One aspect of literacy, writing, has been the subject of a series of studies carried out by Levin and her colleagues. These studies examined the development of writing among three- to seven-year-old Hebrew-speaking Israelis from five perspectives: the emergence of the graphic features of writing; the strategies used in representing meaning in writing; developmental scales of writing; the representation of vowels versus consonants; and the correlations between level of writing and other aspects of literacy in pre-school, and their contributions to reading, writing and language in school.

The emergence of graphic features of writing

Tolchinsky-Landsmann and Levin (1985) asked three- to six-year-olds to write short phrases ('red flower'). Each written product was examined for whether it exhibited a number of general features: linearity, segmentation into written units, constricted size of units, and controlled number of units written per phrase. Likewise, each piece of writing was examined with respect to two Hebrew-specific features: writing in Hebrew letters and in the conventional direction, from right to left. All features increased with age, with general ones used consistently by most children from age four, and Hebrew-specific features from age five. The acquisition of general features has also been documented in the writing of children in other orthographies (Brenneman, Massey, Machado and Gelman, 1996; Gombert and Fayol, 1992; Sulzby, Barnhart and Hieshima, 1989).

Turning to Hebrew-specific features, Israeli children are exposed to symbols written from both right to left and left to right. While Hebrew is written from the right, other orthographies, such as English and numbers, are written from the left. The acquisition of the Hebrew direction indicates a specific distinction between writing in Hebrew and writing in other languages or marking numerals. Two steps were discerned: three- to four-year-olds often mixed directions; four- to five-year-olds wrote in a single direction, though not necessarily the conventional one; and five- to six-year-olds adopted the conventional direction of writing.

Strategies used to represent meaning in writing

Children who know that writing is different from drawing (Brenneman *et al.*, 1996; Tolchinsky-Landsmann and Levin, 1985) are not necessarily aware of the symbolic relation between the signifiers and the signified. When asked to write a spoken phrase, they have to solve the problem of how to represent it in writing. Two main strategies were observed: referential and phonological. Children who use a referential strategy introduce into their writing various features of the referent. For example, when asked to write pairs of words whose referents differ in quantity, such as 'elephant' *pil*, and 'ant' *nemala*, there are children who systematically write longer strings standing for the bigger objects. This phenomenon can be explained as resulting from children's puzzling over the fact that different words are written using different numbers of letters. Not knowing what the number of letters signifies, they exploit this feature to represent quantifiable features of the referent (Ferreiro and Teberosky, 1982).

Use of the referential strategy representing quantity has often been observed among Israeli pre-schoolers (Levin, Korat and Amsterdamer, 1996; Levin and Tolchinsky-Landsmann, 1989; Tolchinsky-Landsmann and Levin, 1985, 1987). A variety of other features emerged as well. When asked to write pairs of words differing in colour ('tomato' and 'cucumber'), children who were offered a variety of colours chose to write in colours characteristic of the referents. A modest proportion of children were also found to use features of the object's form. For example, when asked to write 'a child playing with a ball' one child used a circle as one of his pseudo-letters explaining that it was the ball. The use of referential features appeared throughout the pre-school (four to seven) years. However, the use of form decreased and that of number and colour increased with age.

The referential strategy is used by children less consistently across writings than the phonological strategy, perhaps because the latter converges with conventional writing. A child using the phonological strategy writes longer sounding words with more letters or uses letters that carry the required sound values. The phonological strategy, while rarely found among children younger than five, is quite frequent among older kindergarten children.

Although the referential and phonological strategies are incommensurate, children frequently mix both. Levin and Korat (1993) asked pre-schoolers to write pairs of words that differed both in referential quantity and in phonological length. When asked to write a pair of words, one sounding longer, the other standing for the larger referent ('sea' *yam* vs. 'drop' *tipa*), some children systematically wrote the pairs with the same number of letters, thus trading off both factors. Other children wrote a few pairs referentially, and a few pairs phonologically.

Overall, the phonological strategy became more dominant with age relative to the referential one. Levin and Korat (1993) also found a morphological strategy among the most advanced pre-schoolers. Children were asked to write pairs of mono-morphemic words ('tree' *etz* vs. 'forest' *ya'ar*), and pairs consisting of one mono-morphemic and one bi-morphemic word ('tree' *etz* vs. 'trees' *etzim* with the *-im* suffix denoting plurality). The tendency to write more signs was more pronounced when the longer sounding word was bi-morphemic than when it was mono-morphemic. The morphological strategy was less prevalent than either the referential or phonological strategies.

Finally, a substantial number of pre-schoolers made no use of any of the above strategies. They wrote words as strings of random letters, often including letters from their own names. They seemed to ignore the meaning and form of the words they were asked to write, focusing on letter formation (Levin, Korat and Amsterdamer, 1996; Levin, Share and Shatil, 1996).

Parallel strategies were used by pre-schoolers for word identification. Levin and Korat (1993) presented pairs of printed words and asked children to match spoken with printed words, and to explain their decision. Explanations were classified into five levels: reading or letter naming, phonological (explaining that the longer sounding word is written longer), referential (explaining that the word naming the bigger referent is written longer), phonological–referential (mixing two explanations), and a contextual or egocentric explanation. The referential explanation decreased, while reading and letter naming increased with age. The mixture of both strategies was frequent throughout pre-school.

Developmental scales of writing

Levin, Korat and Amsterdamer (1996) classified pre-schoolers' writing into five levels: scribbling, pseudo-letters or text, random strings of letters, phonetic writing and orthographic writing. *Scribbles* carried no feature of writing and could not be distinguished from scribbles produced for drawings. *Pseudo-letters or pseudo-text* included arbitrary signs often constricted in size and displayed linearly. *Random letters* were Hebrew letters unrelated to the phonological structure of the word. *Phonetic writing* included letters representing the sounds of the word. *Orthographic writing* included words that reflected the orthographic rules of Hebrew script. The transition from one level to the next was found to be gradual; children mixed different levels of writing. Some combined pseudo-letters with Hebrew letters, others wrote some words with random letters and other words phonetically. It was not a rare occurrence for children to choose the first letter of a word phonetically and write the rest in random letters. Nevertheless, the writings of most pre-schoolers could be classified at a single predominant level.

All levels, except the orthographic, were used by children throughout the entire age range (four to seven), although the mean age of children increased from the lower to the higher levels, thus supporting the developmental status of this scale. The orthographic level was exclusively used by the older children. Levin, Share and Shatil (1996) also found that their level of writing was related to children's socio-economic status.

The trends found for writing have parallels in the strategies used for word identification. Share and Jaffe-Gur (in press) investigated strategies employed by pre-schoolers when identifying printed names. While four-year-olds relied mainly on contextual cues such as location or pictorial information, five-year-olds were found to be attending to print, using logographic, partly phonetic or alphabetic strategies. There was a developmental transition from pre-phonetic to phonetic strategies, although many children used different strategies in their attempts to identify different names in different circumstances. An experimental training study by Share and Jaffe-Gur (in press) found that progress appeared to be attributable to the acquisition of phonemic awareness and letter-sound knowledge, rather than to the understanding of the functions and conventions of print.

The representation of vowels versus consonants

Levin et al. (in press) assessed children's level of representation of consonants and vowels in word writing. Writing of consonants was significantly more advanced than that of vowels in kindergarten and in first grade. Kamii (1986) reported a similar trend in English. In Spanish and Italian, pre-schoolers showed the opposite trend, representing more fully vowels than consonants (Ferreiro and Teberosky, 1982; Pontecorvo and Zucchermaglio, 1990; Tolchinsky and Teberosky, in press). Hence, the difference in pace in mastering vowels versus consonants is language specific.

The discrepancy in the acquisition of consonants as opposed to vowels in Hebrew can be explained by the principally consonantal orthography. Recall that consonantal phonemes are fully represented in Hebrew by letters, while vowels are represented in a deficient manner. The difference between consonants and vowels is also reflected in the oral language of Hebrew speakers who often exchange vowels in their pronunciation of words (Ravid, 1995a, b; 1996). In addition, the developmental lag in writing vowels can be attributed to the major role of consonants which constitute the roots carrying the core meaning of words.

Correlations between writing and literacy in kindergarten and school

Kindergarten children's level of writing has been found to correlate with 'concepts about print' (Clay, 1986), vocabulary and non-verbal IQ (Levin, Share and Shatil, 1996), as well as with mastery of morphological structures in oral language (Levin, Ravid and Rapaport, in press).

Levin, Share and Shatil (1996) found that writing level, concepts about print and vocabulary in kindergarten predicted first graders' decoding, comprehension and spelling. Moreover, the level of writing in kindergarten still accounted for significant variance in spelling and reading in first grade after removing the variance explained by other variables. These data suggest that children's writing level plays an important part in their early learning of spelling and reading.

Levin *et al.* (in press) found that writing level in kindergarten predicted mastery of oral morphology in first grade and, conversely, kindergarten children's oral morphology predicted spelling in first grade. Most importantly, writing in kindergarten still accounted for significant variance in oral morphology in first grade, after removing the influence of kindergarten morphology. Similarly, morphology in kindergarten accounted for spelling in first grade after removing the variance of morphology in kindergarten. These findings support a bootstrapping model, according to which learning to write enhances mastery of oral morphology and vice versa.

In sum, pre-schoolers develop an understanding of the written system – its graphic and representational aspects – in phases that can be measured reliably, unfold gradually and are related to both age and socioeconomic status. Representation of Hebrew consonants develops faster than that of vowels. Writing level is also related to concurrent levels of linguistic and literacy-related skills, and contributes to the later formal learning of reading and spelling, as well as to linguistic development in school. The development of writing in Hebrew exhibits both commonalities with other languages and Hebrew-specific characteristics.

Learning to read and write in school

Rapid mastery of decoding

Perhaps the most conspicuous fact about learning to read Hebrew in the formal school setting is its rapid mastery. In a representative sample of over 300 Israeli children, Shatil (1997) reported 82 per cent decoding accuracy at the end of grade 1. Geva and Siegel (1991) arrived at a very similar figure (79 per cent) in their study of the word recognition skills of a large sample of Canadian children from primarily English-speaking homes attending a bilingual English–Hebrew day school. Accuracy of decoding pointed Hebrew in grade 1 (79 per cent) already matched the level achieved in English in grade 5 (78 per cent). Pseudo-word reading in Hebrew approaches similarly high levels of accuracy at relatively early ages (Birnboim, 1995; Geva, Wade-Woolley and Shany,

1993; Meyler, 1993; Shatil, 1997). When one considers the markedly lower levels of spelling performance in these early grades (see below), it is clear that grapheme–phoneme regularity provides a straightforward explanation of the rapid mastery of Hebrew decoding. The Hebrew data, therefore, are consistent with a variety of cross-linguistic investigations showing that reading acquisition is facilitated in orthographies in which relationships between orthography and phonology are simple and invariant (Feitelson, 1988; Mason, Anderson, Omura, Uchida and Imai, 1989; Thorstad, 1991; Venezky, 1973; Wimmer, 1993).

As noted in the introduction, phoneme-to-grapheme correspondence in Hebrew is quite a different matter from grapheme-to-phoneme correspondence. Since most Hebrew words have at least one interchangeable letter, both word-specific knowledge and general knowledge of Hebrew's orthographic conventions are essential for accurate spelling. In their multi-lingual sample, Geva *et al.* (1993) found that spelling performance in Hebrew (25 per cent and 48 per cent accuracy in grades 1 and 2 respectively) consistently lagged behind that of English (35 per cent and 72 per cent). These data clearly bear out the problem of inconsistent phoneme–grapheme relations.

Reading vowel diacritics

Our introductory observations regarding Hebrew morphology and orthography suggest that vowel diacritics might be expected to facilitate early decoding by reducing phonological ambiguity. Alternatively, owing to its complexity, this system may constitute a source of difficulty for the beginning reader (Feitelson, 1989).

Shimron and Navon (1981–82) found that fourth graders named pointed words faster than unpointed words. Words which were pointed incorrectly but which preserved sound were also named faster than unpointed items but more slowly than correctly pointed items. Points also benefited adult readers, but purely graphemic changes in diacritics (homophonic substitutions) did not slow naming times. These data indicate that vowel diacritics assist isolated word pronunciation for both skilled and unskilled readers and, furthermore, that pointing may be integral to the orthographic representations of children but not adults.

Rothschild-Yakar (1989) also reported superior naming accuracy for pointed (84 per cent) relative to unpointed items (66 per cent). Furthermore, the absolute difference between pointed and unpointed items was greater for younger children (24 per cent in grade 1, and 23 per cent in grade 2) than for older children (6 per cent in grade 4) or adults (6 per cent). The contribution of pointing to reading accuracy, as might be expected, was chiefly via a reduction in the number of vowel errors (cf. Birnboim, 1995). Rothschild-Yakar also found a significant effect for pointed words when preceded by a neutral but not predictable sentence context. This context by pointing interaction is analogous to the well-established English-language interaction between context effects and visually degraded versus undegraded stimuli (Stanovich, 1980). In Hebrew, unpointed words can be regarded as phonologically 'degraded' relative to fully pointed words, and hence more dependent on context.

Similar benefits of pointing were also reported by Birnboim (1995) in a small sample of second-grade readers. An error analysis also revealed that the overwhelming majority of oral reading errors were vowel errors: 79 per cent of the errors in unpointed script and 62 per cent in pointed script. This suggests that diacritics do assist in resolving the ambiguity of unpointed script, but remain a source of difficulty, probably owing to the complexity of this vowelling system. This bears out Feitelson's (1988) claim that a major source of difficulty in mastering Hebrew decoding is the diacritical system.

Eshel (1985) reported that pointed text was read aloud more quickly and more accurately than unpointed text by children but not adults. A second study examined the role of both context and pointing in reading homographs embedded in a meaningful sentence. In unpointed text with neutral context, both adults and children frequently misinterpreted the homographs. Pointing significantly reduced these confusions. In predictable context, the advantage of pointing was smaller but still significant for both groups. These results suggest that pointing makes a significant contribution to the disambiguation of homographs which are endemic in Hebrew text.

Thus far, the picture is fairly consistent regarding the benefits of pointing when reading aloud isolated words, sentences or short passages. Only two studies have investigated the role of pointing on children's *silent* reading comprehension.

Even (1995) investigated the contribution of diacritical marks both to silent reading speed and text comprehension among grade 2 and 4 children. No differences were found either in speed or comprehension when comparing pointed to unpointed text. This finding suggests that the additional vocalic information supplied by the points (over and above that already supplied by the mothers of reading) may be insignificant when reading connected text.

Kahn-Horowitz (1994) also failed to find any overall effect for pointing on children's silent reading comprehension of three-sentence passages. There was, however, a significant advantage of pointing for one sub-set of passages consisting of short sentences with relatively few relational terms. Kahn-Horowitz suggested that this sub-set was characterised by poor contextual redundancy. If correct, this interpretation would align with both Eshel's and Rothschild-Yakar's findings regarding the effects of pointing in non-predictable (neutral) contexts.

To sum up, there is no dispute regarding the value of points when reading aloud or their role in the disambiguation of homographs (Frost and Bentin, 1992; Shimron, 1993). When reading text silently, however, the contribution of pointing is less clear.

No study has yet examined whether children can *learn* to read when the points are dispensed with altogether, although some educators have called for the total abolition of diacritics in school texts. Conclusions reached regarding the role of points in the reading of skilled adults have questionable value in explicating their role for the beginner reader because skilled visual/orthographic reading may have been acquired via initial phonologically based decoding skill. The problem here is that all words are novel orthographic strings at one point. Given that context alone does not supply sufficient information for accurate identification of specific lexical items (Share, 1995), the ability to decode print to sound may well be essential for efficient acquisition of the abstract, root-based orthographic representations on which skilled visual Hebrew word recognition depends. Points, therefore, should assist novice readers because they reduce phonological ambiguity. While it is not difficult to imagine a simplified system of Hebrew vowel diacritics facilitating the beginner's mastery of decoding, we would doubt that the same could be said for a complete abolition of vowel points. Speculations aside, the feasibility of learning to read without any pointing whatsoever awaits a direct empirical test.

Morphology

In her second-grade sample, Birnboim (1995) observed superior oral reading accuracy with (pointed) pseudo-words that conformed to, as opposed to diverged from, a regular morphological pattern (MISHKAL). Rothschild-Yakar (1989) found a consistent increase across age in the extent to which unpointed pseudo-words were pronounced in conformity with a legal vowelling pattern. There was also a growing tendency across age to (mis)read incorrectly pointed items in accordance with the correct vowelling pattern, attesting to a growing influence of lexico-morphological knowledge. Ravid (1996) examined first and fourth graders' oral reading of sentences containing normative/literate morphological forms that differed from standard spoken forms. First graders pronounced the pointed forms *more* accurately than fourth graders, suggesting greater reliance on bottom-up ('assembled') grapheme–phoneme translation. The younger readers' oral reading was characteristically slow with extensive self-repairs. Fourth graders tended to disregard the points and produce standard forms. They read both pointed and unpointed versions fluently, with few self-repairs, and with the same level of accuracy. Ravid, like Rothschild-Yakar, concluded that older children's oral reading is characterised by greater reliance on direct ('addressed') orthographic retrieval of phonological forms.

Phonological awareness

A small number of longitudinal/predictive and training studies have examined the role of phonological awareness in Hebrew reading acquisition.

Bentin and Leshem (1993) assessed the phonemic segmentation abilities of over 500 kindergarten children. The lowest scoring children were then randomly assigned to one of four matched training groups ($n = 25$). Interventions consisted of phoneme segmentation alone (recognising and segmenting phonemes), phoneme segmentation plus letter identity, general language skills, and non-specific training (additional regular kindergarten activities). A fifth no-treatment control group included seventeen children scoring at the top end of the phoneme segmentation distribution. At the conclusion of ten weeks of training, both groups trained in recognising and segmenting phonemes, but not the other groups, had improved significantly in phonemic segmentation and, by post-test, matched the initially high-scoring segmenters. At the end of grade 1, the two groups trained in phonemic awareness were well ahead of the other groups in both word and pseudo-word reading. In fact, both groups read almost twice as many words correctly as the control groups and, moreover, were not significantly different from the initially high-scoring group.

Kozminsky and Kozminsky (1993/94) randomly assigned two entire kindergarten classes ($n = 35$) comparable in age and phonemic awareness to experimental and control groups. Training in the experimental group focused on syllabic, sub-syllabic and phonemic awareness, while the control class received a programme of visuo-motor integration. Significant and durable gains in phonemic awareness for the experimental group were accompanied by superior reading comprehension both at the end of grade 1 and again at the end of grade 3.

Lapidot, Tubul and Wohl (1995–96) examined the ability of kindergarten phonological awareness to predict grade 1 reading difficulties in a group of 100 children. Of the eighteen children with poor kindergarten phonological awareness, nine were correctly classified as having reading difficulties in grade 1. All children who scored above the kindergarten cut-off were correctly classified as having no reading problem in grade 1.

These few investigations of phonological awareness in Hebrew concur with the English-language findings: access to phonemes is a significant predictor of later reading and, when trained, has a significant and durable impact on later reading ability. But is the relationship as powerful at that observed in English?

How strong is the relationship between phonological awareness and early reading?

In her longitudinal study, Shatil (1997) included several tests of phonological awareness for children in kindergarten. Correlations with end of first grade decoding and comprehension were significant but substantially smaller than those reported in the English literature (e.g. Stanovich, Cunningham and Cramer, 1984; Yopp, 1988), ranging from 0.31 to 0.42 with a median of 0.36. In fact, the correlations were very similar to those reported by Bentin and Leshem (1991) at the end of grade 1 (0.35). Geva et al. (1993) found the correlation between grade 1 syllable and phoneme deletion (the Rosner test) and grade 1 Hebrew word recognition to be significantly weaker (0.32) than between phoneme deletion and English word recognition (0.62).

If, indeed, phonemic awareness is a weaker predictor of early reading in Hebrew than in English, several alternative explanations might be postulated. The first simply suggests that most children have attained mastery in decoding by the end of grade 1, hence the correlation is attenuated by range restriction. This account is consistent with the strong correlation (0.55) reported by Bentin and Leshem (1993) at the *middle* of grade 1 when most children are still learning basic letter–sound correspondences. At this time, decoding skill may be more comparable to those of English speakers later in the year. This implies that the intrinsic relationship between phonological awareness and reading may be equally strong in both languages, the only difference being one of timing.

A second possible explanation invokes basic differences between English and Hebrew orthography in grapheme-to-phoneme consistency. The unambiguous pronunciation of Hebrew pointed script may demand less skill and flexibility at manipulating phoneme strings. A third factor possibly making phonemic manipulation skill less critical in Hebrew is the language's relatively simple syllable structure. Yet another speculation regarding the attenuated correlation between phonemic awareness and early reading in Hebrew proposes that awareness at the phoneme level may be less critical in Hebrew reading than in English because other units may offer a viable alternative route to proficient Hebrew reading.

Which units of phonology are important for learning to read in Hebrew?

The most common response on the kindergarten phoneme segmentation tasks in Bentin and Leshem's (1993) training study was a sub-syllabic CV segment (36 per cent), the same unit represented in pointed Hebrew by the basic syllable block (consonant letter with appended diacritic). This response occurred twice as often as both correct phoneme responses (19 per cent) and syllable-level responses (12 per cent). CV responses, moreover, correlated significantly with middle of grade 1 reading (0.36) but not end of grade 1 reading (0.19). In view of the substantially larger corresponding correlations obtained for phonemic segmentation (0.55 and 0.35) there can be no mistaking that access to phonemic rather than sub-syllabic units of speech is of primary importance in early reading. Nevertheless, these data are also compatible with the conjecture that CV units, too, play a role in Hebrew reading acquisition.

In the cross-sectional phoneme segmentation study by Bentin, Hammer and Cahan (1991), over one-quarter of the errors committed in kindergarten were again found to be sub-syllabic CV units compared to only 12 per cent syllable errors. In grade 1, both these figures declined but significantly more so for syllabic errors. Thus, in contrast to English language studies, the preferred break-up of the syllable may not coincide with the onset/rhyme division believed to be characteristic of English (see Goswami and Bryant, 1990; Treiman, 1992). This issue was directly addressed by Ben-Dror, Frost and Bentin (1995).

In a cross-language comparison, native Hebrew-speaking and native English-speaking adults were asked to delete the initial sound (left unspecified) in CVC strings. Hebrew speakers deleted the initial consonant significantly less often (79 per cent) than the English speakers (97 per cent). Additionally, response latencies for 'correct' deletions of initial phonemes among the Hebrew speakers were significantly slower. Finally, the percentage of initial phoneme deletions for CVC words in which the medial vowel is normally represented by a mother of reading (קיר, KIR 'wall') was significantly higher than for CVC words in which the medial vowel is not represented by a vowel letter (גן, G(a)N, 'kindergarten') (84 per cent versus 65 per cent). The authors concluded that 'The basic subword phonological unit induced by exposure to Hebrew letters may take the form of a CV phonological unit' (Ben-Dror, Frost and Bentin, 1995, p. 181). Another factor may be the simple (CV) open structure of Hebrew spoken syllables, as discussed in the introduction. It remains to be established whether the preference among Hebrew speakers for dividing a CVC string *after* rather than *before* the vowel has its source in spoken Hebrew phonology and/or in orthographic factors.

Another possibly unique feature of phonological awareness in Hebrew relates to morphology. As discussed above, the semantic core of a word is consonantal, not vocalic: the vowels supply mainly grammatical information. Consistent with the salience of consonants, Lapidot *et al.* (1995–96) found that kindergarten children more easily identified and isolated consonants than vowels. Insensitivity to vowels was also revealed in errors such as stating that ESHKOLIT (grapefruit) and SHULKHAN (table) begin with the same sound. Children also experienced greater difficulty identifying a common terminal vowel (e.g. TMUN*A* (picture)/KHULTZ*A* (shirt)) than a terminal consonant (GEZE*R* (carrot)/ SI*R* (pot)). The greater significance of consonants in Hebrew was also demonstrated by Tolchinsky and Teberosky (in press) in a study of segmentation strategies used by Israeli second graders. When asked to divide words into 'little parts', many pronounced only consonants. This strategy was absent among a matched Spanish cohort.

The developmental course of phonological awareness

Bentin, Hammer and Cahan (1991) investigated the effects of age and first-grade schooling on the development of phonological awareness in a sample of over 1,000 kindergarten and grade 1 children. Both schooling and age significantly improved children's performance on tests of initial and final phoneme isolation, but the effect of schooling was four times greater than the aging effect (cf. Liberman, Shankweiler, Fischer and Carter, 1974). Share and Breznitz (1997) also found little or no awareness of phonemes among Arabic-speaking non-literates (adult illiterates and kindergarten pre-literates), suggesting that phonemic awareness is primarily determined by the experience of learning to read an alphabetic orthography. It appears that the developmental course of phonological awareness observed in both European, Chinese and Japanese investigations (see Morais, Alegria and Content, 1987 for a review) also applies to Semitic languages.

Cognitive correlates of reading ability

A small number of studies have investigated the cognitive and psycholinguistic factors accounting for individual differences in early reading ability.

A longitudinal study by Meyler and Breznitz (in press) examined the role of visual and verbal short-term memory (STM) in early reading. Factor analysis of a battery of six tests in kindergarten produced two distinct visual and verbal factors. While both kindergarten verbal and visual STM significantly predicted later decoding accuracy (real and pseudo-word reading) in grade 1, pre-reading visual STM was the stronger predictor. Visual STM alone predicted decoding speed. Pre-reading performance on the WISC-R block design test also predicted later decoding ability. In attempting to explain their findings regarding visual short-term memory, the authors cited the uniformity of letter architecture, word length and word shape, as well as the complexity of the visual array in pointed Hebrew in which information is arrayed in several parallel axes. Meyler and Breznitz also speculated that Hebrew may bias the reader towards visual/orthographic processing (relative to English), owing to the unique and highly consistent way in which the orthography codes morphology (see Frost and Bentin, 1992; Katz and Frost, 1992).

The most comprehensive study to date of the cognitive and psycholinguistic factors associated with early reading achievement is Shatil's (1997) longitudinal study of a representative sample of over 300 children. In the final months of kindergarten, a battery of thirty measures was administered covering four domain-specific sets of variables (visual-orthographic processing, phonological awareness, phonological memory and early literacy) and three domain-general sets (general ability, metacognitive functioning and oral language). Collectively, the domain-general block explained a borderline 5 per cent of the variance in grade 1 word recognition skill attesting to what Shatil termed the 'cognitive modularity' of decoding. In contrast, domain-specific factors collectively explained a significant 33 per cent of the variance in word recognition. Both domain-specific and domain-general blocks contributed significant and substantial portions of variance to the prediction of grade 1 reading comprehension. Individual domain-specific sets of variables each accounted for significant portions of decoding variance (visual-orthographic processing – 11 per cent; phonological awareness – 11 per cent; phonological memory – 16 per cent; and early literacy – 19 per cent).

Of particular interest is the confirmation of Meyler and Breznitz's finding that visuo-spatial factors significantly predicted early reading in Hebrew. Shatil suggested that the contribution of visuo-spatial ability may be attributable to multiple factors such as the peculiar lack of orthographic redundancy in Hebrew script, and the fact that the reader is constantly obliged to segment multi-morphemic strings into constituent morphemes.

Interestingly, Shatil found that the strongest single variable among the early literacy set was a task which required children to memorise three spoken CV labels for letter-like symbols, then read and write words which combined these elements. This result reinforces the view that CV units have a special significance in Hebrew reading acquisition.

Ben-Dror, Bentin and Frost (1995) compared the semantic, phonological and morphological skills of fifth-grade disabled readers to both age-matched normal readers and a younger vocabulary-matched group of normal readers. Children were asked to judge phonemic identity, semantic relatedness and morphological relatedness. In the morphological task, in which children decided whether two words shared a common root, reading-disabled children were significantly below both control groups. On the phonological and semantic tests, however, the disabled readers were significantly inferior only to the age-matched group.

Also consistent with the notion that phonology is less of a stumbling block in Hebrew than in English are reports that the proportion of developmental dyslexics in Hebrew displaying difficulties in phonology is relatively low. In Lamm and Epstein's (1994) sub-typing study of 320 dyslexics, only 4 per cent of the sample were classified as phonological dyslexics with basic symbol-sound difficulties as evident in consonant reading errors and non-phonetic spelling errors.

The transition from pointed to unpointed orthography

As stated above, children begin learning to read with pointed text, but are gradually exposed to unpointed text in a systematic manner around grade 3. By grade 4, a child is expected to be competent in both scripts. Understanding this transition from a phonologically transparent to a phonologically opaque script is important not only for the study of Hebrew reading acquisition but it also has broader implications for similar transitions both within and across orthographies (e.g. learning English as a second language).

Only a single study appears to have addressed the unique difficulties associated with the transition from pointed to unpointed script. Bentin, Deutsch and Liberman (1990) hypothesised that some poor readers may have difficulties making this transition owing to weaknesses in exploiting contextual information assumed to be critical for reading phonologically ambiguous unpointed text.

Bentin et al. compared a sub-group of nineteen disabled readers (aged eleven years) to a younger control group. A third group, labelled 'poor context' readers, matched the good readers on accuracy of decoding pointed pseudo-words and IQ, but were poorer at reading without vowel diacritics.

Sensitivity to syntactic context was examined by presenting subjects with short spoken sentences containing a noise-masked target word which was either syntactically congruent or syntactically incongruent with the sentence. The authors hypothesised that if either the disabled or 'poor context' readers have impoverished syntactic knowledge or are less able to use this efficiently, then the effect of syntactic congruity should be attenuated relative to good readers. Bentin *et al.* also examined the extent to which syntactically incongruent targets were 'corrected' to conform to the context. Several months later, subjects heard the same spoken sentences and were asked to correct the violations (syntactic correction task).

As predicted, the differences between congruous and incongruous contexts were smaller for disabled readers. Controls also committed fewer syntactic 'corrections' than disabled readers. Explicit syntactic correction also revealed a significant decrement in the disabled group.

In contrast, both the 'poor context' group and the good readers showed the same syntactic congruity effect, but the percentage of syntactic 'corrections' was higher among the good readers. Although these two groups did not differ when explicitly identifying syntactic violations, the good readers were better at repairing the violations. Thus, both groups were equally sensitive to deviant syntactic structures but differed in their ability to correct these violations. Bentin *et al.* ascribed the performance deficits among disabled readers to a genuine linguistic deficit. Deficits in syntactic correction in the 'poor context' group pointed to impairments in the ability to use syntactic knowledge in a productive way.

These conclusions, however, must be tempered by the fact that neither the disabled nor the 'poor context' group were matched to the good readers on basic decoding ability. The disabled readers fell well below the good readers on all reading measures including pseudo-word reading, while the 'poor context' group were matched on pseudo-word decoding *accuracy* but not *speed*. The effects of syntax are therefore confounded with decoding skill. Nonetheless, these data are important in suggesting that at least some children may experience difficulties bridging the gap between pointed and unpointed text because of inadequate syntactic knowledge and/or inefficient use of this knowledge.

It seems likely that problems exploiting context are restricted to unpointed text. Shatil's longitudinal study found negligible correlations between kindergarten syntactic measures (syntactic correction 0.21 and oral cloze test 0.16) and grade 1 decoding of pointed script.

Another source of difficulty in negotiating the transition to the deeper unpointed orthography may be a failure to acquire the root-based orthographic representations necessary for efficient reading without vowel points. A reader who has difficulties establishing orthographic representations in memory may still cope satisfactorily with pointed print, albeit in a strictly bottom-up manner, but would be at a loss with unpointed script.

Summary and conclusions

Our review has highlighted both universal and language-specific aspects of learning to read and write in Hebrew. By virtue of the fact that a productive orthography must code sub-lexical phonological units, whether syllables, sub-syllables or phonemes, phonology may well be a universal and inescapable feature of early reading and writing. The Hebrew data regarding the transition from pre-phonetic to phonetic writing and word identification among pre-schoolers, the contribution of vowel diacritics to early word decoding, the rapid mastery of a script with simple and invariant grapheme–phoneme relationships, the predictive significance of kindergarten phonological skills and, finally, the causal influence of phonological awareness training, collectively affirm that phonology is a universal aspect of becoming literate in phonographic writing systems. Within this broad-brush picture, however, some of the finer detail emphasises language-specific and orthography-specific features.

Unique to Hebrew may be the putative secondary role of phonological units other than phonemes (e.g. CV), a possibly attenuated relationship between phonemic awareness and phonological factors in early reading owing perhaps to a shallow orthography which diminishes the cognitive complexity of early decoding.

Scattered data on the reading processes of both normal and disabled readers, together with morphological influences on early writing and phonological awareness suggest that Semitic morphology and its corollary – a primarily consonantal orthography – have a special significance in learning to read and write in Hebrew. The primacy of consonants over vowels finds expression in pre-school writing, in the phonological awareness literature and also in a diminishing reliance on and attention to vowel diacritics among older and more proficient readers whose reading becomes based less on symbol-to-sound translation and more on recognition of orthographically invariant consonantal roots.

Another unique feature of early Hebrew literacy learning appears to be the complex diacritical system for marking vowels. This complexity is manifest in the fact that although pointed text reduces oral reading errors, the incidence of vowel (diacritic) errors exceeds consonant errors. One possible source of these inefficiencies may be the considerable demands imposed by Hebrew diacritics on the processing of spatial location. Supporting evidence for this speculation can be found in the predictive value of pre-school visual processing competencies, which may be language-specific.

The transition from the shallow pointed script to the deeper unpointed script represents another issue requiring further attention. Data on homograph confusions and the difficulties certain readers seem to experience in utilising context to resolve decoding ambiguity suggest that the transition from the shallower pointed script to the deeper unpointed script is another potential troublespot in attaining written-language proficiency in Hebrew. This issue also has broad implications for similar deep-to-shallow transitions both within and across orthographies.

REFERENCES

Ben-Dror, I., Bentin, S. and Frost, R. (1995). Semantic, phonologic, and morphologic skills in reading disabled and normal children: evidence from perception and production of spoken Hebrew. *Reading Research Quarterly*, 30, 876–93.

Ben-Dror, I., Frost, R. and Bentin, S. (1995). Orthographic representation and phonemic segmentation in skilled readers: a cross-language comparison. *Psychological Science*, 6, 176–81.

Bentin, S., Bargai, N. and Katz, L. (1984). Orthographic and phonemic coding for lexical access: evidence from Hebrew. *Journal of Experimental Psychology: Learning, Memory and Cognition*, 10 (3), 353–68.

Bentin, S., Deutsch, A. and Liberman, I. Y. (1990). Syntactic competence and reading ability in children. *Journal of Experimental Child Psychology*, 48, 147–72.

Bentin, S. and Frost, R. (1987). Processing lexical ambiguity and visual word recognition in a deep orthography. *Memory and Cognition*, 15, 13–23.

Bentin, S., Hammer, R. and Cahan, S. (1991). The effects of aging and first year schooling on the development of phonological awareness. *Psychological Science*, 2, 271–4.

Bentin, S. and Leshem, H. (1993). On the interaction of phonologic awareness and reading acquisition: it's a two-way street. *Annals of Dyslexia*, 43, 125–48.

Berman, R. (1985). Hebrew. In D. I. Slobin (ed.), *The Crosslinguistic Study of Language Acquisition*. Hillsdale, NJ: Erlbaum.

Birnboim, S. (1995). Acquired surface dyslexia: the evidence from Hebrew. *Applied Psycholinguistics*, 16, 83–102.

Brenneman, K., Massey, C., Machado, S. F. and Gelman, R. (1996). Young children's plans differ for writing and drawing. *Cognitive Development*, 11, 397–419.

Eshel, R. (1985). Effects of contextual richness on word recognition in pointed and unpointed Hebrew. *Reading Psychology*, 6, 127–43.

Even, D. (1995). Trumat hanikud lehavanat hanikra velemehirut hakri'a etsel talmidim mekitot bet vedalet halomdim beshitot hora'a shonot. [The contribution of diacritical marks in Hebrew script to reading comprehension and reading speed among grade 2 and grade 4 pupils taught by two different instructional methods.] Unpublished master's thesis, University of Haifa.

Feitelson, D. (1988). *Facts and Fads in Beginning Reading*. New York: Ablex.
(1989). Reading education in Israel. In W. Ellis and J. Hladez (eds.), *International Handbook on Reading Education*. Westport, CT: Greenwood Praeger Press.

Ferreiro, E. and Teberosky, A. (1982). *Literacy before Schooling*. Exeter, NH: Heinemann International.

Frost, R. and Bentin, S. (1992). Reading consonants and guessing vowels: visual word recognition in Hebrew orthography. In R. Frost and L. Katz (eds.), *Orthography, Phonology, Morphology, and Meaning*. Amsterdam: North Holland.

Gelb, I. J. (1963). *A Study of Writing*, second edn. Chicago: University of Chicago Press.

Geva, E. and Siegel, L. (1991). The role of orthography and cognitive factors in the concurrent development of basic reading skills in bilingual children. Paper presented at the meeting of the International Society for the Study of Behavioral Development, Minneapolis, MN.

Geva, E., Wade-Woolley, L. and Shany, M. (1993). The concurrent development of spelling and decoding in two different orthographies. *Journal of Reading Behavior*, 25, 383–406.

Gombert, J. E. and Fayol, M. (1992). Writing in preliterate children. *Learning and Instruction*, 2, 23–41.

Goswami, U. and Bryant, P. (1990). *Phonological Skills and Learning to Read*. Hove, East Sussex: Erlbaum.

Henderson, E. (1985). *Teaching Spelling*. Boston: Houghton Mifflin.

Kahn-Horowitz, J. (1994). Megamot hitptchutiot shel hama'avar lekri'at tekstim lo minukadim. [Developmental trends in the transition to reading unpointed texts.] Unpublished MA thesis, University of Haifa.

Kamii, C. (1986). Spelling in kindergarten: a constructivist analysis comparing Spanish and English speaking children. Unpublished manuscript.

Katz, L. and Frost, R. (1992). In R. Frost and L. Katz (eds.), *Orthography, Phonology, Morphology, and Meaning*. Amsterdam: North Holland.

Kozminsky, L. and Kozminsky, E. (1993/94). Hahashpa'a shel ha'imun bemudaut fonologit begil hagan al hahatslacha berechishat hakri'a bevet hasefer. [The effects of phonological awareness training in kindergarten on reading acquisition in school.] *Chelkat Lashon*, 15–16, 7–28.

Lamm, O. and Epstein, R. (1994). Dichotic listening performance under high and low lexical work load in subtypes of developmental dyslexia. *Neuropsychologia*, 32, 757–85.

Lapidot, M., Tubul, G. and Wohl, A. (1995–96). Mivchan eranut fonologit kekli nibui lerechishat hakri'a. [A test of phonological awareness as a predictor of reading acquisition.] *Chelkat Lashon*, 19–20, 169–88.

Levin, I. and Korat, O. (1993). Sensitivity to phonological, morphological and semantic cues in early reading and writing in Hebrew. *Merrill-Palmer Quarterly*, 39, 213–32.

Levin, I., Korat, O. and Amsterdamer, P. (1996). Emergent writing among kindergarteners: Cross-linguistic commonalities and Hebrew-specific issues. In G. Rijlaarsdam, H. van der Bergh and M. Couzijn (eds.), *Current Trends in Writing Research: Theories, Models and Methodology* (pp. 398–419). Amsterdam: Amsterdam University Press.

Levin, I., Ravid, D. and Rapaport, S. (in press). Developing morphological awareness and learning to write: a two-way street. In T. Nunes (ed.), *Integrating Research and Practice in Literacy*. Amsterdam: Kluwer.

Levin, I., Share, D. L. and Shatil, E. (1996). A qualitative-quantitative study of preschool writing: its development and contribution to school literacy. In M. Levy and S. Ransdell (eds.), *The Science of Writing* (pp. 271–93). Hillsdale, NJ: Erlbaum.

Levin, I. and Tolchinsky-Landsmann, L. (1989). Becoming literate: referential and phonetic strategies in early reading and writing. *International Journal of Behavioral Development*, 12, 369–84.

Liberman, I. Y., Shankweiler, D., Fischer, F. W. and Carter, B. (1974). Explicit syllable and phoneme segmentation in the young child. *Journal of Experimental Child Psychology*, 18, 201–12.

Mason, J. M., Anderson, R. C., Omura, A., Uchida, N. and Imai, M. (1989). Learning to read in Japan. *Journal of Curriculum Studies*, 21, 389–407.

Meyler, A. and Breznitz, Z. (in press). Developmental associations between verbal and visual short-term memory and the acquisition of decoding skill. *Reading and Writing*.

Morais, J., Alegria, J. and Content, A. (1987). The relationships between segmental analysis and alphabetic literacy: an interactive view. *Cahiers de Psychologie Cognitive/European Bulletin of Cognitive Psychology*, 7, 415–38.

Navon, D. and Shimron, Y. (1984). Reading Hebrew: how necessary is the graphemic representation of vowels? In L. Henderson (ed.), *Orthographies and Reading: Perspectives from Cognitive Psychology, Neuropsychology, and Linguistics*. London: Lawrence Erlbaum Associates.

Pontecorvo, C. and Zuccbermaglio, C. (1990). A passage to literacy: learning in a social context. In Y. M. Goodman (ed.), *How Children Construct Literacy* (pp. 59–98). Newark, DE: International Reading Association.

Ravid, D. (1995a). *Language Change in Child and Adult Hebrew: A Psycholinguistic Perspective*. New York: Oxford University Press.

(1995b). The acquisition of morphological junctions in modern Hebrew: the interface of rule and rote. In H. Pishwa and K. Maroldt (eds.), *The Development of Morphological Systematicity: A Cross-linguistic Perspective* (pp. 55–77). Tubingen: Gunter Naar.

(1996). Accessing the mental lexicon: evidence from incompatibility between representation of spoken and written morphology. *Linguistics*, 34, 1219–46.

Read, C. (1986). *Creative Spelling*. London: Routledge and Kegan Paul.

Rothschild-Yakar, L. (1989). Bedikat tahalichei kri'a be'ivrit mitoch perspectiva hitpatchutit etsel talmidim halomdim beshtei shitot hora'a shonot. [A study of reading processes in Hebrew from a developmental perspective among children learning in two different instructional methods.] Unpublished doctoral dissertation, University of Haifa.

Share, D. L. (1995). Phonological recoding and self-teaching: sine qua non of reading acquisition. *Cognition*, 55, 151–218.

Share, D. L. and Breznitz, Z. (1997). Awareness of phonemes among Semitic-speaking nonliterates. Unpublished manuscript.

Share, D. L. and Jaffe-Gur, T. (in press). How reading begins: A study of preschoolers' print identification strategies. *Cognition and Instruction*.

Shatil, E. (1997). Predicting reading ability: evidence for cognitive modularity. Unpublished doctoral dissertation, University of Haifa.

Shimron, J. (1993). The role of vowels in reading: a review of studies of English and Hebrew. *Psychological Bulletin*, 114, 52–67.

Shimron, J. and Navon, D. (1981). The distribution of information within letters. *Perception and Psychophysics*, 30, 483–91.

(1981–82). The dependence on graphemes and on their translation to phonemes in reading: a developmental perspective. *Reading Research Quarterly*, 17, 210–28.

Shimron, J. and Sivan, T. (1994). Reading proficiency and orthography: evidence from Hebrew and English. *Language Learning*, 44, 5–27.

Stanovich, K. E. (1980). Toward an interactive-compensatory model of individual differences in the development of reading fluency. *Reading Research Quarterly*, 16, 32–71.

Stanovich, K. E., Cunningham, A. E. and Cramer, B. B. (1984). Assessing phonological awareness in kindergarten children: issues of task comparability. *Journal of Experimental Child Psychology*, 38, 175–90.

Sulzby, E., Barnhart, J. and Hieshima, J. (1989). Forms of writing and rereading from writing: a preliminary report. In J. Mason (ed.), *Reading-Writing Collection* (pp. 31–63). Neeham Heights, MA: Allyn and Bacon.

Thorstad, G. (1991). The effect of orthography on the acquisition of literacy skills. *British Journal of Psychology*, 82, 527–37.

Tolchinsky L. and Teberosky, A. (in press). The development of word segmentation and writing in two scripts. *Cognitive Development*.

Tolchinsky-Landsmann, L. and Levin, I. (1985). Writing in preschoolers: an age-related analysis. *Applied Psycholinguistics*, 6, 319–39.

Tolchinsky-Landsmann, L. and Levin, I. (1987). Writing in four to six year olds: representation of semantic and phonological similarities and differences. *Journal of Child Language*, 14, 127–44.

Treiman, R. (1992). The role of intrasyllabic units in learning to read. In P. B. Gough, L. C. Ehri and R. Treiman (eds.), *Reading Acquisition* (pp. 65–106). Hillsdale, NJ: Erlbaum.

Venezky, R. L. (1973). Letter-sound generalizations of first-, second-, and third-grade Finnish children. *Journal of Educational Psychology*, 64, 288–92.

Wimmer, H. (1993). Characteristics of developmental dyslexia in a regular writing system. *Applied Psycholinguistics*, 14, 1–33.

Yopp, H. K. (1988). The validity and reliability of phonemic awareness tests. *Research Reading Quarterly*, 23, 159–77.

7 Different morphemes, same spelling problems: cross-linguistic developmental studies

Peter Bryant, Terezinha Nunes and Athanasios Aidinis

The links between morphology and spelling

Learning to read and spell is not just a matter of representing sounds by letters and vice versa. Another fundamental element in learning to read and spell is the link between morphemes and script. According to the *Oxford Dictionary* morphemes are linguistic units which have a meaning or syntactic function and which cannot be further sub-divided in this way. For example, the word 'kissed' has two morphemes: the stem 'kiss', which has meaning, and the inflectional morpheme 'ed', which has the syntactic function of marking the past tense of a verb. Stems are significant units of meaning – words with the same stem are usually related in meaning – but stems do not have syntactic functions. Other morphemes convey meaning and also have a syntactic function – the 'ed', for example, has the function of marking the past tense of regular verbs.

Both types of morpheme have a particular form. For example, 'cars' and 'feet' are both plural words but they do not have the same morpheme marking the plural: in 'cars' the plural morpheme is 's' but in 'feet' there is a phonological transformation from the singular form. These two words are similar syntactically (plural forms) and in meaning but they do not have the same morpheme. Inflectional morphemes, like the 'ed' in past-tense verbs and the 's', do not determine the syntactic category of a word but they are used only with words of particular categories – the 'ed' with verbs, the 's' with nouns.

Another type of morpheme with a syntactic function, the derivational morpheme, is attached to a stem to generate words of a particular syntactic category: for example, 'hood' is a derivational morpheme that generates abstract nouns (e.g. child – childhood, neighbour – neighbourhood); 'ly' generates adverbs (cold – coldly, mad – madly), etc.

112

Thus morphology is not independent of either syntax or meaning: *it involves both syntax and meaning expressed in a particular form*. Because of this constancy of form, morphemes are fundamental in learning to read and write in many scripts that are commonly referred to as 'alphabetic', but could perhaps more appropriately be termed 'morpho-phonic'.

In many languages children learning to read and write must take morphology into account because of spelling patterns which represent morphemes in a way that cannot be reduced to phonology. We can take the case of the spelling of two inflectional morphemes in English, one of which may not make any demands on children's morphological know-ledge whereas the other definitely does make such demands. The two morphemes – both verb endings – are 'ing' and 'ed'. It is, in principle, possible to learn to read and write the 'ing' morpheme purely on the basis of phonology. The letter sequence 'ing' readily translates into the morpheme's usual pronunciation whether it is the morpheme 'ing' at the end of a verb or not: 'testing' and 'string' end with exactly the same letters and the same sound even though these letters represent a morph-eme in the first word but not in the second.

In contrast the 'ed' ending in regular past-tense verbs cannot be reduced in this way to letter–sound correspondence rules. We do not pronounce these letters when they represent the inflectional morpheme in past verbs: we write 'helped' and 'hired' and 'hated' but we pro-nounce the endings of these three words – the part represented by the 'ed' spelling as /t/, /d/ and /id/ respectively. As well as this, the letter string 'ed' at the end of words is pronounced quite differently in words which are not past-tense verbs: we clearly pronounce the 'ed' when we say 'bed' and 'biped' and we just as clearly do not when we say 'combed' and 'piped'. This link between morphology and spelling is easy to illustrate in several alphabetic languages.

Our hypothesis is that the psychological processes involved in learn-ing to spell these morphemes are similar across languages. Of course the actual instances of this link – the particular morphemes, the sounds and the spelling patterns – vary tremendously from script to script.

The role of morphemes in adult reading has been documented in a variety of languages including English (Fowler and Liberman, 1995; Kelliher and Henderson, 1990; Morton, 1982; Murrel and Morton, 1974; Taft, 1985; 1991), Danish (Elbro, 1990), Italian (Caramazza, Laudana and Romani, 1988) and Hebrew (Bentin and Frost, 1995), to list just a few examples. Taft (1991), for example, proposed a multi-level model of processing in reading according to which different orthographic units are visually processed, ranging from single letters to whole words passing through other units smaller than a word such as syllables and morphemes.

Much of this evidence comes from lexical decision tasks, where subjects are asked to decide whether a visually presented string of letters is a word or not. Morphological effects are demonstrated in that the decision takes significantly longer when real morphemes are components of the pseudo-words than when the letter strings do not contain real morphemes. This result suggests that, when real morphemes are identified, the subjects still need to consider whether, when put together, the morphemes form a word or not. Stimuli that contain units which do not coincide with any morpheme can be rejected more quickly because they do not coincide with units of processing. Lexical decision is also influenced by the violation of syntactic relationships between morphemes in pseudo-words. For example, Caramazza, Laudana and Romani (1988) presented Italian adults with two types of stimuli. In one type of stimulus, the letter string was composed of a real stem and a real inflectional morpheme in a plausible syntactic combination (the correct inflection for the type of verb that the pseudo-word could have been); in the second type, the stimulus contained a real stem and inflectional morpheme but the combination was not appropriate syntactically. Lexical decisions took significantly longer when the combination was syntactically plausible than when it was not, suggesting that the syntactic violation abbreviated the decision process, although both types of stimuli only contained real morphemes.

Although there is such rich evidence from diverse languages regarding the use of morphemes by adults in reading, little is known about children's use of morphemes in reading and spelling. Research on children's understanding of the connection between morphology and spelling in a variety of scripts is quite recent. We shall argue that this research shows that children learn about the connection between morphology and spelling in strikingly similar ways across the different languages.

Three kinds of link between morphology and writing

In our view there are three broad ways in which morphology can determine spelling. In some orthographies one can find all three types, but other orthographies contain instances of only one or two of them.

Deciding between two or more acceptable spelling sequences

The first and probably the most common way in which spelling depends on syntax is in specifying a choice of one particular spelling pattern when there are two or more perfectly acceptable spellings for the same sound. In English, for example, whenever the ending of a written word is /ks/, it is spelled with either 'x' or 'cks'. So far as we know, there is no exception to this correspondence which means that both forms of spelling are legitimate and consistent. How then are we to know which of these endings to use? The answer lies in morphology. If the word is a singular noun ('tax') or an adjective ('lax'), it has the 'x' ending; if it is a plural noun or a verb in the third person singular, present tense, the ending is 'cks' ('cracks', 'licks'). In other words, the presence of either the morpheme 's' for the plural of nouns or the 's' for the present third person singular of verbs determines the 'cks' spelling for the /ks/ sounds (of course, the rule can be wilfully flouted for effect as it is by the American football team 'The Red Sox').

The same phenomenon occurs in many other scripts. In Portuguese the sequence of sounds /ise/ can be spelled as 'isse' or 'ice' but there is a morphological difference between the two spellings: 'isse' is an inflectional morpheme for the subjunctive and 'ice' is a derivational morpheme used in generating abstract nouns (e.g. the word pair 'menino – menin*ice*' means 'child – childhood'). Another example in Portuguese is the ending /eza/, which can be spelled as 'eza' or 'esa'. The ambiguity is sorted out rather simply: 'eza' is a derivational morpheme used in abstract nouns (e.g. 'pobreza', which means poverty), whereas 'esa' is an inflectional morpheme for the feminine form of noble titles (e.g. 'princesa' means princess) and ethnic classifications (e.g. 'inglesa' is the feminine for 'Englishman').

In Greek, morphemes are the key to deciding between alternative spelling inflections. For example, many Greek words end in the sound /i/ and this ending can be spelled in one of four ways – with single letters [η, ι] or with digraphs [οι, ει]. Feminine singular nouns and adjectives ending with this sound take the first of these spellings, neuter singular nouns and adjectives the second, masculine plural nouns and adjectives the third, and third person singular active verbs in one conjugation take the fourth. It is interesting to note that Greek is an extraordinarily regular script to read. Letter–sound relationships in Greek are completely consistent in the sense that (dialects apart) one can read any word in Greek and know exactly how it is pronounced.[1] Yet it is quite impossible to spell Greek words just on the basis of a thorough knowledge of these letter–sound relationships. One needs to spell with morphological as well as phonological strategies.

Spelling silent morphemes

Many syntactic distinctions are unpronounced. For example, we pronounce and write a word like 'play' in much the same way whether we are using it as a noun or a verb: the context tells its syntactic status. In the example that we have just given, neither speech nor writing reveals a syntactic distinction, but there are also many cases where such distinctions are captured in writing even though they are not pronounced in speech.

It is not hard to find instances where syntactic and morphological distinctions are marked in spelling. In several languages spelling captures the syntactic status of words in an explicit way which is not reflected in the pronunciation of these words. In German, for example, all proper nouns are spelled with a capital letter, and the same letter string can be written with a small or a capital letter depending on its syntactic function. For example, 'Die Kinder lernen Mathematik' (the children learn mathematics) contrasts with 'Das Lernen von Mathematik' (mathematics learning).

In English, apostrophes are used to represent possession but are not pronounced: 'the boys' sail' and 'the boys sail' sound the same, but have different meanings which the apostrophe captures.

The language where this phenomenon is probably at its strongest is French. Here singular and plural nouns are written differently: the plural is marked with an 's' ending ('maison, maisons') but is usually pronounced in the same way; the written 's' ending is typically silent. Verbs also contain spelling distinctions not marked in speech. Third person singular and third person plural verbs in the present tense usually sound exactly the same but are spelled differently ('il mange' – 'ils mangent'). The 'nt' in plural verbs is unpronounced; it too is a morpheme represented in spelling but not in speech (note that the morpheme for the singular is 'e' and for the plural is 'ent').

Conventional spellings for morphemes which flout letter–sound correspondence rules

In our third type of link between morphology and spelling, there is a direct conflict between letter–sound correspondence rules and the way in which morphemes are spelled. We began this chapter with an example – the 'ed' spelling at the end of regular past-tense verbs in English. The final consonant in these verbs is pronounced in three different ways – /t/, /d/, or /id/ – in different verbs and the constant spelling, 'ed', on strict letter–sound correspondence rules does not represent any of these three spoken endings. This does have the advantage that the common morphemic status of words like 'helped' and 'hired' and 'hated' is marked in the spelling of the endings of these words even though they are pronounced differently. Nevertheless, as we shall see, the spelling of this morpheme causes English-speaking children a great deal of difficulty. This difficulty, no doubt, is exacerbated by the fact that not all past-tense verbs are given the 'ed' ending. The endings of 'irregular' past-tense verbs are spelled phonetically ('felt', 'heard').

English-speaking children certainly manage to cope quite well with another instance in which morphologically based spellings flout alphabetic rules. Words which end in /z/ are usually spelled with a 'z' or a 'zz' ending ('quiz', 'buzz') and these spellings clearly conform to letter-sound rules. However, many plural nouns ('cans', 'theses') and third-person singular verbs ('she tans') also have /z/ endings which are invariably spelled with an 's'.

In fact, although this example is worth mentioning, it may have very little bearing on children's learning how to spell. Plural nouns and third-person singular verbs account for the vast bulk of words in the English language that end in /z/, and this means that words written with a 'z' ending are rare. It is possible that children quickly learn that 's' is the commonest way of spelling the /z/ ending, and indeed there is evidence that they do so (Read, 1986). This should give them some difficulty, but only with the few words which do end in 'z' or 'zz'.

The spelling of stems in English – that is, of morphemes defined by meaning rather than syntactic function – often remains constant even though the pronunciation changes when a derivational morpheme is added: for example, in the pairs 'know – knowledge' and 'magic – magician', there are phonological differences but a common spelling. The use of the letter 'c' to represent the sound /sh/ is not common in English but its appearance is not completely unpredictable (electric – electrician, physics – physician, music – musician, mathematics – mathematician). These examples suggest that there is an advantage in understanding connections between words with the same stem over the strategy of treating such spellings as irregular and attempting to learn them all in a rote fashion. Similar examples are found in Hebrew, where words sharing the same stem are spelled with the same three consonants which define their root, even if there are phonological changes when the root is embedded in a word of a different category.

Cross-linguistic questions about the development of children's understanding of the links between syntax and spelling

Children may have to go through the same steps in learning about the connection between morphology and spelling in different languages despite considerable surface differences in the form that these connections take. The best way to see whether there are such similarities is to ask a series of simple questions which follow almost automatically from the phenomena that we have already described.

The first question: where there are alternative spellings for the same sound, do children start by adopting mostly one of these spelling patterns?

In each instance of the first and the third types of syntactic connection described above, there are two or more spellings for the same sound and the morphological status of the words involved decides the correct spelling sequence. Our first question is whether children at first adopt both spelling patterns (where there are two) either appropriately or inappropriately, or whether they start by using just one of the alternative spelling patterns and later adopt the second (and third and fourth, where these exist).

The answer is simple. At first children tend to show a marked preference for one of the alternative spellings. Later on, and usually after a year or more of experience with reading and writing, they adopt and use the alternative spelling patterns as well. In Portuguese, for example, the nasal diphthong /~au/ can be spelled as '~ao' or 'am' at the end of words. The majority of the children in their first two years of schooling use only the '~ao' spelling pattern at the end of words. They can be 100 per cent correct when the words ending in this phonological sequence are spelled '~ao' and 100 per cent wrong when they are spelled as 'am'. From about their second or third year of schooling they start to use the 'am' ending (Nunes Carraher, 1985; Nunes, 1992).

In English too, where there are two alternative and phonetically acceptable spellings for a particular sound, children begin by using just one spelling and only later adopt the alternative one as well. Da Mota (1995) looked at children's spellings of singular and plural nouns which end in /cs/ and found that younger children simply used one spelling for the ending both of singular and of plural nouns ('fox' and 'sox') whereas older ones varied how they spelled these words.

In Greek, it is the same. We have found that beginning spellers show a marked preference for one spelling of a sound even when there are plain alternatives. As they grow older, they increasingly use alternative spelling patterns. We examined three examples of alternative spellings in Greek, the final /o/, /e/ and /ı/. The first two can be represented in one of two ways whereas the third has four alternative spellings. The level of difficulty of these alternative spellings varies because the phoneme is represented by one letter in some cases and by a digraph in others. With respect to the final /o/ sound, where both alternatives are single letters and there are only two possibilities, [ω and o], we identified as single-letter users those children who spelled fifteen out of the sixteen words which we had dictated with the same letter. Approximately one-third of the second graders were single-letter users who spelled the endings of words consistently with o. With the final /e/ sound, the number of children who spelled the endings using only one alternative (by the same fifteen of sixteen criterion) was even greater, probably because one spelling uses a single letter and the alternative is a digraph: about 45 per cent of the second graders spelled the final /e/ sound with ε only. We also considered the case of final /ɪ/ sounds, which can be spelled in four different ways, and here we used, as the criterion for a marked preference, the use of a single spelling in 80 per cent of the words. According to this criterion, approximately 20 per cent of the second graders ignored alternative spellings, although there were three other possibilities.

Much the same conclusion can be drawn from research on children's learning about the second and third types of morphological connection. What happens with the second type of connection where spelling represents a silent morpheme is easy to understand and easy to predict. At first, children simply leave these spellings out. Fayol, Thevenin, Jarousse and Totereau (1998, in press) have shown that French children at first leave out the 's' and 'nt' spellings for plural nouns and plural verbs, which means that their spellings of these plural words are usually a tolerable representation of the sounds of the words but are essentially unsyntactic. Only when they reached about their third year of school did they start marking the plurals in their spelling.

English children's dealings with the apostrophe are much the same. Many read and write for approximately four years before they even begin to use it, and, when they finally do adopt this spelling device, they tend to do so quite erroneously, as we shall see later (Bryant, Devine, Ledward and Nunes, 1997).

When we come to the third type of syntactic connection, in which conventional spellings transgress alphabetic rules, we also find that children begin by adopting one and ignoring the alternative spelling pattern for a particular sound. But here there is a rationale for the spelling pattern which they initially select and for the one which they initially ignore. Almost without exception, they start by choosing the phonetic spelling. Read (1986) showed, and Treiman (1993) and ourselves (Nunes, Bryant and Bindman, 1997) have since amply confirmed, that beginning spellers write the endings of regular past-tense verbs phonetically. 'Halpt' for 'helped' and 'wotid' for 'wanted' are two instances from Read's collection which illustrate that children begin by avoiding the correct 'ed' ending for these words. Initially children spell the endings of non-verbs and of irregular past-tense verbs much more successfully than those of regular verbs, e.g. the endings of 'field' and 'held' better than the endings of 'called' and 'filled' (Nunes, Bryant and Bindman, 1997). We also found, and so did Treiman (1993), that as children grow older they increasingly add the 'ed' spelling to their repertoire.

Thus whenever there are alternative spellings for different sounds and at least one of these spellings is the conventional spelling for a morpheme, beginning spellers adopt one spelling pattern and ignore alternatives, failing in many cases to take account of morphology in their spellings. Later on – in some cases many years later on – they also adopt and use the alternative spelling.

> *The second question: when children add the alternative spelling to their repertoire, do they assign the right spellings to the right syntactic categories?*

We turn now to older children who are beginning to use the alternative spellings – for example, to English children who spell the /cs/ ending as 'x' in some words and as 'cks' in others and to Greek children who started by writing all /o/ and /e/ endings in one way but have since begun to use alternative spellings. Do they put these spellings at the ends of the morphologically appropriate words straightaway? Do English children immediately write 'x' at the end of singular and 'cks' at the end of plural nouns? Do Greek children adopt ω for verbs and o for singular, neuter nouns?

The answer, which has extremely important implications for any theory about how children learn the connection between morphology and spelling, is clearly 'no'. Children do not at first assign the alternative spellings to the right types of words. In several different languages they start by using the newly adopted spelling pattern or patterns without making the necessary morphological connection. They apply the new pattern to inappropriate words as well as to appropriate ones. Apparently children must go through an intermediate stage in which they learn alternative spellings for particular sounds without at first understanding the morphological basis for these different spellings.

Greek spellings provide an example of children starting with a preferred spelling and then going through this intermediate stage where an alternative representation is adopted but its appropriate use is not understood. In our study we found that those children who wrote exclusively or almost exclusively o for the /o/ endings (mean age = 7.4 years) were, as a group, correct 99 per cent of the time they spelled o ending words and approximately 95 per cent wrong when spelling the words ending in ω. Slightly older children (mean age = 8.1 years) had started to adopt the ω spelling as well as the o, which significantly increased the probability of writing ω word endings correctly (52 per cent correct spellings, a percentage that does not differ from chance level) but also significantly decreased the probability of spelling o endings correctly: they were now correct in only 93 per cent of the words ending in o. Although this may appear a small difference, a *t*-test for the significance of the difference between independent means ($N = 107$) showed that the mean number of correct responses for the younger group was significantly higher than that for the older group. It was only the third group of older children (mean age = 9.3 years) who correctly spelled both o and ω endings in the correct way.

It was the same with words that end in /e/. Younger children (mean age 7.4 years) use the ε spelling for almost all of these word endings and are 99 per cent correct in ε words and 99 per cent wrong when the words end in the digraph αι. The intermediate group of children (mean age = 8.6 years), who used two spellings, spelled the words ending in ε correctly 82 per cent of the time and those ending in the digraph αι 47 per cent of the time correctly. Their improvement was significant in the latter group of words (although their performance is not above chance level), but so also was the fall in the percentage of correct spellings of ε words. Again, a group of older children (mean age = 9.6 years) spelled words with both endings systematically correctly.

Turning to the second type of syntactic connection, where the children mark a distinction in spelling which is not present in the oral language, we find further evidence for this intermediate stage, but with some complications. When English children eventually begin to use the apostrophe, they do so without much heed to its syntactic basis (Bryant, Devine, Ledward and Nunes, 1997). Many nine-year-old children place apostrophes at the ends of nominative and accusative plural words (they write sentences like 'the boy's eat') as well as in possessives and are as likely to omit apostrophes from possessives as from plural words which are not possessives. Over the next two years they become more discriminating. So they go through an intermediate stage when they use this new spelling device without at first understanding its morphological rationale. That understanding comes later.

The complication that we mentioned comes from some extraordinarily interesting data gathered by Fayol, Thevenin, Jarousse and Totereau (1998, in press) on silent morphemes for plural nouns and verbs in French. They found that French children who initially leave out both plural spellings eventually begin to adopt the 's' spelling which they put at the end of plural, and not of singular, nouns. To that extent this result departs from the other results that we have presented in this section: these children seem to make the relevant distinction in meaning between singular and plural as soon as they use the 's' ending. However, they do not get the morphological rationale completely right, for they also begin to use the 's' ending for plural third-person verbs as well: they write the plural ending in 'les maisons' correctly, but they also incorrectly write 'ils manges' instead of 'ils mangent': they have made the right distinction between singular and plural but they ignore the distinction between nouns and verbs. Later on they add the 'nt' ending to their repertoire but here again they show a remarkable confusion between nouns and verbs: they begin to make the reverse error, giving the plural verb ending to plural nouns ('les timbrent' instead of 'les timbres'). These confusions are more likely to appear in words which can either be nouns or verbs than in words which belong to only one of these syntactic categories. Eventually, both confusions are overcome. The French children too go through an intermediate stage in which they adopt new spelling patterns without at first completely understanding their basis, but they seem at the time to have a partial understanding of the syntactic function of the morpheme.

Morphologically based spelling rules which flout letter–sound correspondences provide us with another striking example of this intermediate stage. The study by Nunes, Bryant and Bindman (1997) was longitudinal and followed a large number of children, whose ages at the start of the project were six, seven or eight years, over a three-year period. At various times during this study the children had to spell the same list of words, all of which ended either in a /d/ or in a /t/ sound. These words fell into three categories – regular past-tense verbs, irregular past-tense verbs, and non-verbs.

As we have already remarked, the younger children tended to spell these words' endings phonetically, and as they grew older they changed by adopting the 'ed' spelling as well. However, we found that when the children first adopted this new spelling they often used it with wrong words as well as with the right ones. They generalised the 'ed' ending to irregular past-tense verbs, writing 'feled' for 'felt' and 'heared' for 'heard'. This is not necessarily a morphological mistake: after all these irregular words are past-tense verbs too and, if the children had learned the rule that past-tense verbs end in 'ed' spellings, they might only be applying this rule when writing 'feled'. However, they also made an altogether more surprising mistake: they often wrote the 'ed' ending for non-verbs as well, writing 'soft' as 'sofed' for example, and 'ground' as 'grouned'. Indeed they over-generalised the 'ed' ending in this way nearly as often as with irregular past-tense verbs. Thus they appeared to have no real understanding of the morphological basis for the 'ed' spelling.

Later on, these children went through a second intermediate stage in which they continued to make the first kind of generalisation, writing 'ed' at the end of irregular past-tense verbs, but no longer showed the overgeneralisation to non-verbs. We suggest that in this second intermediary stage children understand one aspect of the morpheme 'ed', that is, that the morpheme is used for past-tense verbs. The problem now is to deal with further syntactic complexities related to the exceptions to this rule.

To conclude, the answer to our second question is that children go through a stage when they use conventional spellings for morphemes without understanding their morphological basis. Eventually they restrict the new spellings to appropriate words.

Do children genuinely understand the morphological basis for the conventional spellings of morphemes when they use these spellings appropriately?

Our hypothesis is that children's understanding of when to use these new spelling patterns is based on their growing awareness of morphemes. This predicts correlations (a) across different types of morphological spelling patterns and (b) between these spelling patterns and children's morphological awareness. Both types of evidence have already been obtained in English and in Greek and we will consider each in turn.

Evidence from English   In our longitudinal study (Nunes, Bryant, and Bindman, 1997) we asked over 300 children, in their second, third or fourth years of school at the start of the project to spell: (1) interrogatives; (2) regular past-tense verbs (e.g. 'killed', 'stopped'); (3) irregular past-tense verbs (e.g. 'held', 'slept'); and (4) non-verbs (e.g. 'cold', 'except') ending with the same phoneme as the verbs. The children spelled these lists of words amongst other, unrelated words in three sessions which covered a period of twenty-one months (session B eight months after A: session C twelve months after B). They were also given an IQ test and tests of morphological awareness.

Relationships between different morphological spelling patterns   Interrogative words begin with one of two sounds /w/ and /h/, but, with the exception of 'how', interrogatives are spelled with 'wh'. Children might learn this limited set of spellings by rote but we hypothesised that this is not the case. We predicted that children would use the 'wh' spellings consistently only when they developed morphological spelling strategies and, consequently, that the consistent use of 'wh' spellings in interrogatives would correlate with the use of 'ed' spellings, which also depend on the same type of strategy.

We found strong relationships between 'ed' and 'wh' spelling. We carried out three multiple regressions, one for each session, in which the outcome measure was the correct spelling of regular verb endings, and age and IQ were the first two steps. In spite of these stringent controls, the relationship between 'wh' and 'ed' spelling remained significant in each session.

Relationships between morphological spelling patterns and morphological awareness   The second part of our hypothesis was that children's understanding of morphologically based spellings depends on their morpho-syntactic awareness: so we investigated the relationship between children's use of the 'ed' spelling and their awareness of morphology.

We found that we had to design two new morpho-syntactic awareness tasks because previous measures did not clearly meet our criterion for this awareness. We argue that a task measures children's awareness only when they have to manipulate language intentionally (Gombert, 1992). One previous measure is the sentence completion task (see, for example, Carlisle, 1995) in which children are provided with a simple word and asked to finish a sentence with an inflected or derived form. This task confounds syntactic and semantic awareness and does not meet the requirement of using language for a function other than speaking. Another is the morpheme-reversal task (for example, changing 'mailbox' to 'box mail') and the morpheme completion task (for example, completing the word 'overwhelm' when the subject just heard 'whelm'; Elbro, 1989). These tasks do not include such confounding but they deal only with stems: they do not include morphemes with a syntactic function and thus do not measure morpho-syntactic awareness.

Our two new tests of morpho-syntactic awareness, which were entirely oral, were both based on the analogy paradigm where the children must identify a relationship between one pair of stimuli and apply the same relationship to complete the second pair, following the model a:b::c:d (Piaget, Montangero, and Billeter, 1977; Sternberg, 1977). The children manipulated sentences (sentence analogy) in one task and single words (word analogy) in the other. Both tasks were presented with the support of two puppets. In each trial the first puppet 'said' the first stimulus and then the second puppet 'said' the second member of

Table 7.1   *Sample questions from the two morpho-syntactic awareness tasks.*

The sentence analogy task			
1. Tom helps Mary Tom sees Mary	Tom helped Mary ————————		
2. Jane threw the ball Jane kicked the ball	Jane throws the ball ————————		
The word analogy task			
1. anger strength	angry ————	2. teacher writer	taught ————
3. walk shake	walked ————	4. cried drew	cry ————

the pair; then the first puppet 'said' the third stimulus, which was the first member of the second pair in the analogy, and the child was asked to play the role of the second puppet and to say the last element. There were eight trials in each task. Table 7.1 gives several examples. We gave the children both tasks in session A and one of them (word analogy) in an intervening session between sessions B and C.

We found that the patterns of the children's spelling fell into five different categories which could readily be seen as different developmental stages. The children were assigned to *stage 1* when their spelling of the endings of the irregular past-tense verbs and non-verbs was not an acceptable phonetic spelling in at least 50 per cent of the cases. This means that end sounds in /d/ should be spelled systematically with a 'd' and end sounds in /t/ should be spelled with a 't' for children to be assigned to any other stage beyond stage 1.

Stage 2 children were those who met this 50 per cent criterion but did not yet use the 'ed' spelling systematically. We set a criterion of a maximum of two words spelled with the 'ed' ending in any of the thirty words for the children to be classified in this stage because we reasoned that isolated instances of the 'ed' spelling might be observed simply from rote memory.

We classified as *stage 3* those children who used the 'ed' ending in at least 10 per cent of the words (three out of thirty endings). Considering the trends discussed earlier about children's initial use of morphological spelling patterns, we assumed that some of the children were still likely to be unaware of the significance of the 'ed' ending when they first adopted it and to use it inappropriately. Thus we also classified the

Table 7.2   *The mean ages and scores in each morpho-syntactic awareness task by spelling stage for the use of 'ed' in English.*

Stage groups in Session A	N	Mean age	Mean score word analogy (out of 8)	Mean score sentence analogy (out of 8)
Stage 1	58	7.0	1.03	1.67
Stage 2	78	7.2	1.44	2.83
Stage 3	86	7.9	2.27	3.84
Stage 4	52	8.0	2.62	4.65
Stage 5	63	8.1	3.08	5.07

children as being in stage 3 if they used at least one 'ed' spelling in a non-verb.

Stage 4 children were those who satisfied the two previous positive criteria (50 per cent appropriate phonetic spellings for non-verbs and irregular verbs and use of the 'ed' spelling at least three times) and had started to understand the syntactic significance of the 'ed' ending: they used 'ed' spellings in verbs only. However, they had not achieved completely correct performance because they used the 'ed' ending in irregular verbs as well as regular verbs. Finally, *stage 5* children met the previous positive criteria of adequate phonetic spellings and use of at least three 'ed' endings and confined these endings to regular verbs.

Table 7.2 gives details of the children assigned to these five stages. It shows a relationship between the stages and morpho-syntactic awareness. The children in the more advanced stages also had higher scores in the morpho-syntactic awareness tasks.

We did discriminant function analyses to test the association between morpho-syntactic awareness scores in the first session (session A) and the spelling stages in sessions A, B and C. In these analyses we controlled for age and verbal IQ by putting them into the equation before entering morpho-syntactic awareness scores. Thus there were six analyses in all (two morpho-syntactic tests in session A, and the stage groups in sessions A, B and C as outcome measures).

In each analysis only one discriminant function was significant, and age and IQ were always significantly related to this function. The session A sentence analogy (Wilks' lambda 0.588; $p < 0.001$) and word analogy scores (Wilks' lambda 0.593; $p < 0.001$) both predicted the stages assigned to the children in session A. They both predicted the stages in session B as well (sentence analogy – Wilks' lambda 0.721; $p < 0.001$ and word analogy – Wilks' lambda 0.710; $p < 0.001$). Finally the session A sentence analogy scores (Wilks' lambda 0.757; $p < 0.001$) but not the word analogy scores predicted the stages in session C twenty-one months later.

It is worth noting that in each analysis the relationship between the spelling stage groups and the canonical discriminant function was entirely orderly. The higher the stage group, the greater the function: the functions were always negative for stage groups 1 and 2, around zero for stage 3 and positive for stages 4 and 5.

Thus these analyses showed a close relationship between the sentence and word analogy scores and the spelling stages both at the time that we gave these analogy tests and in subsequent sessions, even after controls for differences in age and IQ. The sentence analogy test successfully predicted the membership of the stage groups over a twenty-one-month period. This is strong support for the hypothesis that children in the later stages grasp the reason for the conventional spellings for morphemes and that their mastery is founded on morpho-syntactic awareness.

Evidence from Greek   The evidence that we have from Greek children concerns the choice for morphological reasons of alternative but acceptable spellings. We worked with three different end sounds, /o/, /e/ and /ι/, which have alternative spellings that cannot be distinguished phonologically but can be discriminated on the basis of morphology. The final /o/ sound is spelled with o when the word is a neutral noun in the singular, nominative, and with ω when the word is a verb in the first-person singular, active voice. The final /e/ sound is spelled with ε when the word is a verb in the first-person plural, active voice, and with the digraph αι when it is a verb in the third-person singular, passive voice. Finally, there are four alternative spellings for /ι/ sounds, which mark (1) feminine nouns and adjective in the singular, nominative form [η]; (2) neuter nouns in the singular, nominative form [ι]; (3) masculine nouns and adjectives in the plural, nominative form [οι]; and (4) a verb in the third-person singular, active voice [ει]. The first two of these spellings are single letters, whereas the latter two are digraphs.

We argued that a connection in Greek, as in English, across different types of morphological spelling and also between morphological spelling and morpho-syntactic awareness, would be evidence that there are similar developments in learning about very different orthographies.

Our data on Greek spelling are cross-sectional. Over 200 Greek children ranging from seven to ten years (school grade levels 2 to 4) spelled a total of sixty-four words ending in one of three vocalic sounds, /o/, /e/

or /ɪ/. The children also answered two tasks that assessed their awareness of morphemes, a word analogy and a sentence analogy task, adapted for use with Greek children from the paradigm developed by Nunes, Bryant and Bindman (1997).

Also, following the Nunes, Bryant and Bindman model, the children were classified independently for the spelling of each final sound into stages that reflected their growing understanding of when to use the alternative spellings. We used two criteria to define the stages: the number of alternative spellings of each sound and whether the spellings were appropriate for the morpheme in question. These criteria produced three categories of performance for the words ending in /o/ and /e/ sounds, where only two spellings are correct, and five categories of performance for the words with final /ɪ/ sounds, where four different spellings were possible. In each of the three cases (for /e/, /o/ and /ɪ/ end sounds), children whose performance was classified as stage 1 used only one spelling 80 per cent of the time or more.

The criterion for stage 2 was that a single spelling pattern should not be used more than 80 per cent of the time and that the children should still be making many generalisation errors. Although these children knew that there were alternative spellings, they still did not know how to chose between these alternatives. Most of the time the children still showed a strong preference for one spelling (or two, in the case of final /ɪ/ sounds where four spellings are possible), but correctly spelled at most one word type systematically (i.e. more than 80 per cent of the time). In this stage the children's marked preference for one spelling results in frequent correct spelling of the word type where that spelling happens to be correct. This stage is taken to reflect progress beyond stage 1 because the children show some knowledge of the possibility of using different spellings for the same sound.

In stage 3, two categories of words are spelled systematically correctly. This is the last possible stage when only two types of word are considered (the final /o/ and /e/ sounds). For the spelling of the final /ɪ/ sound, where there were four word types, we defined stage 3 performance as involving the use of at least three spelling patterns and writing systematically correctly (80 per cent of the time or more) two types of word.

Stage 4 performance was defined by the use of at least three alternative spellings and the systematic correct spelling of three categories of words.

Finally stage 5 performance was defined by the correct spelling of all four types of word (and consequently the use of all alternative spelling patterns).

Table 7.3 *Number of children with mean ages and mean scores in the word and sentence analogy tasks by spelling stage in the three examples from Greek.*

	N	Mean age	Mean score word analogy	Mean score sentence analogy
Stages for final /o/ sounds				
1	22	7.8	6.7	4.1
2	85	8.3	8.8	6.5
3	107	9.2	13.1	11.8
Stages for final /e/ sounds				
1	29	7.8	7.4	5.4
2	133	9.2	10.3	8.3
3	49	9.6	14.3	13.0
Stages for final /ı/ sounds				
1	9	7.5	6.7	4.4
2	80	7.8	7.9	5.3
3	21	8.7	11.0	9.0
4	23	8.7	10.9	9.4
5	69	9.6	14.2	13.0

The results of the classification into stage groups (which was done by the computer) are presented in table 7.3.

Relationships across different morphological spelling patterns and between these and morpho-syntactic awareness If the stages describe the children's understanding of the morphological basis for the different spellings, there should be a significant relationship (1) between the stages that the children are allocated with the different spellings, i.e. a child who is advanced in spelling /o/ should also do well in spelling /ı/ appropriately, and (2) between the children's morpho-syntactic aware-ness scores and their spelling stages.

We looked for these two kinds of connection with partial correlations controlling for age and verbal IQ (table 7.4). Some were low, but all were significant. We also carried out three discriminant function ana-lyses to see whether the two morpho-syntactic scores predicted the children's stages with each of the three sounds. In each analysis, age and IQ were the first two steps and the third and fourth steps were word and sentence analogy scores. The outcome measure in one ana-lysis was the children's spelling stage with the /o/ sound, in another with the /ı/ sound and in the third with the /e/ sound.

In the analyses of the spellings of the /o/ and the /ı/ sound, only one discriminant function was significant and all the variables were significantly

Table 7.4   *Partial correlations between the stages in spelling and grammatical awareness tasks (N = 195).*

	Spelling /e/ sound	Spelling /o/ sound	Spelling /ı/ sound	Word analogy
Spelling /o/ sound	0.21 $p = 0.003$			
Spelling /ı/ sound	0.20 $p = 0.005$	0.56 $p = 0.000$		
Word analogy	0.16 $p = 0.020$	0.20 $p = 0.004$	0.30 $p = 0.000$	
Sentence analogy	0.14 $p = 0.046$	0.34 $p = 0.000$	0.39 $p = 0.000$	0.63 $p = 0.000$

correlated with this function in both analyses. The word analogy scores (Wilks' lambda 0.52; df = 3; $p < 0.001$) and the sentence analogy scores (Wilks' lambda 0.49; df = 4; $p < 0.001$) predicted the stages that the children achieved with the /o/ spellings. In the analysis of the spellings of the /ı/ endings also, both the word analogy scores (Wilks' lambda 0.40; df = 4; $p < 0.001$) and the sentence analogy scores (Wilks' lambda 0.37; df = 4; $p < 0.001$) predicted the children's spelling stages.

This strong connection between the children's morpho-syntactic awareness and their spelling stages was repeated in the analysis of the /e/ sound spellings with the word analogy but not with the sentence analogy task. This analysis produced two discriminant functions but only the first ($X^2 = 107.10$; df = 6; $p < 0.0001$) was interpretable because all four variables were significantly related to it, whereas none was significantly related to the second. Word analogy scores significantly predicted the children's assignment to the stages (Wilks' lambda = 0.59; df = 3; $p < 0.0001$) even after controlling for age and verbal IQ, but sentence analogy scores did not add significantly to this prediction after the word analogy scores had been entered into the equation.

We conclude that the evidence about English and Greek is remarkably similar. In both cases children do not grasp the significance of morphological spelling patterns when they first start to use them but come to do so later. In Greek as well as in English the children's understanding of morphological spellings is significantly and specifically correlated across different instances of these spellings ('wh' and 'ed' in English; the three sounds in Greek). Finally, in both languages, there is a strong connection between morpho-syntactic awareness and the children's morphological spellings.

Conclusions

The rich evidence from different languages with respect to adults' use of morphemes as units in reading indicates that morphemes continue to be important throughout a reader's development. Our studies show that the ability to use these units in processing is the result of development, at least as far as spelling is concerned.

The studies which we have reviewed here demonstrate that the acquisition of morphological strategies by children is not accomplished in a single step but develops over at least two years from the time that children start to learn to read and write. Children concentrate initially on mastering phonological aspects of spelling and only after they have conquered these to a reasonable extent do they incorporate morphological strategies into their repertoire. When they start to use morphemes as spelling units, they do not seem at first to understand their function but later come to understand when to use morphemes as a spelling unit. Our results in English and Greek show that there is a strong and specific association between children's morpho-syntactic awareness and their adoption of morphemes as spelling units: this relationship remains significant even after controls for age and IQ are taken into account. The results of the longitudinal study in English suggest a causal connection: children's morpho-syntactic awareness at an earlier age is a significant predictor of their understanding of when to use morphemes in spelling.

We consider these results a solid beginning for further research on how children develop literacy beyond the first stages. They also indicate a striking similarity in processes across languages. A broader lesson can be learned from such cross-linguistic similarities: it is that learning to read and spell are intelligent activities and children must come to understand the 'logic' of the writing system if they are to master it truly.

NOTE

1 We do not mean that all words can be read by simple one-to-one correspondence rules. Written Greek also includes digraphs and complex conditional rules.

REFERENCES

Barber, C. (1993). *The English Language: A Historical Introduction*. Cambridge: Cambridge University Press.
Bentin, S. and Frost, R. (1995). Morphological factors in visual word identification in Hebrew. In L. B. Feldman (ed.), *Morphological Aspects of Language Processing* (pp. 271–92). Hillsdale, NJ: Erlbaum.

Bryant, P., Devine, M., Ledward, A. and Nunes, T. (1997). Spelling with apostrophes and understanding possession. *British Journal of Educational Psychology*, 67, 93–112.

Caramazza, A., Laudana, A. and Romani, C. (1988). Lexical access and inflectional morphology. *Cognition*, 28, 297–332.

Carlisle, J. (1995). Morphological awareness and early reading achievement. In L. B. Feldman (ed.), *Morphological Aspects of Language Processing* (pp. 189–210). Hillsdale, NJ: Lawrence Erlbaum.

da Mota, M. (1995). The role of grammatical knowledge in spelling. Unpublished D.Phil. thesis, University of Oxford.

Elbro, C. (1989). Morphological awareness in dyslexia. In C. von Euler (ed.), *Wenner-Gren International Symposium Series: Brain and Reading*. Hampshire, England: Macmillan.

   (1990). *Differences in Dyslexia. A Study of Reading Strategies and Deficits in a Linguistic Perspective*. Copenhagen: Munksgaard International Publishers.

Fayol, M., Thevenin, M. G., Jarousse, J. P. and Totereau, C. (1998, in press). On learning written French morphology. In T. Nunes (ed.), *Learning to Read: An Integrated View from Research and Practice*. Dordrecht, Holland: Kluwer.

Fowler, A. E. and Liberman, I. Y. (1995). The role of phonology and orthography in morphological awareness. In L. B. Feldman (ed.), *Morphological Aspects of Language Processing* (pp. 157–88). Hillsdale, NJ: Erlbaum.

Gombert, J. E. (1992). *Metalinguistic Development*. New York: Harvester.

Kelliher, S. and Henderson, L. (1990). Morphologically based frequency effects in the recognition of irregularly inflected verbs. *British Journal of Psychology*, 81, 527–39.

Morton, J. (1982). Disintegrating the lexicon: an information processing approach. In J. Mehler, E. C. T. Walker and M. Garrett (eds.), *Perspectives on Mental Representation* (pp. 89–110). Hillsdale, NJ: Lawrence Erlbaum.

Murrel, G. and Morton, J. (1974). Word recognition and morphemic structure. *Journal of Experimental Psychology*, 102, 963–8.

Nunes, T. (1992). Leitura e escrita: processos e desenvolvimento [Processes and development in reading and spelling]. In E. S. de Alencar, *Novas contribuicoes da psicologia aos processos de ensino e aprendizagem* [New contributions from psychology to teaching and learning] (pp. 13–50). Sao Paulo: Cortez Editora.

Nunes Carraher, T. (1985). Exploracoes sobre o desenvolvimento da competencia ortografia em portugues [Exploring the development of competence in orthography in Portuguese]. *Psicologia: Teoria e Pesquisa*, 1, 269–85.

Nunes, T., Bryant, P. E. and Bindman M. (1997). Morphological spelling strategies: developmental stages and processes. *Developmental Psychology*, 33, 637–49.

Piaget, J., Montangero, J. and Billeter, J. (1977). Les correlats. In J. Piaget, *L'Abstraction Réfléchissante*. Paris: PUF.

Read, C. (1986). *Children's Creative Spelling*. London: Routledge and Kegan Paul.

Sternberg, R. J. (1977). Component processes in analogical reasoning. *Psychological Review*, 84, 353–78.

Taft, M. (1985). The decoding of words in lexical access: a review of the morphological approach. In D. Besner, T. G. Walker and G. E. MacKinnon (eds.), *Reading Research: Advances in Theory and Practice*, vol. V (pp. 83–124). New York: Academic Press.

(1991). *Reading and the Mental Lexicon*. Hillsdale, NJ: Lawrence Erlbaum.

Treiman, R. (1993). *Beginning to Spell*. New York: Oxford University Press.

8 The relationship between phonological awareness and orthographic representation in different orthographies

Usha Goswami

Phonological awareness – a child's awareness that spoken words can be broken down into smaller units of sound – is now known to be an important predictor of learning to read in virtually every orthography that has been studied. The relationship between phonological awareness and reading holds for highly transparent orthographies, such as German and Spanish, for less transparent orthographies, such as English and French, and for orthographies that are wholly or partly logographic, such as Chinese and Japanese (e.g. Caravolas and Bruck, 1993; Cossu, Shankweiler, Liberman, Tola and Katz, 1988; Gombert, 1992; Huang and Hanley, 1995; Lundberg, Olofsson and Wall, 1980; Mann, 1986; Naslund and Schneider, 1991; Porpodas, 1993; Schneider and Naslund, in press; Wimmer, Landerl, Linortner and Hummer, 1991; Wimmer, Landerl and Schneider, 1994). In this chapter I will address three related questions concerning the developmental connection between phonological awareness and reading. The first is whether the same sequence of phonological development can be observed in children who are growing up in different linguistic environments. The second is whether awareness of the same phonological units predicts reading development in these different linguistic environments, and the third is whether the kinds of connections that children make between phonology and orthography differ depending on the phonology of the language that is being learned and the orthographic units that this phonology makes salient. These are all questions that, so far, have only partial answers. However, as the research reviewed in this chapter (and in this book) will show, they are questions that are receiving increasing interest in the literature on learning to read.

The sequence of phonological development

Levels of phonological awareness

When psychologists first began to measure phonological awareness, they began at the level of the *phoneme*. Phonemes are the smallest sounds that change the meanings of words: *hop* and *top* differ by a single phoneme (the initial phoneme), and so do *hop* and *tip* (the medial phoneme). We now know that phonological awareness can be measured at more than the phonemic level. Two other important levels of phonological awareness have also been distinguished. These are the level of *syllables*, and the level of *onsets* and *rimes*.

Syllabic awareness refers to children's ability to detect constituent syllables in words. For example, a word like *gasoline* has three syllables, and a word like *wagon* has two. *Onset-rime awareness* is the ability to detect that a single syllable is made up of two units, the onset, which corresponds to any phonemes before the vowel, and the rime, which corresponds to the vowel sound and to any following phonemes. Words like *bay*, *play* and *spray* have onsets consisting of one, two and three phonemes respectively (corresponding to the spelling patterns *b*, *pl* and *spr*). All of these words have a single phoneme rime (corresponding to the spelling pattern *ay*). Words like *tea* and *tree* also have single-phoneme rimes, words like *beak* and *light* have two-phoneme rimes, and words like *cold* and *help* have three-phoneme rimes. As these examples make clear, onset-rime awareness and phonemic awareness are not always distinct. Onsets are often single phonemes, and so, less frequently, are rimes. However, many rimes and a number of onsets correspond to phonological units that consist of more than one phoneme.

Measuring phonological awareness

In order to measure the development of phonological knowledge, psychologists have devised a number of different tasks. To select just three examples, they have used the *tapping* task, in which children are required to tap out the number of sounds in words, the *oddity* task, in which children have to select the word that has a different sound from other words in a group, and the *same/different judgement* task, in which children have to judge whether two words share a sound or not. These tasks can be administered at any or all of the three phonological levels: syllable, onset-rime and phoneme.

Liberman and her colleagues used the *tapping* task to measure the development of phonological awareness at the syllable and phoneme levels (Liberman, Shankweiler, Fischer and Cater, 1974). They asked children aged from four to six years to tap once with a wooden dowel for each of the syllables or phonemes in spoken words. These words had either one syllable or phoneme (*fix, i*), two syllables or phonemes (*wagon, at*), or three syllables or phonemes (*gasoline, cup*). Liberman *et al.* set a criterion of six consecutive correct responses as evidence for segmentation ability. They found that 46 per cent of the four-year-olds in their study could segment the words into syllables, whereas 0 per cent of this age group reached criterion for phonemes. For the five-year-olds, the figures were 48 per cent and 17 per cent, respectively. High levels of success on the phoneme task were only observed in the six-year-olds, who had been learning to read for about a year (the mean age of this group was six years, eleven months). Ninety per cent of the six-year-olds succeeded in the syllable task, and 70 per cent could segment the stimuli into phonemes.

The *oddity* task was first used to measure the development of onset and rime awareness by Bradley and Bryant (1983). They devised two versions of the oddity task, one (based on sets of three words) for four-year-olds, and one (based on sets of four words) for five-year-olds. The children were asked to spot the word in the group that differed in either its initial sound (bus, bun, *rug*), its medial sound (*pin*, bun, gun) or its final sound (*doll*, hop, top). Although these triples of words differed in terms of single phonemes, the oddity judgements could be made on the basis of shared onsets (the initial sound task) or rimes (the medial and final sound tasks, see Kirtley, Maclean, Bradley and Bryant (1989) for evidence that children solve the oddity task by thinking about onsets and rimes). Bradley and Bryant reported that four- and five-year-olds performed at above-chance levels on all versions of the oddity task, with rime awareness being easier than onset awareness. In later work, Bryant and his colleagues have shown that even three-year-olds are aware of rimes (e.g. Maclean, Bradley and Bryant, 1987).

Finally, the *same/different judgement* task was used to measure the development of syllable, onset-rime and phoneme awareness by Treiman and Zukowski (1991). They asked children aged four, five and six years to say whether two words spoken by the experimenter shared a sound at either the beginning or the end. The beginning task could be performed on the basis of either shared syllables (*hammer, hammock*), shared onsets (*broom, brand*) or shared initial phonemes (*steak, sponge*). The end task could be performed on the basis of either shared final syllables (*compete, repeat*), shared rimes (*spit, wit*) or shared final phonemes (*smoke, tack*). Treiman and Zukowski followed Liberman *et al.* in using a criterion of six consecutive correct responses as evidence that the children could perform the different tasks. They found that criterion on the syllable tasks was reached by 100 per cent of four- and six-year-old children, and by 90 per cent of the five-year-olds. The different age groups were also successful in the onset-rime version of the task, with 56 per cent of the four-year-olds reaching criterion, 74 per cent of the five-year-olds and 100 per cent of the six-year-olds. However, the younger children had considerable difficulty with the phoneme version of the task. Here criterion was reached by 25 per cent of the four-year-olds, 39 per cent of the five-year-olds and 100 per cent of the six-year-olds. So only the six-year-olds, who had been learning to read for about a year, showed equivalent levels of performance at the three phonological levels.

These studies present a consistent picture of the development of phonological skills. The development of phonological awareness appears to progress from the syllabic level via the onset-rime level to the phonemic level (see also Goswami and Bryant (1990) for further evidence regarding this developmental progression). An awareness of syllables, onsets and rimes appears to develop long before children go to school and begin learning to read. An awareness of phonemes appears to develop via tuition in reading. However, as noted earlier, the development of onset-rime awareness in itself involves the development of some phoneme awareness, as many words have single-phoneme onsets. Although a number of studies have shown that onset-rime awareness precedes phonemic awareness in most English-speaking children (Kirtley, Maclean, Bradley and Bryant, 1989), this general conclusion refers to the *awareness of every constituent phoneme in words*, rather than to the awareness of particular phonemes, such as the initial phoneme.

The studies discussed here suggest that syllable, onset and rime awareness is present by at least age four, and phoneme awareness by about age six. However, the age of the emergence of phonemic skills is probably relative, depending on the onset of tuition in reading. Even adults tend to lack phoneme awareness if they have never been taught to read. For example, Morais, Cary, Alegria and Bertelson (1979) studied a group of illiterate adults in Portugal who had never been taught to read, and found that their phonemic skills were extremely weak. If phoneme awareness depends on reading tuition in school, then it should emerge somewhat later in children who begin school when they are older than children in England and America, and somewhat earlier in children who begin being taught to read earlier than children in England and America.

Cross-linguistic studies

This hypothesis can be examined by cross-linguistic studies of the development of phonological awareness. So far, however, relatively little work on the development of phonological awareness has been conducted in languages other than English. Perhaps surprisingly, the studies that have been carried out to date suggest that the developmental sequence of syllabic and onset/rime awareness preceding an awareness of phonemes is consistent across linguistic environments. This seems surprising as it would seem plausible to propose that differences in the phonological input provided by different languages should affect the development of children's awareness of the different phonological levels. We will consider three examples of such work, from Italian, German and Czech.

Cossu, Shankweiler, Liberman, Tola and Katz (1988) replicated the tapping study carried out by Liberman *et al.* with Italian children. The pre-school Italian children were aged four and five years, and the school age sample were seven- and eight-year-olds. The procedures were modelled as closely as possible on those of Liberman *et al.* (1974). The children were given a small wooden dowel, and were asked to tap once for each syllable in words like *gatto, melone* and *termometro*, and once for each phoneme in words like *mi, per* and *sale*. The percentage of children reaching the criterion of six consecutive correct responses at the syllable level was 67 per cent for the four-year-olds, 80 per cent for the five-year-olds, and 100 per cent for the school-age sample. The equivalent figures for the phoneme task were 13 per cent, 27 per cent and 97 per cent, respectively. Thus Italian children, too, show good syllabic awareness prior to entering school. Phonemic awareness, in contrast, appears to emerge as reading is taught.

An oddity task was used to measure the development of onset and rime awareness in German children by Wimmer, Landerl and Schneider (1994). Their onset task consisted of sets of words like Bach, Bahn, *Dach*, and Bad. Their rime tasks consisted of sets of words like Mund, rund, *Mond*, Hund (middle sound different) and Meer, *Mehl*, sehr, leer (end sound different). The children tested were aged on average six years, eleven months, and were in their first month of schooling. Wimmer *et al.* found that the onset task (40 per cent correct) was more difficult than the rime tasks (60 per cent correct), in line with Bradley and Bryant's findings for English children. They also found that performance levels on all of the tasks were well above chance. Thus for German children, as for English children, onset and rime awareness is present before reading is taught.

Finally, Caravolas and Bruck (1993) used a same/different judgement task to measure the development of onset and phoneme awareness in English-speaking (Canadian) and Czech-speaking children. In their task, the children had to judge whether two spoken nonsense words shared the same initial phoneme when the phoneme either *was* the onset (*semp*, *soold*), or was part of the onset (*krin*, *klav*). We will call the first task the onset task, and the second task the phoneme task. Three age groups of children were tested in each language, four-year-olds, five-year-olds and seven-year-olds. Caravolas and Bruck found that both the English-speaking and the Czech children were significantly better at the onset task than at the phoneme task, although the performance differences were small in magnitude. The number of items solved correctly in each task for the four-year-old English-speaking children was 50 per cent and 48 per cent (onset task and phoneme task, respectively, both at chance level), 66 per cent and 61 per cent (5-year-olds, onset task and phoneme task), and 96 per cent and 91 per cent (seven-year-olds, onset task and phoneme task). Corresponding figures for the Czech children were 46 per cent and 43 per cent (four-year-olds), 59 per cent and 54 per cent (five-year-olds), and 94 per cent and 91 per cent (seven-year-olds). Thus similar levels of overall performance were found in the different languages, and both language groups followed the developmental pattern of onset awareness being easier than phoneme awareness.

These three studies suggest that the sequence of phonological development is similar for children who are growing up in different linguistic environments. However, the study by Caravolas and Bruck is particularly interesting with respect to this question, as they had initially hypothesised that Czech children would show a greater awareness of complex onsets than English children. This was because complex (= two-phoneme) onsets are more frequent in Czech than in English. As we have seen, no such evidence emerged. However, Caravolas and Bruck *did* find that Czech children had a greater ability to manipulate complex onsets in a sound isolation task, in which they had to isolate the first sound in nonsense words like *saul* and *slau*. Caravolas and Bruck suggested that the same/different judgement task may be less reliable than other phonological awareness measures, as it proved insensitive to subtle cross-language differences. It is thus important to identify the phonological awareness tasks that are most sensitive to subtle cross-language differences, and to use these tasks in future research. The possibility that differences in the phonological input provided by different languages affect the development of phonological awareness at different phonological levels is a fascinating one for researchers, and one that has hardly begun to be pursued.

Predictive relationships between phonological awareness and reading in different orthographies

Rime awareness and reading in English

The second question that was posed at the beginning of this chapter was whether awareness of the *same* phonological units predicts reading development in different linguistic environments. For example, it is quite possible that the sequence of phonological development could be the same across different linguistic environments, but that the relationship between phonological awareness at the different levels and progress in reading and spelling could differ depending on the phonology of the language that is being learned and the orthographic units that this phonology makes salient. We will focus here on rime awareness, as a number of studies carried out in English have demonstrated that early rime awareness is an important predictor of later progress in reading and spelling. Whether the same predictive relationship holds in other languages is less clear.

Perhaps the most cited study of the importance of rime awareness for reading progress in English is the longitudinal project carried out in Oxford by Bradley and Bryant (1983). This project began with 403 children aged four and five, and followed up reading progress in 368 of them approximately three years later. The four- and five-year-olds were given the oddity task described above, and their reading and spelling progress was measured using standardised tests when they were seen again at eight and nine. Strong and significant relationships were found between the oddity measures taken prior to schooling and the children's reading and spelling performance three years later. Furthermore, these relationships remained strong even when the influence of intellectual level at the time of the initial and final tests and of differences in memory were removed.

The most convincing aspect of Bradley and Bryant's data, however, lay in the results of the training study that they conducted at the same time. The training study was done with a sub-set of sixty-five of the children, and concentrated on those with the poorest oddity scores at the beginning of the study. These children were divided into four groups, two of which were given phonological training about onsets and rimes for a period of two years, and two of which acted as control groups. The phonological training was either oral in nature, requiring children to sort pictures on the basis of shared sounds (e.g. putting a cat, a rat, a hat and a bat together), or combined this oral training with additional tuition in spelling (via plastic letters). One control group received the same picture-based training with semantic rather than phonological categories (e.g. farmyard animals), and the other group were an 'unseen' control.

At the end of the two years of training, the reading and spelling progress of the children was measured. The two experimental groups (phonological training) were both ahead of the children in the critical *seen* control group, and were also ahead of the children in the unseen control group. The group which had received oral training were on average four months ahead of the seen control group in reading and spelling, and eight to ten months ahead of the unseen control group. The group which had received phonological training combined with spelling tuition were on average eight months ahead of the seen control group in reading, and an astonishing seventeen months in spelling. Their gains compared with the unseen control group were even more remarkable, being twelve months in reading and twenty-three months in spelling. Bradley and Bryant's conclusion that there was a causal connection between onset-rime awareness and learning to read and spell in English has since been replicated in other English studies (e.g. Maclean, Bradley and Bryant, 1987; Holligan and Johnston, 1988; Ellis and Large, 1987).

Rime awareness and reading in other orthographies

However, a similar relationship between onset-rime awareness and reading has not been found in comparable studies conducted in other languages (although see Lundberg *et al.*, 1980). For example, in the study discussed earlier by Wimmer *et al.* (1994) carried out with German children, the predictive relationship between performance on the oddity task and reading and spelling progress was investigated in the same way as in Bradley and Bryant's study. Follow-up measures of reading and spelling were taken both one year after administration of the oddity task, and three years later. Wimmer *et al.* found that performance on the oddity task was only minimally related to reading and spelling progress in German children in the one-year follow-up, when they were seven to eight years old (the same age as the children in Bradley and Bryant's study). However, significant predictive relationships *were* found in the three-year follow-up, when the children were aged on average nine years, nine months. At this point rime awareness (although not onset awareness) was significantly related to both reading and spelling development.

This data suggests that rime awareness only becomes an important predictor of reading progress *later* in development for German children.

This pattern differs from that found in studies carried out in English, where the predictive strength of rhyme measures appears to drop out after the age of around six years (e.g. Stanovich, Cunningham and Cramer, 1984). Other studies of the relationship between different levels of phonological awareness and reading carried out in more transparent orthographies support Wimmer *et al.*'s general conclusion, although such studies have not been longitudinal ones. For example, Cardoso-Martins (1994) questioned whether a special relationship existed between early rhyme awareness and initial progress in learning to read in Portuguese, and while a recent study in Norwegian found a significant relationship between rhyming and reading in children who were in their first year of schooling (seven-year-olds), the same study found a much larger correlation between phoneme awareness and reading in these children (Hoien, Lundberg, Stanovich and Bjaalid, 1995).

Cross-linguistic findings such as these raise the interesting possibility that the level of phonological awareness that is most predictive of reading development may vary with the phonology of the language that is being learned and the orthographic units that this phonology makes salient to the learner. In particular, a strong connection between rhyming and early reading may not hold for alphabetic orthographies other than English. English is orthographically 'non-transparent', as letters can represent more than one phoneme. Most alphabetic languages are 'transparent', with each letter representing only one phoneme. Different levels of phonological awareness may thus be predictive of reading development in transparent and less transparent orthographies, with phoneme awareness being more important in transparent orthographies. Although the spelling units that offer *the most consistent mappings to phonology* reflect the rime in English, they reflect the phoneme in more transparent orthographies such as German and Portuguese.

The spelling system of English

Evidence that the spelling units that offer *the most consistent mappings to phonology* reflect the rime in English comes from a statistical analysis of English orthography carried out by Treiman, Mullennix, Bijeljac-Babic and Richmond-Welty (1995). Treiman *et al.* calculated how many times individual letters had the same pronunciations when they occurred in the same positions across different words for all of the consonant–vowel–consonant (CVC) monosyllabic words of English (e.g. 'c' in *cat*, *cup*, *cold*, etc.; 'p' in *cup*, *top*, *help*, etc.). The CVC words in this analysis included words spelled with vowel digraphs, like *rain* and *beak*, and words with 'rule of e' spellings, like *cake* and *lane*. Treiman *et al.*

reported that the pronunciation of the initial and final consonants was reasonably consistent across different words. The first consonant (C_1) was pronounced the same in 96 per cent of CVC words, and the final consonant (C_2) was pronounced the same in 91 per cent of CVC words. However, the pronunciation of vowels turned out to be far less consistent. Individual vowels were only pronounced the same in 51 per cent of CVC words. This analysis shows that the lack of transparency in written English is largely due to the vowels.

Treiman *et al.* then went on to look at the spelling–sound consistency of larger spelling units in the words, namely the C_1V and the VC_2. When the consistency of the initial consonant and the vowel was considered as a unit (C_1V, for example *bea* in *beak* and *bean*), then only 52 per cent of CVC words sharing a C_1V spelling had a consistent pronunciation. A far greater gain in consistency occurred for spelling units corresponding to rimes. When the consistency of the vowel and the final consonant was considered as a unit (VC_2, for example, *eak* in *peak* and *weak*), then 77 per cent of CVC words sharing a VC_2 spelling had a consistent pronunciation. This statistical analysis of the properties of English orthography shows very clearly that the spelling–sound consistency of written English is greatest for initial consonants (onsets), final consonants and rimes. This may help to explain the robust finding that onset-rime awareness is an important early predictor of learning to read in English.

Although similar statistical analyses of languages like Portuguese and German have not (to my knowledge) been done, it seems likely that such analyses would result in a rather different picture concerning spelling–sound consistency at the level of the individual letter (C_1, V, C_2). The consistency of different initial and final consonants and vowels across different words in these orthographies should be close to 100 per cent. From this perspective, it is interesting to note that in countries with very transparent orthographies, like Austria, there is little debate about how to teach initial reading. In Austria, the sequence in which the letters and their sounds are taught in school is decided by the government, and all schools follow the same teaching sequence. This lack of debate about how to teach reading is probably a consequence of the high orthographic transparency of German. Although the alphabet does *not* consistently represent the phonemes of spoken English, it probably does consistently represent the phonemes of spoken German.

The question that we wish to pursue here, however, is whether the kinds of connections that children make between phonology and orthography depend to some extent on the phonology of the language being learned and the orthographic units that this phonology makes salient.

If differences in orthographic transparency lead children to focus on different spelling units as they are learning to read, particularly in the early stages of reading development, then we can predict that attention to spelling units that reflect rimes should be far greater in children who are learning to read English than in children who are learning to read orthographically transparent scripts like German. We will consider two lines of evidence that are relevant to this hypothesis. The first concerns the spontaneous focus on spelling patterns for rimes that is adopted by children who are learning to read English. The second concerns cross-linguistic comparisons of children's ability to read nonsense words that contain either familiar or unfamiliar rimes.

The nature of the orthography and the development of orthographic representations

Orthographic analogies and rime units in English

Evidence that children who are learning to read English show a spontaneous focus on spelling units that correspond to rimes comes from research into children's use of orthographic *analogies* in reading. An orthographic analogy involves using a shared spelling sequence to make a prediction about a shared pronunciation. For example, a child who knows how to read a word like *beak* could use this word as a basis for reading other words with shared spelling segments such as *peak*, *weak* and *speak*, or *bean*, *bead* and *beat*. Notice that in order to use a word like *beak* as a basis for reading a new word like *peak*, the child needs to make a prediction about the pronunciation of the new word that is based on the shared spelling sequence for the *rime* (VC_2). In order to use *beak* as a basis for reading *bean*, however, the child needs to make a prediction about the pronunciation of a shared spelling unit that crosses the onset-rime boundary. The shared spelling sequence *bea-* in *beak* and *bean* corresponds to the onset and part of the rime (C_1V).

In order to measure children's ability to use a word like *beak* as a basis for reading analogous words like *peak* and *bean*, my early experiments used the 'clue' word technique (Goswami, 1986, 1988, 1991; see figure 8.1). Young readers (five-, six- and seven-year-olds) were taught to read a 'clue' word, such as *beak*, which was printed on a card. They then retained this card as their clue while reading a series of other words, also printed on cards, some of which were analogous to their clue word. A pre-test had established that the children could not read these other words prior to learning their clue word. The results showed that words like *peak* were easier to read by analogy to the clue word

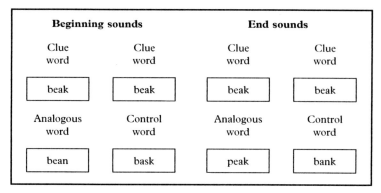

Figure 8.1   The 'clue word' analogy technique (Goswami and Bryant, 1990).

than words like *bean*. This finding was particularly marked for the younger children. From this work I concluded that rime analogies were more frequent than analogies based on the onset and part of the rime, and that they emerged first developmentally. At that time, I interpreted this developmental pattern with respect to the sequence of phonological development. Rime analogies required an early-developing form of phonological awareness (onset-rime awareness), whereas analogies based on the onset and part of the rime required phonemic awareness (segmentation of the rime).

Further research apparently supported this developmental explanation. I found that analogies based on rimes were typically the *only* analogies made by very young readers, and I also found that analogies between the onset and part of the rime (*beak–bean*), and analogies between shared vowel digraphs (*beak–heap*) were not typically observed until a child had been reading for a period of around six to eight months (Goswami, 1993). Rime analogies showed a specific connection to measures of onset-rime awareness, while onset and part of the rime analogies were more strongly related to phonemic awareness (Goswami, 1990a; Goswami and Mead, 1992). Finally, rime analogies really did seem to result from some orthographic analysis. I found that if children were taught to read a clue word like *head*, which was analogous in spelling to a rhyming word like *bread* but not analogous in spelling to a rhyming word like *said*, then analogies like *head–said* were relatively rare (Goswami, 1990b). This experiment established that rime analogies indeed depended on shared spelling patterns, and were not the result of a simple form of 'rhyme priming'.

The evidence from these 'orthographic analogy' studies that rimes were functionally important units for young readers of English has now received support from a number of related studies using converging methods (e.g. Bowey and Hanson, 1994; Bruck and Treiman, 1992; Ehri and Robbins, 1992; Muter, Snowling and Taylor, 1994; Treiman, Goswami and Bruck, 1990; Greaney and Tunmer, 1996; Wise, Olson and Treiman, 1990). More recently, however, I have become interested in the possibility that the salience of the rime spelling unit in English is not simply due to the fact that onset-rime awareness develops relatively early. While this is no doubt important in helping children to use rime analogies, greater importance may lie in Treiman *et al.*'s recent demonstration that the spelling patterns for rimes in English offer a greater degree of spelling–sound consistency across words than a C-V-C ('phonics') analysis (Treiman *et al.*, 1995), and in Kessler and Treiman's (in press) demonstration that the rime is a highly salient unit in English phonology. The importance of the phonology of a language and the orthographic units that this phonology makes salient for reading development can be assessed by cross-linguistic studies.

Orthographic analogies in more transparent orthographies

If the phonology of a language and the statistical characteristics of its orthography which reflect this phonology – its transparency – help to determine children's propensity to use rime analogies in reading, then we can predict that rime analogies should be most frequent in non-transparent orthographies like English and French, and least frequent in highly transparent orthographies like Spanish and Greek. It is important to note that analogy is being conceived of as an automatic process, driven by the level of a child's phonological knowledge and by the nature of the orthographic–phonological relations that operate in a particular orthography (see also Goswami, Gombert and De Barrera, 1998). From this perspective, analogies should operate in every writing system. However, analogies in a very transparent orthography would reflect grapheme–phoneme relations, and analogies in English would reflect rime-based coding.

One way of comparing the salience of rime units in languages other than English is to study nonsense word reading. Nonsense words can be matched in terms of the phonological assembly processes that they require, but be spelled in such a way that they either have rimes that are familiar from real words, as in the English example *dake* (cake, make), or unfamiliar (*daik*). A focus on rime units will only help in reading the first kind of nonsense word, as children can read a nonsense word like *dake* either by using a rime analogy or by assembling grapheme–phoneme correspondences. In contrast, as the rime spelling pattern *-aik* does not occur in any real words in English, children can only read the matched nonsense word *daik* by assembling grapheme–phoneme correspondences. In order to compare the salience of rime units in reading for children who are learning different orthographies, we need to derive similar matched pairs of nonsense words in other languages. We can then measure the magnitude of the difference in reading accuracy and reading speed between nonsense words with familiar rimes (e.g. *dake*) and nonsense words with unfamiliar rimes (e.g. *daik*) in different orthographies.

Along with a number of colleagues, I have been using this matched nonsense word technique to compare the importance of spelling units that correspond to rimes for learning to read in English, French, Spanish and Greek (Goswami, Gombert and De Barrera, 1998; Goswami, Porpodas and Wheelwright, 1997). Although it is difficult to devise nonsense words with unfamiliar rimes (like *daik*) in more transparent orthographies, we have managed by studying words of more than one syllable (Greek), thereby focusing on the entire unit following the onset (the spelling pattern for the *rhyme*), or by studying nonsense words that are unfamiliar in terms of rhyme phonology as well as rime orthography (Spanish). I will briefly describe each study in turn. However, to preview our results, the salience of rime units seems to vary in a direct way with the degree of transparency of the orthography that is being learned. Spelling units corresponding to rimes are most salient to young readers of English, fairly salient to young readers of French, and not salient at all to young readers of Spanish and Greek. This set of findings implies that children who are learning to read different orthographies do indeed develop somewhat different orthographic representations. Children who are learning non-transparent scripts develop orthographic representations that are partly underpinned by larger phonological units like rimes. Children who are learning to read transparent scripts develop orthographic representations that are underpinned by phonemic units, and do so from the *beginning* of learning to read.

Nonsense word reading in English vs. French

As noted above, the logic behind the cross-linguistic comparisons that we made depended on generating different types of nonsense words in the different orthographies. In order to study the importance of rime units in learning to read English vs. French, two types of nonsense word were devised. One type reflected the orthographic–phonological relations in

Table 8.1   *Accuracy of nonsense word reading: English vs. French O+P+ words vs. O–P+ words (percentage correct).*

Language	List type		Age (years)
	O+P+	O–P+	
English	56.3	36.2	7
	64.1	48.2	8
	91.7	78.9	9
French	83.1	77.9	7
	89.8	84.6	8
	94.3	87.8	9

French and English at *both* the onset-rime and the grapheme–phoneme level, as in *dake* and *fenche*. These nonsense words could either be decoded by using rime units from real word neighbours in the two orthographies (*cake, manche*) or via knowledge of grapheme–phoneme correspondences. Such nonsense words will be referred to as O+P+ words, as they share both orthography (O) and phonology (P) at the level of the rime with real words. A second type of nonsense word was matched for phonology with real words at the level of the rime (P+), but used orthographic rime spellings that were not found in real words (O–). These were O–P+ words, like *daik* and *fenche*. If children find O+P+ nonsense words like *dake* and *fanche* easier to read than matched O–P+ nonsense words like *daik* and *fanche*, this would support the idea that their orthographic representations represent information about rime units.

To test this idea, we gave O+P+ and O–P+ nonsense words like *dake* and *daik* to English and French seven-, eight- and nine-year-old readers (Goswami, Gombert and De Barrera, 1998). The O+P+ and O–P+ words were matched as closely as possible for orthographic familiarity using mean positional bigram frequency measures, and the English and French children were matched by reading age (using standardised reading tests from the two countries). They were also matched as closely as possible for their reading knowledge of the real words that had been used as a basis for the O+P+ words (i.e. the children's knowledge of real word analogues like *cake* and *manche* was matched across orthographies). The results of this cross-linguistic comparison are given in table 8.1.

Inspection of the table shows that an advantage in reading the O+P+ nonsense words was found in both English and French readers. Reaction time data showed that a similar advantage existed for reading speed, with O+P+ words being read faster than O–P+ words in both orthographies. However, the size of the O+P+ advantage was much larger in English. The younger English children read around 20 per cent more of the O+P+ nonsense words correctly compared to the O–P+ nonsense words, and were on average 0.5 seconds faster in reading the O+P+ words. This implies that rimes are more salient units in the orthographic representations developed by young English readers than in the orthographic representations developed by young French readers. However, rime units also have a privileged status for young readers of French, as the French children also showed a significant advantage in reading the O+P+ words. The younger French children read around 5 per cent more of the O+P+ nonsense words correctly compared to the O–P+ nonsense words.

Nonsense word reading in English vs. Greek

As both English and French are non-transparent orthographies, the finding that rime units have functional significance for beginning readers of these orthographies is not really a surprising one. The statistical characteristics of French orthography show a smaller advantage for rime units compared to that demonstrated in English by Treiman *et al.* (see Peereman and Content, 1996), but orthographic constraints on the possible VC_2 units in French mean that spelling–sound consistency is increased by focusing on these units, just as in English. The finding that French children are sensitive to these orthographic units thus makes sense in terms of the statistical characteristics of the orthography. In a highly transparent orthography such as Greek, however, rime units would not be expected to confer any functional advantage. This is because the relationship between graphemes and phonemes is so predictable: the phonology of the Greek language can be unambiguously represented by a 1:1 correspondence between phonemes and graphemes. As nothing is gained in terms of decoding accuracy by focusing on rime units, children learning to read Greek would not be expected to find O+P+ nonsense words like *dake* easier to read than O–P+ nonsense words like *daik*.

The same logic of comparing children's reading of O+P+ and O–P+ nonsense words was thus used to compare children's orthographic representations in English and Greek (Goswami, Porpodas and Wheelwright, 1997). Groups of seven-, eight- and nine-year-old readers from the two countries were given lists of O+P+ and O–P+ nonsense words to decode, and reading accuracy and reading speed were compared across orthographies. Although the very transparency of Greek made O–P+ stimuli difficult to create, we managed this by using bi- and

Table 8.2 *Accuracy of nonsense word reading: English vs. Greek O+P+ words vs. O–P+ words (percentage correct).*

Language	List type		Age (years)
	O+P+	O–P+	
English	38.8	23.2	7
	72.4	56.3	8
	86.5	75.0	9
Greek	88.8	89.9	7
	84.9	85.4	8
	94.5	90.9	9

tri-syllabic words that incorporated the few Greek phonemes that could be represented by more than one letter. Examples of the Greek stimuli are χλεει (hlei, O+P+ for *plei*) and χλαιυ (hlei, O–P+). Examples of the English stimuli are *bomic* (O+P+ for *comic*) and *bommick* (O–P+).

The results of this cross-linguistic comparison are given in table 8.2. As can be seen, the English children found the O+P+ words much easier to read than the O–P+ words, whereas the Greek children showed equivalent decoding accuracy for both word types. Inspection of the reaction time data showed that the English children were again significantly faster in decoding the O+P+ words. The Greek children showed no significant difference in speed between the two word types. Thus whereas nonsense words that share familiar spelling segments with real words (O+P+ words) are decoded faster and with greater accuracy by children who are learning to read a non-transparent orthography like English, the same is not true of children who are learning to read a transparent orthography like Greek. This implies that the orthographic sequences that reflect rhymes are not salient units in the orthographic representations developed by young readers of Greek.

Nonsense word reading in English, Spanish and French

Spanish, like Greek, is a highly transparent orthography. Unlike Greek, its transparency is such that O–P+ nonsense words are impossible to devise. However, a third type of nonsense word can be created to measure orthographic representations in Spanish, by varying orthographic and phonological familiarity *together*. Logically, O–P– words are also possible. These nonsense words are unfamiliar in terms of *both* orthography and phonology at the level of the rime. For example, English

O–P– nonsense words would be stimuli like *faish* and *zoip*. No real English word rhymes with these nonsense words, and no real English word is spelled with the rime units *-aish* or *-oip*. Although these nonsense words can be decoded by using grapheme–phoneme correspondences, just like O–P+ words, if we compare O+P+ nonsense words like *dake* with O–P– nonsense words like *faish*, we can find out whether young children are learning something *specific* about the orthographic–phonological relations that operate in their particular orthography.

Comparisons between O+P+ and O–P– nonsense words were made across three orthographies, English, French and Spanish (Goswami, Gombert and De Barrera, 1998). Of course, an advantage for O+P+ nonsense words over O–P– nonsense words would be expected in all orthographies. However, our interest was in whether this advantage would be *greater* in orthographies with low transparency, like English and French, compared to orthographies with high transparency, like Spanish. Even phonologically unfamiliar sequences of graphemes that are not found in the traditional orthography will have a very predictable pronunciation in a highly transparent orthography like Spanish. This will be less true in English and French.

In our study, English, French and Spanish seven-, eight- and nine-year-old readers were given lists of O+P+ and O–P– nonsense words to decode. Examples of the English stimuli are *fape* (O+P+ for *tape*) and *faish* (O–P–); examples of the French stimuli are *fanche* (O+P+ for *manche*) and *chenfe* (O–P–); and examples of the Spanish stimuli are *duez* (O+P+ for *juez*) and *muet* (O–P–). The O+P+ and O–P– nonsense words were equated across lists for their constituent grapheme–phoneme correspondences. Decoding accuracy and reading speed were again used as dependent measures. The accuracy data from this third cross-linguistic comparison are shown in table 8.3.

As is clear from the table, an advantage in reading the O+P+ nonsense words compared to the O–P– nonsense words was found in all three orthographies. However, the size of the O+P+ advantage varied with orthographic transparency. The effect was extremely small and non-significant (0–3 per cent) in Spanish, and was relatively large and highly significant (10–30 per cent) in English and French. The Spanish children did show a significant effect of orthographic and phonological familiarity in reading *speed*, however, as they took significantly longer to read the O–P– nonsense words than the O+P+ nonsense words. Taking these results together, it seems that *all* of the children were learning something *specific* about the orthographic-phonological relations that operated in their particular orthography, whether this orthography was transparent or not.

Table 8.3   *Accuracy of nonsense word reading: English, French and Spanish O+P+ words vs. O–P– words (percentage correct).*

Language	List type		Age (years)
	O+P+	O–P–	
English	28.7	11.8	7
	66.2	33.3	8
	59.9	50.7	9
French	71.4	52.9	7
	80.5	68.5	8
	82.0	73.4	9
Spanish	95.8	94.3	7
	94.3	94.3	8
	94.8	92.2	9

Nonsense word reading in more and less transparent orthographies

Considering all of the different cross-linguistic comparisons discussed above together, it seems that the orthographic representations that are developed by children who are learning to read less transparent orthographies are *more* specific than those that are developed by children who are learning to read more transparent orthographies. Children who are learning to read less transparent orthographies like English and French develop orthographic representations that encode specific sequences of grapheme–phoneme correspondences, such as specific spelling sequences for rimes, and reading *accuracy* varies with rime familiarity. Children who are learning to read more transparent orthographies like Greek and Spanish develop orthographic representations that encode individual grapheme–phoneme correspondences, and although they are still sensitive to the sequential constraints between these correspondences that characterise their orthography, this sensitivity only affects reading *speed*. It is also clear that nonsense word reading accuracy overall varies remarkably with orthographic transparency. Despite our efforts to match the children in our different studies for reading age and real word knowledge, the younger Spanish and Greek children were far more accurate in our nonsense word reading tasks than the younger English and French children. If nonsense word reading is accepted as a useful means of comparing code acquisition across different orthographies, then code acquisition in highly transparent orthographies appears to be much more rapid than code acquisition in less transparent orthographies.

The orthographic–phonological relations in Spanish and Greek appear to be acquired to a high level of accuracy during the first year of learning to read, whereas the orthographic–phonological relations in English and French are acquired at a slower developmental pace.

Conclusion

In this chapter, I set out to answer three related questions concerning the developmental connection between phonological awareness and reading. The first question was whether the same sequence of phonological development would be observed in children who were growing up in different linguistic environments. The answer to this question at the moment appears to be that it is. Despite some variation in the phonological input provided by different languages, the development of phonological awareness in all languages studied so far appears to proceed from an awareness of syllables to an awareness of onsets and rimes, and then to an awareness of phonemes. However, it is important to point out that little cross-linguistic research of this kind has been done, and that future research using more sensitive phonological awareness tasks may change this picture.

The second question that I set out to answer was whether awareness of the *same* phonological units would predict reading development in different linguistic environments. The answer to this question at the moment appears to be that it does not, at least in terms of whether the same phonological units predict reading development at the same developmental time points. For example, the special connection between rhyming and early reading development currently appears to be restricted to learning to read in English. No similar relationship is found for Portuguese, and although rhyme awareness does predict reading development in German, it does so at a later developmental time point.

The third question that I began with was whether the kinds of connections that children make between phonology and orthography depend on the phonology of the language being learned and the orthographic units that this phonology makes salient. The answer to this question at the moment tentatively appears to be that they do. The cross-linguistic nonsense word reading studies discussed above suggest that rimes are only functional units in the reading development of children who are learning to read less transparent orthographies, such as English and French. Children who are learning to read more transparent orthographies, such as Greek and Spanish, appear to make more fine-grained connections between graphemes and phonemes from the beginning of learning to read. However, it is important to emphasise that this tentative conclusion depends on only one line of research, which is in turn based on a set of assumptions about nonsense word reading.

Nevertheless, if this tentative conclusion were to receive support from future research studies, then it would fit nicely with the differences in the methods that are adopted for teaching reading in these different countries. As noted earlier, Austria uses a traditional 'phonics' programme for teaching reading, in which the different grapheme–phoneme correspondences are taught in a fixed order. The same kind of programme is used in Greece, and in fact the same initial reading book is used in all Greek schools. In England, an eclectic mixture of approaches is used to teach initial reading, and there is no fixed teaching sequence or single reading book. Instead, there is a national debate about whether 'whole language' methods, which avoid phonics, are more useful than a decoding approach based on teaching children grapheme–phoneme correspondences. It is difficult to avoid the conclusion that teaching initial reading is a straightforward matter in highly transparent orthographies. It is a less straightforward matter in less transparent orthographies. The growing evidence for the importance of rime units in learning to read in these less transparent orthographies may go some way towards redressing this balance (Goswami, 1996).

NOTE

I would like to thank the teachers and children of the many primary schools in Cambridge who participated in this research, and also Jean Emile Gombert, Costas Porpodas and the teachers and children of participating schools in France, Greece and Venezuela for fruitful collaborations. Support for this research was partly provided by a Medical Research Council Project Grant (G9326935N).

REFERENCES

Bowey, J. A. and Hanson, J. (1994). The development of orthographic rimes as units of word recognition. *Journal of Experimental Child Psychology*, 58, 465–88.

Bradley, L. and Bryant, P. E. (1983). Categorising sounds and learning to read: a causal connection. *Nature*, 310, 419–21.

Bruck, M. and Treiman, R. (1992). Learning to pronounce words: the limitations of analogies. *Reading Research Quarterly*, 27 (4), 374–89.

Caravolas, M. and Bruck, M. (1993). The effect of oral and written language input on children's phonological awareness: a cross-linguistic study. *Journal of Experimental Child Psychology*, 55, 1–30.

Cardoso-Martins, C. (1994). Rhyme perception: global or analytical? *Journal of Experimental Child Psychology*, 57, 26–41.

Cossu, G., Shankweiler, D., Liberman, I. Y., Tola, G. and Katz, L. (1988). Awareness of phonological segments and reading ability in Italian children. *Applied Psycholinguistics*, 9, 1–16.

Ehri, L. C. and Robbins, C. (1992). Beginners need some decoding skill to read words by analogy. *Reading Research Quarterly*, 27 (1), 12–28.

Ellis, N. C. and Large, B. (1987). The development of reading: as you seek, so shall ye find. *British Journal of Psychology*, 78, 1–28.

Gombert, J. E. (1992). *Metalinguistic Development*. Hemel Hempstead, Herts: Harvester Wheatsheaf.

Goswami, U. (1986). Children's use of analogy in learning to read: a developmental study. *Journal of Experimental Child Psychology*, 42, 73–83.

(1988). Orthographic analogies and reading development. *Quarterly Journal of Experimental Psychology*, 40A, 239–68.

(1990a). A special link between rhyming skills and the use of orthographic analogies by beginning readers. *Journal of Child Psychology and Psychiatry*, 31, 301–11.

(1990b). Phonological priming and orthographic analogies in reading. *Journal of Experimental Child Psychology*, 49, 323–40.

(1991). Learning about spelling sequences: the role of onsets and rimes in analogies in reading. *Child Development*, 62, 1110–23.

(1993). Toward an interactive analogy model of reading development: decoding vowel graphemes in beginning reading. *Journal of Experimental Child Psychology*, 56, 443–75.

(1996) (ed.). *The Oxford Reading Tree Rhyme and Analogy Programme*. Oxford, England: Oxford University Press.

Goswami, U. and Bryant, P. E. (1990). *Phonological Skills and Learning to Read*. Hillsdale, NJ: Lawrence Erlbaum.

Goswami, U., Gombert, J. E. and De Barrera, L. (1998). Children's orthographic representations and linguistic transparency: nonsense word reading in English, French and Spanish. *Applied Psycholinguistics*, 19, 19–52.

Goswami, U. and Mead, F. (1992). Onset and rime awareness and analogies in reading. *Reading Research Quarterly*, 27 (2), 152–62.

Goswami, U., Porpodas, C. and Wheelwright, S. (1997). Children's orthographic representations in English and Greek. *European Journal of Psychology of Education*, 12, 273–92.

Greaney, K. T. and Tunmer, W. E. (1996). Onset/rime sensitivity and orthographic analogies in normal and poor readers. *Applied Psycholinguistics*, 17, 15–40.

Hoien, T., Lundberg, L., Stanovich, K. E. and Bjaalid, I. K. (1995). Components of phonological awareness. *Reading and Writing*, 7, 171–88.

Holligan, C. and Johnston, R. S. (1988). The use of phonological information by good and poor readers in memory and reading tasks. *Memory and Cognition*, 16, 522–32.

Huang, H. S. and Hanley, R. J. (1995). Phonological awareness and visual skills in learning to read Chinese and English. *Cognition*, 54, 73–98.

Kessler, B. and Treiman, R. (in press). Syllable structure and phoneme distribution. *Journal of Memory and Language*.

Kirtley, C., MacLean, M., Bradley, L. and Bryant, P. (1989). Rhyme, rime and the onset of reading. *Journal of Experimental Child Psychology*, 48, 224–45.

Liberman, I. Y., Shankweiler, D., Fischer, F. W. and Carter, B. (1974). Explicit syllable and phoneme segmentation in the young child. *Journal of Experimental Child Psychology*, 18, 201–12.

Lundberg, I., Olofsson, A. and Wall, S. (1980). Reading and spelling skills in the first school years predicted from phonemic awareness skills in kindergarten. *Scandinavian Journal of Psychology*, 21, 159–73.

MacLean, M., Bradley, L. and Bryant, P. E. (1987). Rhymes, nursery rhymes and reading in early childhood. *Merrill-Palmer Quarterly*, 33, 255–82.

Mann, V. A. (1986). Phonological awareness: the role of early reading experience. *Cognition*, 24, 65–92.

Morais, J., Cary, J., Alegria, J. and Bertelson, P. (1979). Does awareness of speech as a sequence of phones arise spontaneously? *Cognition*, 7, 323–31.

Muter, V., Snowling, M. and Taylor, S. (1994). Orthographic analogies and phonological awareness: their role and significance in early reading development. *Journal of Child Psychology and Psychiatry*, 35, 293–310.

Naslund, J. C. and Schneider, W. (1991). Longitudinal effects of verbal ability, memory capacity and phonological awareness on reading performance. *European Journal of Psychology of Education*, 6 (4), 375–92.

Peereman, R. and Content, A. (1996). Orthographic and phonological neighbourhoods in naming: not all neighbours are equally influential in orthographic space. *Journal of Memory and Language*, 37, 382–410.

Porpodas, C. (1993). The relation between phonemic awareness and reading and spelling of Greek words in the first school years. In M. Carretero, M. Pope, R. J. Simons and J. I. Pozo (eds.), *Learning and Instruction*, vol. III, (pp. 203–17). Oxford: Pergamon Press.

Schneider, W. and Naslund, J. C. (in press). The impact of early phonological processing skills on reading and spelling in school: evidence from the Munich Longitudinal Study. To appear in F. E. Weinert and W. Schneider (eds.), *Individual Development from 3 to 12: Findings from the Munich Longitudinal Study*. Cambridge: Cambridge University Press.

Stanovich, K. E., Cunningham, A. E. and Cramer, B. R. (1984). Assessing phonological awareness in kindergarten: issues of task comparability. *Journal of Experimental Child Psychology*, 38, 175–90.

Treiman, R. and Zukowski, A. (1991). Levels of phonological awareness. In S. Brady and D. Shankweiler (eds.), *Phonological Processes in Literacy*. Hillsdale, NJ: Erlbaum.

Treiman, R., Goswami, U. and Bruck, M. (1990). Not all nonwords are alike: implications for reading development and theory. *Memory and Cognition*, 18, 559–67.

Treiman, R., Mullennix, J., Bijeljac-Babic, R. and Richmond-Welty, E. D. (1995). The special role of rimes in the description, use and acquisition of English orthography. *Journal of Experimental Psychology*, *General*, 124, 107–36.

Wimmer, H., Landerl, K., Linortner, R. and Hummer, P. (1991). The relationship of phonemic awareness to reading acquisition: more consequence than precondition but still important. *Cognition*, 40, 219–49.

Wimmer, H., Landerl, K. and Schneider, W. (1994). The role of rhyme awareness in learning to read a regular orthography. *British Journal of Developmental Psychology*, 12, 469–84.

Wise, B. W., Olson, D. K. and Treiman, R. (1990). Subsyllabic units as aids in beginning readers' word learning: onset-rime versus post-vowel segmentation. *Journal of Experimental Child Psychology*, 49, 1–19.

9   Learning to read in Scandinavia

Ingvar Lundberg

Introduction

Is reading acquisition an easier task for an Italian child than for an English child? A reasonable answer seems to be, yes it is. Italian is by all standards a far more regular language in terms of the correspondence between phonemes and graphemes (see the chapter by Cossu in this volume). However, the issue of the importance of linguistic factors in early reading acquisition may be more complicated than one is inclined to believe.

The purpose of the present chapter is, with reference to a comparison of Scandinavian countries, to raise some of the problems involved and demonstrate how difficult it may be to isolate the impact of orthographic regularity on reading acquisition.

Although orthographic-linguistic factors might have some importance in the process of reading acquisition, it is extremely difficult in practice to demonstrate their contribution in explaining the variation in reading achievement. One basic problem is related to the fact that linguistic variation in most cases is confounded with cultural-historical, socio-economic and educational factors, and these factors seem, as will be demonstrated, to contain as much explanatory power as the linguistic ones. Age of school start, patterns of informal literacy socialisation, social value systems, literacy culture, exposure to print, etc. are factors to be controlled if one wants to capture the pure impact of orthography. This is certainly not an easy task.

The educational scene in Scandinavia

The Scandinavian countries, Denmark, Norway, Sweden and Finland,[1] are often perceived as a homogeneous group of nations unified not only by their geographical neighbourhood on the northern periphery of Europe but also by similar languages, common historical and cultural traditions, similar political patterns, high priorities for social welfare systems and high egalitarian ambitions.

157

A view of the educational scene in Scandinavia is, for the purpose of this chapter, complicated by the fact that the conditions for reading instruction are now in a dramatic transitional stage in most Scandinavian countries. The transitions concern the change of age for school entrance, decentralisation of school systems, changes in the national syllabus, the influx of immigrants, and the increasing impact of alternative arenas for literacy socialisation outside school.

Up till now, compulsory education has started in the August of the year of the child's seventh birthday and has lasted for a period of nine years. However, important steps have been taken towards an earlier school start in most countries. Most schools are public, and teaching is regulated by a national syllabus common to all schools in the country. However, the level of detail varies considerably from country to country. As far as reading is concerned, the Swedish master plan, for example, contains only a few general goals and no prescriptions of method. It is the responsibility of local schools, and in the end individual teachers, to decide how these general goals are to be attained. In all countries there is the same clear tendency towards decentralisation of authority to local school boards. Teachers are trained in state colleges with uniform admission policies and uniform standards of quality.

The homogeneity of the school system is further promoted by the lack of social stratification in most Scandinavian municipalities. With the exception of a few metropolitan districts, residential areas are mixed and contain people from all kinds of social background. Since students are generally recruited from the local neighbourhood, the student population is fairly similar from school to school. Teaching standards and economic resources are also similar across schools. Thus, the intraclass correlations (reflecting small between-school variation in relation to within-school variation) in the Scandinavian countries are lower than in most other parts of the world (Elley, 1994). However, this situation may change in the near future. The influx of immigrants and refugees has created a new situation in many places. In some suburban areas of big cities one can find schools where a majority of students speak a language at home which is different from the instructional language. The multi-ethnic and multi-cultural character of these societies is a fairly new phenomenon in most Scandinavian countries.

Methods of first reading instruction

The relatively shallow orthographies of the Scandinavian countries have led to the inclusion of phonics elements at the beginning of reading instruction. In all countries attempts are made to keep a balance between analytic and synthetic methods. Listening, speaking, reading and writing are integrated from the start, in contrast to many other countries where writing is typically introduced later in the programme. In Scandinavia, writing is supposed to support the acquisition of reading and facilitate the task of breaking the alphabetic code. Phonemic segmentation and sound blending is emphasised early by a majority of teachers. A whole-language approach has inspired many teachers but they still insist on giving explicit instruction in the alphabetic principle.

Lundberg (1993) described the teaching of reading in Scandinavia in grade 3 based on responses from several hundred teachers. Most of the differences observed could be understood as the results of different achievement levels. The practices reported by Finnish teachers were probably well adapted to the high performance level of Finnish students. In Denmark, teachers normally follow their class over many school years, often till the end of compulsory schooling, whereas teachers from the other Scandinavian countries tend to stay with their class only during the first three years in school. Thus, Danish teachers are on the average less experienced as instructors during the first critical stage of reading acquisition.

In addition to the general background or contextual conditions for reading acquisition a few words about the linguistic and orthographic characteristics of the Scandinavian languages are also approporiate before we make a closer comparison of reading achievement.

The Scandinavian orthographies

Danish, Swedish and Norwegian are all North Germanic languages with many similarities in vocabulary and syntax. Finnish, however, belongs to a totally different language family with a different vocabulary and with much of the syntax expressed in a rich inflectional system, making Finnish words on average longer than in the other languages and thereby, probably, placing strain on the beginning reader. Finnish is normally not at all comprehensible to other Scandinavians.

Orthographically, the languages can be ordered along a scale of regularity (shallowness), with Finnish as the most regular system with a close one-to-one correspondence between graphemes and phonemes. On a regularity scale Finnish seems to come close to the Italian language. Swedish and Norwegian are closer to German or Dutch, whereas Danish might be said to have a somewhat deeper orthography. At least it seems to Swedes and Norwegians that Danes tend to underarticulate when they are speaking, making oral Danish a bit harder to understand for Swedes and Norwegians. Underarticulation, poorly specified vowels, assimilations, etc. in spoken Danish give the impression that the well-specified Danish orthography, because of its distance from spoken Danish, involves more difficulty for the beginner than the orthographies of the other Scandinavian languages. However, there are dialectical variations within all the countries which create wide variations in the distance between the spoken and written forms of the language.

The possible impact of dialect on reading and spelling acquisition has attracted the interest of some Scandinavian researchers (Bull, 1985; Österberg, 1961; Wiggen, 1992). However, the confounding of factors in these studies is quite obvious. Children with non-standard dialects and with very limited knowledge of the standard national language are mostly also at a socio-economic disadvantage which in itself may be a serious obstacle to reading acquisition. Undoubtedly, however, there are regions in Scandinavia, particularly in Norway and Sweden, where the discrepancy between the local oral language and the national language norm is considerable, implying an extra obstacle for the beginning reader.

Although the Scandinavian languages basically have a rather shallow orthography, there are clear problems for a beginning reader or speller. Take, for example, the /ʃ/ sound in Swedish which can be spelled in the following ways: *stj, sj, skj, sk, sch, ch, sh, g, si* or *ti*. The /j/ sound is spelled as *j, g, gj, hj, lj* or *dj*. Vowels such as /o/ are quite randomly spelled *o* or *å*, and /ɛ/ is spelled *e* or *ä*. The morpho-phonemic character of the orthography can be illustrated by *hög* (high) and *högt* (highly) where *gt* is pronounced *kt* but spelled according to the morphemic relationship, i.e. the stem is preserved (*hög*) despite the clear change in pronunciation /hö̲k̲t/ in the inflection. Similar examples can be found in Danish and Norwegian.

Especially difficult hurdles for beginning spellers in all three languages are the principles for doubling consonants. The rules are very complicated and include many exceptions. The normal case is that consonants are doubled to indicate a preceding short vowel. In unstressed syllables, however, short vowels do not need double consonants. A number of other exceptions are governed by morphological rules. In Finnish there are also rules for doubling vowels to mark the value of consonants.

Like many other German languages, the three Scandinavian languages, but not Finnish, are also characterised by heavy clusters of consonants in initial as well as in final positions (e.g. in Swedish *struts, skälmskt*) or in middle positions in compound words such as *falsktskrikande*. Phonotactic reductions and assimilations are common in normal oral language (e.g. Lundberg is often pronounced Lu*m*ber*j*) which in Scandinavia, as in most other countries, contributes to widening the gap between spoken and written language and creates difficulties in the beginning stages of literacy development.

Scandinavian research on the relationship between phonological processes and learning to read

As in many fields of inquiry, reading research has been heavily dominated by the USA, Canada, Australia and Great Britain. The generality of insights gained from this impressive work might, however, be hampered by concentration on a single language, a specific orthography, specific school traditions and specific cultural patterns. Fortunately, a more balanced situation is now developing which is also reflected in the present volume. Over the last couple of years, the activity level in reading research has increased remarkably in some European countries, most notably in the Netherlands, Belgium, Germany, Austria, Italy, Spain, Greece and the Scandinavian countries. Israel has also made important contributions to the field. In Asia, countries like Japan, China and Singapore show a rapid growth in reading research. In the remaining part of this chapter some aspects of Scandinavian research will be presented and, in particular, research related to the first steps in literacy where the relationship between phonological awareness and reading is highlighted.

Scandinavian reading research is surprisingly well coordinated in functional networks with nodes in Copenhagen, Stavanger, Umeå (Göteborg) and Turku (Jyväskylä). In Norway, Torleiv Höien is the founder of a well-recognised Centre for Reading Research in Stavanger. More recently Carsten Elbro has established a very active Centre for Research on Reading Disability in Copenhagen. The Swedish scene used to be dominated by the Umeå group under my own leadership, but after my move to Göteborg a new group is under development there. Turku has been the Finnish centre with Pekka Niemi as the most prominent coordinator. Recently, Jyväskylä has become increasingly important especially with Heikki Lyytinen's strong group on the neuro-psychology of reading disability.

A distinct advantage in doing research on the relationship between phonological awareness and reading in Scandinavia is that one can find perfectly healthy and cognitively well-developed children who, by the age of seven, know only a few letters and cannot read a single word (except for a few logographs). The main reason for this state of affairs is the simple fact that they have not yet enjoyed the benefit of explicit reading instruction. This makes it possible to examine the critical role of phonological awareness independently of reading skill and reading instruction. It is also possible to clarify the role of general cognitive development, i.e. decentration ability, in the development of phonological awareness.

It would appear that the cognitive demands of becoming phonemically aware might, in fact, be rather high. It seems to require a basic ability to shift attention, decentrate, from content to linguistic form. According to Piaget (1952) many seven-year-olds should have reached a stage of cognitive development where the ability to decentrate is present. By studying older, non-literate children the impact of general cognitive development could thus be compared with the effect of having acquired a more restricted phonological module that has been refined by extensive contact with print.

In the research to be briefly reviewed here, utilising this advantage we have in Scandinavia, we have attempted to answer a number of questions discussed in the current literature on the relationship between phonological awareness and reading acquisition.

A commonly held view is that reading instruction is necessary for the development of phonemic awareness. Lundberg (1991b) studied more than 200 non-reading pre-schoolers aged six to seven years and found that not more than about ten children were able to deal with language segments at the phoneme level. Although these cases are exceptional, they demonstrate that it is possible, at least in principle, to develop phonemic awareness outside the context of formal reading instruction in school. The real stimulating force, however, seems to be involvement in the acquisition of reading and spelling.

It has been demonstrated that phonemic awareness can be developed among Scandinavian pre-schoolers without the use of letter or other elements of early reading instruction. Lundberg, Frost and Petersen (1988) designed a Danish programme which required daily games and exercises in group settings over a full pre-school year. The programme included listening games, rhymes and ditties, playing with sentences and words, discovering the initial sounds of words and finally carrying out the full segmentation of words into phonemes.

The effects of this programme were very specific. There were modest or even no effects on general cognitive functions, on language comprehension, vocabulary and rhyming and syllable segmentation, but quite dramatic effects on phonemic skills. Thus, it was concluded that phonemic awareness could be developed among pre-schoolers by training, without introducing letters or written text. A more crucial element seems to be the *explicit* guidance of children when they are trying to access, attend to and extract the elusive, abstract, and implicit segments of language.

Earlier, we had demonstrated the remarkable predictive power of phonological awareness in pre-school for later reading achievement in school (Lundberg, Olofsson and Wall, 1980). What develops later in time (reading) can hardly be the cause of something preceding it. Thus, the longitudinal research has brought us a step closer to an understanding of the causal relationship. The crucial question now is whether explicit training in pre-school also facilitates later reading and spelling acquisition in school. The pre-school children studied by Lundberg *et al.* (1988) were followed up through four school years, and reading and spelling achievement was assessed on several occasions. The trained group outperformed the control group on each of twelve points of measurement, indicating the beneficial effect of the pre-school programme.

Lundberg (1995) presented data from children in pre-school with a high risk of developing reading disability as revealed in a pre-test on phonological awareness and general language development. Risk children who were involved in the training programme had fairly normal reading and spelling development, whereas the control children showed the expected poor literacy development. Thus, it seems to be possible to prevent the development of reading and spelling disabilities in school by a carefully designed pre-school programme which brings the children to a level of phonological awareness that is sufficiently high to meet the demands involved in the alphabetic system. The risk children who did not enjoy the benefit of such training seemed to face serious obstacles on their way to literacy.

Several other Scandinavian studies have also demonstrated the remedial and facilitating power of phonological awareness training in pre-school or school as part of regular teaching or as an important element in special education (Elbro, 1996; Lie, 1991; Tornéus, 1984). The training programme used by Lundberg *et al.* (1988) has become popular and has been incorporated into the pre-school curriculum throughout Scandinavia.

The studies of phonological awareness have also focused on more theoretical issues such as, for example, the dimensionality of phonological awareness or the neurological substrate.

Lundberg (1978) and later Stanovich (1992) have argued that phonological awareness might be viewed as a continuum or hierarchy ranging from 'shallow' to 'deep' sensitivity, where the deeper levels require more explicit analysis of smaller sized phonological units. The task of deciding which words rhyme, for example, seems to require a small amount of conscious awareness of phonemic segments. The attention is more directed to global similarity between words. One should then not be surprised to find rhyming ability among non-reading children. Syllables are also accessible units of the speech signal, more able to be isolated, more salient and less abstract than the phoneme units. To attend to and become aware of syllables, the child does not have to ignore the natural unity of the articulatory act, as is the case with attending to phonemes.

A study by Höien, Lundberg, Bjaalid and Stanovich (1995) supported the view that there are different components of phonological awareness corresponding to the different levels of language analysis required by the task. More than 1,500 children in pre-school and grade 1 in Stavanger were tested with a battery of tasks including rhyme recognition, syllable counting, initial phoneme identification, phoneme deletion, phoneme synthesis and phoneme counting. Three basic factors were extracted in a principal component analysis: a phoneme factor, a syllable factor and a rhyme factor. It was demonstrated that the three components of phonological awareness were separate predictors of early word-reading ability, with the syllable factor as the weakest predictor. Not unexpectedly, the phoneme factor proved to be the most powerful predictor of early reading acquisition. Among the various phonemic tasks, the phoneme identification tasks explained the highest proportion of unique variance.

The phonological problems associated with dyslexia have also been examined in several Scandinavian studies (for reviews, see Borström and Elbro, 1997; Lundberg, 1995; Lundberg and Höien, 1991). A step in the direction of finding a neurological correlate to the phonological problems was taken by Larsen, Höien, Lundberg and Ödegaard (1990) in a study of fifteen-year-old dyslexics in Stavanger. Brain scans (MRI) revealed that the planum temporale tended to be of equal size in the two hemispheres more often among dyslexics than among normal controls. More specifically, however, all dyslexics with severe phonological problems had symmetry of the plana temporale. We still do not know, however, how this deviation from the normal pattern in the language cortex affects the development of phonological coding and other processes necessary for fluent reading. Functional studies will certainly reveal more about the neuro-biological basis of dyslexia in the near future.

So far, the focus has been on basic linguistic and cognitive prerequisites for learning to read. In the next section of the chapter, factors related to instruction and cultural-historical conditions will be treated as possible determinants of reading achievement.

The IEA study of reading literacy

The critical importance of reading literacy in post-industrial societies was the primary motivating force behind the large IEA (International Association for the Evaluation of Educational Achievement) study of reading achievement among nine-year-olds and fourteen-year-olds in thirty different countries (Elley, 1994). The study included 210,000 students and some 11,000 teachers. The main data collection took place in 1991. The aim was not only to describe the levels of achievement in different countries. More important was to explain and understand the factors underlying the variation in reading achievement at various levels of aggregation (individuals, classrooms, communities, countries, groups of countries). Thus, reading achievement was related to factors in the home – instructional conditions, school resources, economy, welfare and language.

In terms of achievement (averaged over three scales: narratives, expository texts and documents), Finland had the highest score of all countries in both age groups. Sweden also had a prominent position, ranking third in both age groups. The position of Norway was somewhere in the middle, whereas Denmark had a surprisingly low rank for the younger age group (lowest among the industrialised countries). The rank order among the Scandinavian countries seems to correspond to their relative position on the orthographic regularity scale referred to above, thus apparently confirming the hypothesis of the critical importance of orthographic structure for early reading acquisition. However, the achievement differences seem far too large in relation to the orthographic differences, making the simplistic orthographic interpretation of the country differences in Scandinavia rather implausible.

In fact, it seems as if linguistic differences do not contribute much to explaining the variation in reading achievement of other countries taking part in the IEA study. For example, the difference in achievement between Spain and Venezuela is quite remarkable given the identity of language. Here, of course, the difference in socio-economic development is the most likely explanation of the difference in reading levels. Countries with deep orthographies like France and New Zealand clearly outperform countries with more shallow orthographies, like Italy, Spain or Greece. And, as we saw, despite great similarities in language and socio-economic conditions Sweden, Norway and Denmark occupy very different ranks in reading achievement. Other factors must obviously be considered.

The top positions for Finland and Sweden are remarkable considering the fact that formal reading instruction does not start until the age of seven in these countries. Despite the fact that the Swedish and Finnish children had attended school for little more than two years at the time of testing, they clearly outperformed students from New Zealand, the Netherlands and other countries with an earlier school start and with reading instruction which had lasted for almost double the time.

Another interesting finding was the case of Singapore. Here, the students were tested in English which is also the instructional language from the start. However, more than 75 per cent of the students in the schools of Singapore speak another language at home (Chinese, Malay, Hindi, Tamil), and these languages are mostly very different from English in grammar as well as in vocabulary. Yet the students do learn how to read in English and do it so well that, by the age of nine, they outperform students in other parts of the world where English is the mother tongue of most students (e.g. Ireland).

The Singapore example demonstrates that it is fully possible to learn how to read in a language which is different from your home language. This has also been shown by Wagner, Spratt and Ezzaki (1989) who studied Berber-speaking children in Morocco with Arabic as their reading language. In fact, many children in multi-lingual societies around the world have to meet an instructional language and a written language which is different from their home language.

Does teaching make much difference?

It would be tempting to attribute the high ranks of Finland and Sweden in the international reading competition to the excellent instructional conditions in these countries. Educationalists as well as lay people tend to think that the most critical determinant of student achievement must be the instruction given. However, at least as far as reading is concerned, there is no real empirical support for this idea. In comprehensive multivariate analyses we have tried to capture the possible explanatory power of instructional factors in the variance in reading achievement between school classes within different countries and between countries (Lundberg and Linnakylä, 1992; Lundberg, 1994; Munck and Lundberg, 1994; Lundberg and Rosén, 1997). The somewhat disheartening conclusion of these attempts has been that teaching does not explain much of the variance in student achievement. Far more powerful explanations of student variance are provided by home factors (cultural capital, reading habits) and community resources.

Of course, teaching does make a difference in the sense that a majority of students must be exposed to some systematic instruction to acquire literacy. However, a relatively low threshold value seems to be sufficient for most students. And in most schools this threshold is reached. Then, there are other factors which are far more decisive in creating variation in reading achievement. In most countries, the variation between classrooms is small in relation to the variation that exists between students within classes. In the Nordic countries and some others, variation between classrooms accounts for less than 10 per cent of the total variations. This means that there is almost no scope for teaching factors to operate in the explanation of student variation. The small variation that in fact exists between classes also involves variation in socio-economic levels of homes and communities due to social stratification of schools. The proportion of variance left to be explained by teaching is in fact too small to be of any significance.

A conclusion from this analysis might be that reading is a skill which to a large degree is developed in arenas outside school. Long before school entrance some children may have had thousands of hours of fruitful meetings with written language through story-book reading, messages on the fridge door, shopping lists, postcards from relatives, computer games, playful writing and plastic letters. These children have certainly also experienced and understood the joy of reading and its potential value in life.

Other children may have had a very limited exposure to print when they enter school and very few opportunities to interact with text under the supervision of encouraging and interested adults. In fact, such initial differences between children even tend to increase over the years in a snowballing process known as the Matthew effect in educational development (Stanovich, 1986). It is certainly a hard task to make up for such initial differences. During the first school years teachers may have only a few hundred hours available to compensate for the big differences between students originating from informal literacy socialisation in home settings and from differences in basic abilities related to reading acquisition.

Once the students have broken the alphabetic code they have a powerful instrument available for self-instruction (e.g. Share, 1995). With their recently acquired insight into how the writing system functions they can, on their own, begin to attack new words encountered in the environment, on signs, headlines or packages. With support and encouragement from eager adults and older peers or siblings they soon learn to decode words automatically and can read coherent texts with fluency and enjoyment. The IEA study revealed huge differences between poor and good readers in terms of reading habits outside school. The teacher's role in this process seems to be far less than one would expect.

If teaching does not explain much of the variation in reading achievement, and if linguistic factors seem to have a limited impact on the first steps to literacy, we have to search for other sources of explanation. We will now consider how cultural and historical factors may contribute to national differences.

A cultural–historical perspective on reading

Centuries before a compulsory school system was established in Sweden in 1842 and long before the industrial revolution, the vast majority of the population was literate in the sense that they could pass annual church examinations where oral reading as well as comprehension of religious concepts were assessed by the parish vicar. As early as 1684, in the context of the Counter-Reformation, a royal decree announced that all the inhabitants of Sweden (including Finland which was part of the Swedish kingdom until 1809) were expected to be able to read and see what was written in holy scriptures by themselves (Johansson, 1987; Lundberg, 1991a). It was the responsibility of the head of the household to guarantee that all members of the household, including servants were taught how to read. Manuals for efficient home teaching were soon circulated.

The literacy campaign was on the whole very successful. Social pressure from the community was extremely high. First, failure in the public examination must certainly have been a disgrace. Second, failure also had formal social consequences. Non-readers were not permitted to marry or to witness in court. Thus, illiteracy was punished by loss of civil rights.

Apparently, quite informal tutoring was sufficient to reach a level of literacy where the alphabetic code was broken. As early as the seventeenth century it was possible to massproduce ABC books and the small catechism and distribute them to practically all households. A record of the number of books possessed by the households in Rättvik, a parish of Dalecarlia in mid Sweden, indicated an average of two or three books per family around 1720 (Johansson, 1990). In the IEA study, the number of books at home was the single most powerful predictor of reading achievement in most countries.

The general reading ability in Sweden and Finland during pre-industrial times, when the country was a typical poor agrarian society, shows that there is no simple and necessary relationship between literacy and economic development. In the far more industrialised country of England during the same period the level of literacy was much lower. A look at the world today would reveal quite a high correlation between literacy and economic development. But still, the relationship might be complex and not necessarily causal in a simple sense.

The example of Sweden/Finland also shows that a special value system with deep historical and cultural roots might have developed in a society. Of course, nature, climate and demographic conditions also play a significant role. As a contrast, we can take Mediterranean or many African societies where cultures have a more oral orientation. Here, people come together in streets, in cafés and market places, at public wells, and so forth, in densely populated areas with a mild climate. In the sparsely populated areas of Finland and Sweden with more electric light than sun and where the distance between people outside the circle of close relatives is great, written texts have been a highly valued form of human communication.

The societal and social demands on adult literacy seem to be higher in Finland and Sweden than in some other countries. In relation to the IEA study, similar panels of judges in responsible societal positions, in nine countries (Finland, Greece, Hong Kong, the Netherlands, New Zealand, Slovenia, Sweden, Switzerland, and Venezuela) estimated the requirement of reading competence for various segments of the adult population. The highest demands were expressed by the Finnish and Swedish panels.

In a recent survey of adult literacy (OECD, 1995) which included eight countries (Canada, Germany, Ireland, the Netherlands, Poland, Sweden, Switzerland and the USA), Sweden had the highest average scores in all domains of literacy tested. Certainly, linguistic factors are not sufficient to explain these international differences in literacy. Historical, cultural and socio-economic factors might be better candidates.

Cultural differences related to literacy were manifested by several indicators in the IEA study. Among nine-year-olds, Swedish children reported the largest number of books at home. The access to daily newspapers is another relevant factor. Here, Finland takes the lead with Sweden as the second country. Finnish and Swedish children have the most advanced reading habits outside school among the nine-year-olds, both in amount and frequency of reading, borrowing books from libraries, buying books and receiving books as gifts.

The analysis of historical and cultural factors as sources for explaining national differences in achievement has so far not included Denmark and Norway. It seems, however, that traditions have been quite different in these countries. Norway belonged to the Danish sphere and was part of the Danish kingdom until the beginning of the nineteen century. The successful church campaign for developing general literacy in Sweden (and Finland) was, for many reasons, not at all the same success story in Denmark (and Norway).

Concluding comments

Our focus on phonemic awareness as a critical factor in reading acquisition has been quite natural considering the type of orthography represented by the Scandinavian languages. With a long tradition in reading, instruction letters and speech sounds have been the basic building blocks or stepping stones for the self-teaching process to start.

Intuitively, it seems quite obvious that some orthographies make the first steps into literacy an easier task than others. The code breaking must clearly be simpler when there is a one-to-one correspondence between graphemes and phonemes. However, there must always be a considerable gap between spoken and written language even in the most shallow orthographies (Lundberg, 1996). Underarticulation, assimilations, reductions and dialectical variation contribute towards widening the gap in all languages.

Although orthographies may vary in difficulty it is certainly a challenging task to demonstrate the impact on reading acquisition of this variation. Careful longitudinal case studies of reading and spelling acquisition in different orthographies, sophisticated error analyses of misspellings and misreadings based on detailed linguistic knowledge, and assessments of differential effects of experimentally manipulated orthographic structures on accuracy and speed of word recognition may contribute towards revealing the impact of orthography. Several chapters in this book have given more specific examples of such methods. The microanalysis must, however, be seen in the light of far more powerful determinants of variation in achievement. The present chapter has demonstrated how international comparisons can help to reveal the possible impact of teaching, school conditions and cultural and historical traditions. After all, reading is primarily a cultural practice. Thus, a cross-linguistic perspective inevitably also involves a cross-cultural perspective.

NOTE

1 Iceland is also one of the Nordic countries but is not included in the present analysis.

REFERENCES

Borström, I. and Elbro, C. (1997). Prevention of dyslexia in kindergarten: effects of phoneme awareness training with children of dyslexic parents. In C. Hulme and M. Snowling (eds.), *Dyslexia. Biology, Cognition, and Intervention* (pp. 235–53). London: Whurr.

Bull, T. (1985). *Lesing og barns talemål.* Oslo: Novus.

Elbro, C. (1996). Early linguistic abilities and reading development: a review and a hypothesis. *Reading and Writing. An Interdisciplinary Journal*, 8, 453–85.

Elley, W. B. (ed.) (1994). *The IEA Study of Reading Literacy: Achievement and Instruction in Thirty-two School Systems.* Oxford: Pergamon.

Höien, T., Lundberg, I., Bjaalid, I. K. and Stanovich, K. E. (1995). Components of phonological awareness. *Reading and Writing. An Interdisciplinary Journal,* 7, 1–18.

Johansson, E. (1987). Literacy campaigns in Sweden. In R. J. Arnove and H. Graff (eds.), *National Literacy Campaigns. Historical and Comparative Perspectives* (pp. 65–98). New York: Plenum Press.

(1990). Female literacy in Sweden around 1700 – some examples. Unpublished manuscript, University of Umeå, Sweden.

Larsen, J. P., Höien, T., Lundberg, I. and Ödegaard, H. (1990). MRI evaluation of the size and symmetry of the planum temporale in adolescents with developmental dyslexia. *Brain and Language,* 39, 289–301.

Lie, A. (1991). Effects of a training program for stimulating skills in word analysis in first-grade children. *Reading Research Quarterly,* 26, 234–50.

Lundberg, I. (1978). Linguistic awareness as related to reading. In A. Sinclair, R. J. Jarvella and W. J. M. Levelt (eds.), *The Child's Conception of Language.* New York: Springer-Verlag.

(1991a). Reading as an individual and social skill. In I. Lundberg and T. Hoien (eds.), *Literacy in a World of Change.* Stavanger: Centre for Reading Research/UNESCO.

(1991b). Phonemic awareness can be developed without reading instruction. In S. A. Brady and D. P. Shankweiler (eds.), *Phonological Processes in Literacy. A Tribute to Isabelle Y. Liberman* (pp. 47–53). Hillsdale, NJ: Erlbaum.

(1993). The teaching of reading in the Nordic countries. *Scandinavian Journal of Educational Research,* 37, 43–62.

(1994). The teaching of reading. In W. B. Elley (ed.), *The IEA Study of Reading Literacy: Achievement and Instruction in Thirty-two School Systems.* Oxford: Pergamon.

(1995). Reading difficulties can be predicted and prevented: a Scandinavian perspective on phonological awareness and reading. In C. Hulme and M. Snowling (eds.), *Reading Development and Dyslexia* (pp. 180–99). London: Whurr.

(1996). *Sprog og laesning. Laeseprocesser i undervisningen.* Copenhagen: Munksgaard/Alinea.

Lundberg, I., Frost, J. and Petersen, O.-P. (1988). Effects of an extensive program for stimulating phonological awareness in preschool children. *Reading Research Quarterly,* 33, 263–84.

Lundberg, I. and Höien, T. (1991). Initial enabling knowledge and skills in reading acquisition: print awareness and phonological segmentation. In D. J. Sawyer and B. J. Fox (eds.), *Phonological Awareness in Reading: The Evolution of Current Perspectives* (pp. 73–95). New York: Springer-Verlag.

Lundberg, I. and Linnakylä, P. (1992). *Teaching Reading Around the World.* Haag: IEA.

Lundberg, I., Olofsson, Å. and Wall, S. (1980). Reading and spelling skills in the first school years predicted from phonemic awareness skills in kindergarten. *Scandinavian Journal of Psychology,* 21, 159–73.

Lundberg, I. and Rosén, M. (1997). Two-level structural modeling of reading achievement as a basis for evaluating teaching effects. Submitted for publication.

Munck, I. and Lundberg, I. (1994). Multivariate analyses of Population A data. In W. B. Elley (ed.), *The IEA Study of Reading Literacy: Achievement and Instruction in Thirty-two School Systems*. Oxford: Pergamon.

OECD (1995). *Literacy, Economy and Society*. Paris: OECD.

Österberg, T. (1961). *Bilingualism and the First School Language*. Uppsala: Almqvist and Wiksell.

Piaget, J. (1952). *The Origins of Intelligence in Children*. New York: Norton.

Share, D. I. (1995). Phonological recording and self-teaching. The sine qua non of reading acquisition. *Cognition*, 55, 151–218.

Stanovich, K. E. (1986). Matthew effects in reading: some consequences of individual differences in the acquisition of literacy. *Reading Research Quarterly*, 21, 360–407.

   (1992). Speculations on the causes and consequences of individual differences in early reading acquisition. In P. B. Gough, L. C. Ehri and R. Treiman (eds.), *Reading Acquisition* (pp. 307–42). Hillsdale, NJ: Erlbaum.

Tornéus, M. (1984). Phonological awareness and reading: a chicken and egg problem? *Journal of Educational Psychology*, 76, 1346–58.

Wagner, D. A., Spratt, J. E. and Ezzaki, A. (1989). Does learning to read in a second language always put the child at a disadvantage? Some counter-evidence from Morocco. *Applied Psycholinguistics*, 10, 31–8.

Wiggen, G. (1992). *Rettskrivingsstudier 2. Kvalitativ og kvantitativ analyse av rettskrivingsavvik hos östnorske barneskoleelever*, vols. 1–2. Oslo: Novus Forlag.

10   Learning to read Chinese

J. Richard Hanley, Ovid Tzeng and H.-S. Huang

Introduction

The Chinese people use a writing system that has been in operation for several thousand years. It differs in many important respects from the alphabetic writing systems that are commonplace in the West (Hung and Tzeng, 1981). Whereas an alphabetic system uses a small number of abstract elements (letters) to represent the phonemic structure of the language in writing, Chinese words are represented by a large number of different visual symbols, known as characters. It is estimated that children should have learnt to recognise at least 4,000 different characters by the time they reach twelve years old.

The reason why there are so many of them is that characters in Chinese represent *morphemes* rather than phonemes, where a morpheme is defined as the smallest unit of meaning in a language. Hence it is often claimed that Chinese characters do not directly represent the spoken form of the language. Because, however, morphemes are represented in Chinese by single syllables, there is a sense in which Chinese characters represent units of spoken language (syllables) as well as morphemes. Furthermore, many Chinese characters contain a phonetic element which provides a clue as to how the character should be pronounced. Because these characters can be broken down into smaller components, it is probably not accurate to refer to Chinese as a logographic writing system (see Tzeng, Zhong, Hung and Lee, 1995).

In the next two sections, some of the factors which led to the development of this unique orthographic system will be discussed, and some reasons why this ancient system remains in use today will be outlined. We will then go on to discuss the ways in which children are taught to read Chinese, and consider whether phonological awareness plays any role in the acquisition of Chinese literacy. We will then investigate whether children can make use of the phonetic components that Chinese characters contain when learning to read new words, and conclude by examining the nature of the reading impairment observed in Chinese children who experience difficulties in learning to read.

The Chinese writing system and how it is taught

Spoken Chinese

The language that is spoken in different parts of China varies considerably. For example, Mandarin, the language used in the north of mainland China and in the capital, Beijing, has a number of different regional dialects. There are at least six further languages (Min, Wu, Xiang, Hakka, Gan and Cantonese) that are spoken in the south of China, and these languages are also associated with different regional dialects. Like Mandarin, all of these languages have their origins in Ancient Chinese, but are not mutually comprehensible, having evolved their own vocabularies over the centuries.

One important difference between Chinese and English is that, almost invariably, each morpheme in Chinese is represented by a single syllable (see Chen, 1996, for discussion). In English, many morphemes are represented by words containing more than one syllable (e.g. *tennis, carpet*), but this is not the case in Chinese. As in English, many Chinese words are multi-syllabic (80 per cent according to Li, 1977) but, unlike English, a Chinese word that contains two syllables will always contain two morphemes. This means that in Chinese, a written symbol representing a morpheme inevitably represents a syllable also.

The syllabic structure of Chinese words differs markedly from that found in Indo-European languages such as English in at least two important respects. First, there are no consonant blends in any of the Chinese languages either before or after the vowel. Second, Chinese syllables typically have a consonant–vowel (CV) structure. Although there are some CVC syllables, only two nasal consonants /n/ and /ŋ/ ever follow the vowel in Mandarin. In Cantonese, the language spoken in Hong Kong, /p/, /t/, and /k/ are additional possible endings. It therefore follows, of course, that the number of syllables is much smaller in Chinese than in English. This means that it is in principle much easier to represent spoken Chinese than English in the form of a syllabic writing system; many thousands of different symbols would be necessary if English words were written syllabically.

One consequence of this is that the number of morphemes that can be given a unique representation in spoken Chinese is relatively small. This means that many morphemes share the same syllable. In other words there is a relatively large number of homonyms in Chinese. This number is reduced somewhat by the existence of specific pitch patterns in which words are spoken in Chinese, known as *tones*. There are four different tones in Mandarin (high-level, high-rising, falling-rising, high-falling) and nine different tones in Cantonese. Many syllables represent different morphemes when spoken in different tones. Therefore, the existence of tones greatly increases the number of morphemes that can be represented unambiguously in Chinese. Tones do not help distinguish morphemes in *written* Chinese, however, because there are no symbols in the Chinese writing system that convey information about tone.

Written Chinese

Approximately 5,000 years ago, the first written symbols started to appear in China in the form of ideographs written on tortoise shells. Within 1,500 years of their original appearance, many of these ideographs were accompanied by a phonetic symbol that specified in an ingenious fashion the spoken form of the word that the character represented. In order for this to work, it was, of course, necessary for the reader to be familiar with the pronunciation of the phonetic symbol. Because there are so many homonyms in Chinese, it was possible to use as the phonetic symbol the character for a different word that was pronounced the same way as the ideograph in question. So long as the phonetic symbol was a character that represented a relatively common morpheme, it became possible to indicate the pronunciation of all characters in this way (see Hung and Tzeng, 1981 for further discussion).

The consequence of this is that there is a large number of homophones in Chinese, where one part of the character conveys information about pronunciation (the phonetic), and another part of the character conveys information about the meaning (the radical). Over time, the characters started to diversify in different parts of China; new characters began appearing and some characters changed their pronunciation. Approximately 2,000 years ago, this process of diversification was halted when it was decided to standardise the characters, and the Chinese writing system has remained essentially unchanged ever since.

Over 80 per cent of Chinese characters contain a phonetic component and a radical component and are known as phonetic compounds. Take, for example, the character 洋 which means *ocean* and is pronounced /iaŋ/. The left part 氵 is the semantic radical. When 氵 appears on its own, it means *water* and is pronouncd /sue/. The right part of the character 羊 is the phonetic. When 羊 appears on its own, it means *goat* and is pronouncd /iaŋ/. The radical therefore provides the reader with information about the meaning of the compound character, and the phonetic provides its pronunciation. In many cases, as in the above example, the phonetic component remains a reliable guide to the correct pronunciation of the character. Unfortunately, the phonetic no longer provides a totally reliable guide for many characters, partly because the pronunciations of many words have changed over the centuries such that the phonetic now rhymes with the pronunciation of the entire character instead of being homophonic with it. For some compound characters, the pronunciation of the phonetic no longer resembles the pronunciation of the character at all.

We pointed out in the opening paragraph that the number of visual forms that a Chinese child must master is enormous by comparison with the number of letters that a child reading an alphabetic system must learn. Printing, word processing and the use of dictionaries are also much more convenient in an alphabetic system. Because of this, it has sometimes been suggested that Chinese characters might be completely replaced by an alphabetic writing system. Aside from the literary history, stretching back over many centuries, that would be lost if the characters were replaced by an alphabetic system, the fact that so many Chinese words are homophones would also create problems. As we said above, Chinese compound characters contain a semantic radical component that provides important information about the meaning of homophones. This makes them easily distinguishable from other characters that are pronounced in the same way. Indeed, when speaking a homophone, some Chinese speakers will draw the character in the air in order to disambiguate themselves. In alphabetic systems such as *Pinyin* (see below), this information is not available in the way that the word is written, and these systems are therefore much more ambiguous than the Chinese script itself. There is of course a parallel here with deep alphabetic orthographies such as English where information about the different meanings of homophones such as *tail* and *tale* can be derived from the way they are spelled. The fact that the same phonemic structure can be represented in more than one way in written English and in written Chinese may make life hard for the novice but has clear advantages for the skilled adult reader.

An equally important reason for the retention of the characters has to do with the unity of the Chinese people. However, this is not for the precise reason that is often put forward. Many writers (for a recent example see So and Siegel, 1997, pp. 2–3) have advanced the claim that the characters enable Chinese people to communicate with each other in writing even though they may speak different versions of the Chinese language (e.g. people who speak Cantonese and those who speak Mandarin). That is, because the characters represent morphemes, they can represent the same morpheme in print regardless of the phonemic structure of the corresponding spoken word. In practical terms, however, Mandarin speakers would find it quite difficult to read a newspaper from Hong Kong written in Cantonese because the syntax of the two languages is different. In addition, the meaning of some of the characters is in fact different in Cantonese and Mandarin.

Traditionally, Chinese characters have generally been used as the written form of Mandarin. That is, when children throughout mainland China and Taiwan are taught to read characters, they are taught the pronunciation of the word in Mandarin even if the language spoken locally is Cantonese or Min. In Hong Kong, for example, even before the incorporation of Hong Kong with mainland China in July 1997, only a relatively small set of characters was taught in Cantonese at the start of elementary school. As children get older, they are taught to read in Mandarin. This is certainly not because Chinese characters represent the spoken form of Mandarin any more closely than they represent the spoken form of Cantonese or Min. In fact, it might be argued that the phonetic component of compound characters gives a less reliable guide to the pronunciation of the word in Mandarin because Mandarin, unlike Cantonese and Min, incorporated elements of other languages such as Manchurian after the Chinese writing system was standardised. It is more likely that children are taught to read in Mandarin in order to consolidate the political power of the central government in Beijing by ensuring that their version of the Chinese language remains dominant. If the characters were replaced by an alphabetic script, then versions of the alphabetic script, unintelligible to speakers of Mandarin, might start to appear in parts of the country where other Chinese languages are in common use.

Pinyin and Zhu-Yin-Fu-Hao

The way in which Chinese children are taught to read differs very markedly from one area of China to another. In Taiwan and mainland China, children have been introduced to the reading of Mandarin via a quite separate alphabetic system since the 1950s. All children in the first grade at school (six to seven years) in mainland China are taught to read an alphabetic script (Pinyin) before beginning to learn Chinese characters. Similarly, all pupils in Taiwan learn an alphabetic script known as *Zhu-Yin-Fu-Hao* during the first ten weeks of the first grade before any exposure to Chinese characters takes place. In Hong Kong, Pinyin is not used to teach reading in Cantonese, although a small number of primary schools incorporate Pinyin when the children are subsequently taught to read in Mandarin. The number of schools may well increase rapidly in the coming years following the recent political changes in Hong Kong.

Zhu-Yin-Fu-Hao (which literally means 'symbols of phonetic pronunciation') is a script similar to Pinyin in which a phoneme is represented by a unique character. There are thirty-seven different characters in Zhu-Yin-Fu-Hao, all of which are visually different from any of the characters that comprise the Chinese writing system proper. In Pinyin, the written symbols are letters from the Roman alphabet, but otherwise the two systems are very similar, both of them being shallow alphabetic systems.

Although it is learnt during the first few weeks of the first year in school, most children rapidly become fluent in Pinyin or Zhu-Yin-Fu-Hao and continue to use it throughout most of their primary school years. Whenever a new character appears in a primary school textbook, it is always accompanied by its representation in Pinyin or Zhu-Yin-Fu-Hao. Zhu-Yin-Fu-Hao also contains symbols that represent the tone in which the word is spoken. Knowledge of Zhu-Yin-Fu-Hao thus helps children to pronounce new characters for themselves via sub-lexical phonology without assistance from the teacher or parent. Pinyin and Zhu-Yin-Fu-Hao therefore fulfil one of the main functions of the alphabetic principle in Western writing systems, the provision of a self-teaching mechanism (see Share, 1995).

The Zhu-Yin-Fu-Hao symbols continue to accompany the new character over several pages of the child's reading book until it is considered that the child should have finally learnt the character, and be capable of reading it without help from the Zhu-Yin-Fu-Hao. When writing an essay, a child is encouraged to write in Zhu-Yin-Fu-Hao any word for which he or she does not know the appropriate character. 'Errors' of this kind can be routinely observed in the writing books of Taiwanese children, as can errors where the child produces a character that is homophonic with the character that they should have written. Such responses provide evidence that Chinese children can use the speech production system during writing/spelling (cf. Ellis, 1993).

In Hong Kong (Ho and Bryant, 1997a), children are taught to read as young as three years old in their first kindergarten year. By the end of first grade (seven years old) they should be able to read 460 different characters, and by the end of second grade they should be able to read 960 different characters. Children in Hong Kong are generally taught by rote learning; they learn new characters by copying them many times over. The teacher will outline the meaning and pronunciation of the character, but the children's attention is not specifically directed to the phonetic or the semantic component of compound characters.

In Taiwan, the school year is divided into two semesters each containing sixteen teaching weeks. Children are taught between eight and ten new characters per week, which means that the child will learn as many as 320 new characters in a school year. Although repeated copying of the character plays an important role in the learning process, many teachers in Taiwan do routinely draw the child's attention to the phonetic and the semantic components of compound characters.

Phonological awareness and learning to read

Are children with superior phonological awareness better readers of Chinese?

Although it is clear that Chinese children, just like Chinese adults, can represent visually presented Chinese characters in phonological codes in tests of short-term memory (Tzeng, Hung and Wang, 1977; Hu and Catts, 1993), recent research has started to investigate whether children with superior phonological awareness skills learn to read Chinese more quickly. It is well known that there is a strong correlation between the reading performance of children learning to read English and other European languages (see Goswami, this volume) and their performance on tests of phonological awareness. That is, good readers tend to perform well on tasks such as auditory rhyme detection and counting the number of phonemes in spoken words (for discussion, see Goswami and Bryant, 1990). Given that many Chinese characters contain a phonetic component, and that many Chinese children have learnt an alphabetic writing system, it is important to investigate the relationship between phonological awareness and learning to read Chinese.

Huang and Hanley (1995) examined the relationship between performance on tests of phonological awareness and single-word reading in a cross-sectional study of eight-year-old children from Taiwan, Hong Kong and Britain. They used a phoneme deletion task in which the subject was asked to listen to a spoken word, remove either the first or the last phoneme from the word, and then respond with the word that was left (e.g. *party > part*). They found a highly significant correlation between phoneme deletion test scores and reading test scores in all three groups of children. As in previous research with readers of English (e.g. Tunmer and Nesdale, 1985), these differences remained significant in the British sample even when the effects of variables such as vocabulary and non-verbal intelligence had been accounted for. This was not the case with the Chinese children, however. In the Taiwanese sample, for example, the relationship between Chinese reading ability and phonological awareness was no longer significant when the effect of vocabulary was accounted for. Vocabulary score was also very strongly correlated with Chinese reading ability in a study of eleven-year-old children in mainland China carried out by McBride-Chang and Chang (1995).

So and Siegel (1997) also reported a significant correlation in primary school children from grades 1–4 in Hong Kong between single-word reading and performance on two tasks that they considered to require phonological ability. These were a test in which children were asked to indicate whether auditorily presented homophones were being spoken in the same tone, and a test which required children to indicate whether auditorily presented words rhymed with each other. Once again, however, performance on all of these tasks was heavily correlated with performance on a test requiring knowledge of word meaning.

Somewhat different results were obtained by Ho and Bryant (1997a). They found that there was a significant correlation between performance on a test of auditory rhyme detection and single-word reading in first-grade children from Hong Kong, but only when the reading test was entirely comprised of phonetic compound characters. The relationship remained significant even when the effects of IQ had been accounted for. In second-grade children, however, there was no significant correlation between phonological awareness performance and any of the reading test measures.

In a longitudinal study of six-year-old children from Taiwan, Ko and Lee (1997a) found no significant relationship between pre-school phonological awareness scores and reading of Chinese characters either one or two years later. By contrast, Huang and Hanley (1994, 1997) in a similar study found that there *was* a significant correlation between pre-school phonological awareness scores and reading ability a year later even when the effects of vocabulary and intelligence test scores had been accounted for. This relationship was no longer significant when the Chinese character reading ability of these children was re-examined three years later (Huang, 1996). More worryingly, Huang and Hanley (1994, 1997) observed that the predictive power of early phonological awareness disappeared once the effects of pre-school reading scores had been accounted for. The finding that pre-school reading level was of overwhelming importance in determining subsequent reading performance is reminiscent of results reported by Wagner and Torgesen (1987) with an alphabetic writing system, but this is certainly not always the case with alphabetic orthographies (e.g. Wimmer, Landerl, Linortner and Hummer, 1991).

Ho and Bryant (1997b) have recently performed a longitudinal study of reading development in children in Hong Kong in which this problem did not occur, as none of the 100 subjects used in the study was able to read any Chinese characters on a pre-test when they were three years old. Ho and Bryant found significant correlations between children's scores on a phonological awareness test at age three and their reading ability both two and three years later.

Another particularly interesting aspect of Ko and Lee's (1997a) study was their finding that there was a significant correlation between the ability of children to read words in Zhu-Yin-Fu-Hao and their score on tests of real word reading. This relationship remained significant even when the effects of intelligence test scores were accounted for. This suggests that children with superior skills in Zhu-Yin-Fu-Hao have become better readers of Chinese characters. This important finding, which demonstrates the key role that Zhu-Yin-Fu-Hao plays in the development of Chinese literacy, is well worth further detailed investigation.

Overall, therefore, the relationship between phonological awareness and learning to read Chinese is clearly more complex than is the case with alphabetic orthographies. There is evidence that at least some of the significant correlations between tests of reading and phonological awareness in Chinese children come about because both are related to other variables such as vocabulary test score. Although the results of Ho and Bryant's (1997b) longitudinal study are certainly consistent with the view that children with superior phonological awareness skills do have some advantages in learning to read Chinese, the longitudinal studies from Taiwan do not strongly support this conclusion. As one might have anticipated that the relationship between phonological awareness and subsequent reading development would have been at least as strong in Taiwan as in Hong Kong, the precise reasons for the different findings remain unclear at the present time.

Does knowledge of an alphabetic system increase the phonological awareness of Chinese children?

Read, Zhang, Nie and Ding (1986) claimed that phonological awareness skills develop as a consequence of learning an alphabetic script. They compared two groups of adult subjects from mainland China, one of whom had learned to read Chinese characters via Pinyin while at school. The other group had not learned Pinyin, and were literate only in Chinese characters. The results showed that adults who had never learnt Pinyin found it extremely difficult to add or delete individual consonants in spoken Chinese words. In contrast, subjects in the Pinyin group could perform the same tasks readily and accurately. These differences do not emerge because instruction in Pinyin explicitly teaches phoneme deletion skills; as Read *et al.* pointed out (1986, p. 42), 'there is not a classroom exercise like the deletion task'.

Consistent with this, Huang and Hanley (1995) showed that eight-year-old children from Taiwan, who had been taught Zhu-Yin-Fu-Hao two years earlier, performed significantly better on Chinese phoneme deletion tasks than eight-year-old children from Hong Kong who had not been taught Pinyin or Zhu-Yin-Fu-Hao. These findings are consistent with those of Mann (1986) which revealed relatively poor phoneme deletion ability in Japanese children who had not learnt an alphabetic script.

In a separate study, Huang and Hanley (1994, 1997) showed that the performance of first-grade Taiwanese children aged six years improved significantly on a test of phoneme deletion from 35 per cent (pre-test) to over 60 per cent (post-test) after learning Zhu-Yin-Fu-Hao. This improvement occurred despite the fact that there was a gap of only ten weeks between the two testing sessions. This improvement is likely to be specific to the learning of Zhu-Yin-Fu-Hao rather than to greater maturity because there was no further improvement in performance on the phoneme deletion test when children were re-tested at the end of the school year. Similar results with first-grade Taiwanese children have been obtained by Ko and Lee (1997a).

Ko and Lee (1997b) also investigated this issue by testing illiterate Taiwanese adults undergoing a course of reading instruction. The performance of these subjects on tests of phoneme deletion increased substantially after they had been taught to read words in Zhu-Yin-Fu-Hao. Similarly, Leong (1997) investigated the phonological awareness ability of university students in Hong Kong who could read Cantonese but not Mandarin. Performance on a test of phoneme addition by this group was significantly better after they had been taught Pinyin compared with a group of students who had not received such instruction.

Taken together, the results reviewed in this section demonstrate clearly that the phonological awareness of both Chinese children and Chinese adults immediately increases once they have learnt an alphabetic system.

Phonological awareness skills in Chinese- and English-speaking children

Ho and Bryant (1997c) have investigated the performance of children from Hong Kong on a variety of different tests of phonological awareness. They found that three-year-old children could perform certain tasks with some degree of proficiency. They could indicate when words were homophones even when spoken in different tones, and they were able to indicate when two words rhymed so long as they were similar in tone. However, they were at chance level when asked to judge rhyme in words spoken in different tones, nor could they judge tone in words that did not rhyme. By five years old, they could perform both these tasks with some degree of proficiency. At seven, they could detect onsets in spoken words, but this ability could conceivably have developed earlier, as younger children were not given the onset tests.

Ho and Bryant note that the performance of children from Hong Kong on the rhyme task was somewhat lower than in British children of a comparable age (e.g. Maclean, Bryant and Bradley, 1987). This suggests that rhyme awareness may develop somewhat later in Chinese children. They believe that this may be due to differences in the written language rather than differences in spoken language in that learning to read Chinese is unlikely to encourage children to pay attention to sub-syllabic units such as onset and rhyme. Consistent with this, Huang and Hanley (1995) showed that eight-year-old Taiwanese children who had learnt Zhu-Yin-Fu-Hao performed significantly better on tests sensitive to awareness of rhyme and alliteration than Hong Kong children.

However, there *is* evidence that differences in the syllabic structure of a language *per se* do seem to produce differences in the phonological awareness skills of children who speak that language. Huang and Hanley (1995) reported that British children were significantly better than Hong Kong children (who spoke English as a second language) on first sound deletion from CVCC English words. Conversely, the Hong Kong children were significantly *better* than the British children on first sound deletion from CCVC words. CVCC first sound deletion was significantly more difficult than CCVC first sound deletion for the Hong Kong subjects. For example, to delete /s/ from 'stop' was easier than to delete /t/ from 'task' for the Hong Kong group. In contrast, English children found first sound deletion to be significantly more difficult in CCVC words than in CVCC words.

Relatively poor performance by English subjects when asked to delete a phoneme from an initial consonant cluster is consistent with the findings of Morais, Cluytens and Alegria (1984) and Perfetti, Beck, Bell and Hughes (1987). Treiman (1985) argued that English-speaking children always group the phonemes in a syllable into the onset and the rhyme, and that initial consonant clusters are treated as single units. Therefore, CCVC, CVCC, and CCVCC words would all be parsed as simple CVC strings. Why did items of this kind not pose similar problems for the Hong Kong children? As we said at the start of this chapter, there are no consonant blends in Chinese syllables. As Wang (1973) noted: 'When European words with consonant clusters are represented in Chinese, they are typically broken up so that each consonant has its own syllable' (p. 57). The name 'Clinton', for example, is written with three characters representing three syllables: [kuh]-[lin]-[ton]. Bearing this in mind, it is perhaps not surprising to note that the Hong Kong children performed so well on initial phoneme deletion of words containing consonant clusters. If the Hong Kong children are implicitly adding a vowel between consonants when they hear words with consonant clusters, then the phoneme deletion task in reality becomes a syllable deletion task. As a consequence, this may make it relatively easy for them to parse consonant clusters into separate units.

Findings consistent with these have been reported by Holm and Dodd (1996) who compared the performance of students from mainland China at an Australian university with those of Australian students on a test of phonological awareness. On tests that involved spoonerising English words that started with consonant clusters, the Australian students frequently exchanged both elements of the cluster (e.g. crowd-play > plowd-cray). The Chinese students were much less likely to make an error of this kind, however.

Why did the Hong Kong children in Huang and Hanley's (1995) study perform *worse* than the British children when asked to delete the first phoneme from an English word with a single consonant before the vowel? This may occur because of the large number of Chinese syllables that have a CV structure. It would not be surprising if their experience with words of this kind makes Chinese children who have never learnt Pinyin or Zhu-Yin-Fu-Hao show a tendency to treat a consonant followed by a vowel as a single unit.

Similar results were reported by Leong (1997) in his study of Hong Kong university students who had undergone a course in Pinyin when learning to read Mandarin. These subjects performed much better than the comparison group in segmental analysis of the initial consonant in both English and Chinese words, but showed no corresponding advantage with final consonants. Knowledge of Pinyin or Zhu-Yin-Fu-Hao will confer the experience of decomposing CV syllables into distinct consonant-vowel units. Without such experience, Hong Kong students may be much more likely to consider a Chinese CV syllable to be an indivisible unit.

The effect of learning Pinyin on the reading of English

Holm and Dodd (1996) also examined the performance of Chinese students in Australia at reading English. In particular, they compared a group of students who were residents of mainland China with students who had learnt to read in Hong Kong. This enabled them to determine whether learning Pinyin affected in any way the ability of the Chinese students to read English.

The results were very striking indeed. In terms of their overall ability to read and spell English words, the two groups were well matched. This means that differences between the two groups could not simply be explained in terms of differences in their overall reading level. Students from Hong Kong found it extremely difficult to read and spell English non-words, however. Their ability to perform tests of auditory rhyme judgement and phoneme segmentation on English words was also extremely limited. Holm and Dodd pointed out that the Hong Kong students' performance in reading English was very similar to that of the developmental phonological dyslexic student studied by Campbell and Butterworth (1985), who appeared entirely dysphonetic and had learnt to read by a visual look-and-say strategy. It would therefore appear that the phonological awareness skills fostered by learning Pinyin can be applied successfully by Chinese students when they are subsequently exposed to alphabetic systems that represent other languages in print. Without familiarity with Pinyin or Zhu-Yin-Fu-Hao, the Chinese students seem to lack entirely the ability to develop the knowledge of sub-syllabic phonology that seems to play such an important role in the acquisition of English reading skills (e.g. Share, 1995).

The use of the phonetic component of compound characters

Reading phonetic compounds and pseudo-characters

As explained earlier, over 80 per cent of Chinese characters are known as phonetic compounds and contain a component that provides information about the pronunciation of the entire character. It is estimated that there are approximately 800 different phonetic symbols that appear as part of compound characters (Hoosain, 1991), the vast majority of which are characters in their own right. A common strategy adopted by Chinese readers when they encounter an unfamiliar character is to attempt to give a pronunciation that corresponds to the phonetic element (Fang, Horng and Tzeng, 1986; Wang, 1973). One problem with this is that although the phonetic usually appears to the right of the semantic radical (in approximately 80 per cent of phonetic compounds), this is not always the case. Consequently, the reader may inappropriately attempt to use the semantic radical as the phonetic cue. Secondly, the pronunciation of the phonetic yields the correct pronunciation of only about 40 per cent of compound characters (Zhou, 1978). Nevertheless, deep alphabetic orthographies such as English and French also contain many orthographic irregularities, but English and French children are generally taught information about letter–sound relationships and appear to be sensitive to them from an early age (e.g. Frith, 1985). Is there evidence that Chinese children are sensitive to the phonetic element of compound characters?

The answer appears to be *yes*. Lien (1985) showed that children made more errors when naming characters whose phonetic component did not give a reliable cue to the pronunciation of the character as a whole. Chen and Yuen (1991) showed that seven-year-old children from Hong Kong, Taiwan and mainland China were all able to read aloud pseudo-characters in which the radical and the phonetic components from different words were arbitrarily put together by pronouncing the phonetic. Interestingly, the children from Hong Kong (who had not learnt Pinyin) were significantly worse at this task than the children from Taiwan or mainland China, even though they performed as well as the Taiwanese children on a lexical decision test. These results suggest that phonologial processing of Chinese compound characters may be encouraged by prior exposure to Pinyin or Zhu-Yin-Fu-Hao.

Tzeng *et al.* (1995) investigated the way in which children process the phonetic component of compound characters by asking third- and sixth-grade Taiwanese children to read pseudo-characters. They manipulated the type of pseudo-character by generating compound characters in which the phonetic component had markedly different characteristics. In *regular only* pseudo-characters, the phonetic symbol selected was a phonetic that appeared in real characters that are all pronounced the same way as the phonetic symbol itself when it is written as a separate character. In *irregular only* pseudo-characters, the phonetic symbol was one that appeared as part of real characters that are all pronounced differently from one another. In the *mixed* condition, there were pseudo-characters containing phonetic components that were pronounced consistently in some, but not all, of the real characters in which they appeared. Results showed that the *irregular only* pseudo-characters took longest to read aloud. There were significantly more 'correct' pronunciations (i.e. pronunciations that were the same as the pronunciation of the phonetic symbol when it is written as a separate character) in *regular only* pseudo-characters and fewest correct responses in *irregular only* pseudo-characters. The mixed condition was associated with incorrect responses particularly where the pseudo-character contained a phonetic element taken from a *high frequency* character that is pronounced differently from the way the phonetic is normally pronounced. The majority of incorrect responses were responses that were the same as the pronunciation of a compound character containing that phonetic symbol, but which is pronounced differently from the way the phonetic is normally pronounced.

It is clear from these results that the children were strongly influenced by the presence of the phonetic component when reading these unfamiliar characters. Tzeng *et al.* argued that the children were not simply pronouncing the phonetic part of the pseudo-character. If this had been the case, then there would have been no reason to expect the observed differences between the regular only condition and the mixed condition. It appears that Chinese children are sensitive to the way in which the phonetic component is pronounced in the real words in which it appears. Tzeng *et al.* suggested that such findings are compatible with lexical analogy models of English reading (e.g. Taraban and McClelland, 1987) which claim that the ease with which a word is read aloud is influenced by the way in which the word's visual neighbours are pronounced.

Results that are consistent with those of Tzeng *et al.* (1995) have been reported by Ho and Bryant (1997a) with first- and second-grade children from Hong Kong. Ho and Bryant showed that characters with phonetic components that were identical in pronunciation to that of the character as a whole were associated with more correct pronunciations than characters in which the pronunciation of the phonetic and the entire character differed. This effect was greater in low-frequency than high-frequency characters, indicating that the phonetic is more likely to be used in low-frequency characters. This is presumably because the low-frequency characters are more likely to have been unfamiliar to the children. The effects were also stronger in the grade 2 children than in the grade 1 children, suggesting that the use of the phonetic in reading new words develops as the child gets older. As the Hong Kong children, unlike Tzeng *et al.*'s Taiwanese sample, had not learnt Pinyin or Zhu-Yin-Fu-Hao, these results support Chen and Yuen's (1991) conclusion that the use of the phonetic is not confined to children who are already fluent in an alphabetic writing system.

Evidence that Chinese children are also sensitive to the semantic radical component of phonetic compounds has been provided by Chan and Nunes (1998). They gave children from Hong Kong a choice of six radicals and six phonetics (which did not co-occur in any phonetic compounds) and asked them to use them to create names for six unfamiliar objects. Results showed that children as young as six years old were able to create new compound characters for objects in which the radical that was selected was semantically related to the meaning of the object concerned. The six-year-old children also showed evidence of creating compounds in which the phonetic was on the right and the radical on the left (as in the majority of compound characters). This provides evidence that children at this stage have developed some sensitivity to the relative location of the phonetic and radical components of compound characters.

Children's reading errors

The errors that children make when reading real Chinese words aloud also support the view that the phonetic component of compound characters is of great significance for them. Ho and Bryant (1997a) showed that a common type of error that the children made (25 per cent) was a response in which the pronunciation of the phonetic was used as the pronunciation of the entire character. Also common were errors in which a character was read as a different character that contained the same phonetic component (9 per cent). There were also some errors in which the character was read as a different character that contained the same semantic radical component or else the pronunciation of the radical was given as the pronunciation of the entire word (4 per cent).

Tzeng *et al.* (1995) reported four main types of error when children were reading real words. The most common were derivative errors where a simple character was read as a compound character in which the character serves as the phonetic. However, there were three other main types of errors observed also. These were visual errors where a word was pronounced like a visually similar character, and tonal errors where a character was read in the wrong tone. In addition, there were semantic errors where a character was pronounced like a word of similar meaning. For example, the character that represents the third Heavenly Stem was read as the character that represents the first or second Heavenly Stem. These three symbols do not share a semantic radical and bear no physical similarity to one another. This type of error is of enormous potential interest, as normal children learning to read alphabetic writing systems do not make semantic errors when reading single words (for discussion, see Ellis, 1993). It would be very interesting to know whether such errors are less likely to occur in phonetic compounds than in other types of Chinese character.

Perhaps the largest study of the reading errors that children make was performed by Ko (1992) in a survey of over 37,000 Taiwanese children. Each child was given a character and was asked to add an additional character that would make up a multi-syllabic word. Ko was particularly interested in the responses which did not comprise real Chinese words. By far the most common type of error (57 per cent) in children of all grades (from 1 to 6) was where the child wrote a character that would have made a real word if it had been paired with a character that was visually similar to the original character. This suggests that the child had made a visual error when reading the original character. Visual errors are observed in the reading of English children (e.g. Frith, 1985) but probably not on a scale of this kind. Phonological errors did occur also (approximately 37 per cent) although in many cases the error may have been visual also. There was virtually no evidence of the children making semantic errors.

Reading difficulty and its determinants

Rozin, Poritsky and Sotsky (1971) successfully taught a group of non-readers from the USA to read English written in Chinese characters. Even though the American children were only taught a relatively small set of Chinese characters (thirty), this led to some speculation that developmental dyslexia might be more widespread in countries that use alphabetic orthographies than in countries such as Japan and China that use syllabic or morphemic writing systems. However, such a conclusion is not warranted on the basis of this study. For all we know, it may have been the case that Rozin *et al.*'s poor readers would have been just as successful if they had been taught to read English written in a transparent alphabetic system such as Zhu-Yin-Fu-Hao.

Stevenson, Stigler, Lucker, Lee, Hsu and Kitamura (1982) challenged Rozin *et al.*'s findings in a study that compared reading ability in children from the USA, Japan and Taiwan. They showed that in all three groups there were a considerable number of children whose performance at reading single words was well below what would be expected of children their age. Their results (p. 1173) with fifth-grade readers showed that 8 per cent of the Japanese children, 3 per cent of the American children and 2 per cent of the Taiwanese children 'failed to meet the criteria for success at grades 3, 4 and 5 and were, according to these criteria, more than two grades behind their reading level'. Of course, these results do not indicate that the nature of the writing system plays no role in reading disability, nor do they guarantee that the numbers of children who suffer from reading problems in these three countries are approximately equal. However, they do suggest that Chinese children can suffer severe problems in learning to read characters.

What might be the nature of the cognitive deficit and the reading deficit experienced by Chinese children with reading disability? Stevenson *et al.* (1982) claimed that poor reading performance was significantly correlated with performance on other academic tasks such as arithmetic ability in the Chinese and Japanese poor readers, but not in the American poor readers. This suggests that the basis of the reading deficit may be more specific in children learning to read English. Unfortunately, the explosion of research activity in the last two decades that has been directed at the nature of developmental dyslexia in English-speaking countries has not been matched by an equivalent number of published studies of dyslexia in Chinese-speaking countries. Several recent studies of Chinese reading development have, however, included comparisons of good and poor readers.

The difference in reading skill between the good and poor readers in So and Siegel's (1997) study of Hong Kong children was at least as large as between developmental dyslexics in studies performed in the USA or the UK. Their fourth-grade poor readers performed at a similar level on a reading task to first-grade normal readers. Despite this they performed much worse than the younger normal readers on tests of tone and rhyme discrimination, but no worse than them on other tests of language ability that did not involve reading. This suggests that as in children learning to read English, reading problems may be directly related to phonological processing ability.

Lee (1997) compared poor readers in the fifth grade in Taiwan with third-grade children matched on the basis of reading age. The poor readers read 11.1/50 words correctly on a single-word reading test (the mean for normal fifth-grade children was 22.7/50). Although the reading age comparison group were two years younger, they read 11.7/50 of these words correctly. Lee showed that the poor readers performed worse than the younger comparison group both on a test of phoneme deletion and on a test which involved reading words and non-words written in Zhu-Yin-Fu-Hao. The results are reminiscent of those indicating that dyslexic children in English-speaking countries have greater difficulty in reading non-words than younger normal readers with whom they are matched for reading age (Rack, Snowling and Olson, 1992). The poor readers performed at a similar level to the comparison group on a test of visual memory that involved recognition memory for unfamiliar Greek and Japanese symbols. Huang and Zhang (1997) also found evidence of significant impairments in phonological awareness skills in poor readers in Taiwan when their performance was compared with good readers of the same age.

The results of these studies are certainly consistent with the view that Chinese children with reading difficulties suffer from phonological processing impairments comparable with those found in poor readers of

English (e.g. Snowling, 1995). Whether or not there are also children who suffer from a form of developmental *surface* dyslexia (e.g. Castles and Coltheart, 1993; Hanley and Gard, 1995), as might seem very likely in a writing system such as Chinese, would be an interesting issue for future research to investigate. Further evidence for this could be obtained by observing whether or not there are any systematic differences between the type of reading errors that individual Chinese children with reading impairments make when reading Chinese characters.

The idea that some children might have difficulty in learning to read Chinese because of a deficit in remembering the visual form of a word rather than as a consequence of a phonological processing impairment is consistent with research suggesting that visual skills may play a particularly important role in learning to read Chinese. Huang and Hanley (1995) observed that visual memory skills were significantly correlated with reading ability in eight-year-old children from Taiwan and Hong Kong, but not in children from Britain (for further discussion, see Hanley and Huang, 1997). Similarly, Ho and Bryant (1997b) found that differences in visuo-perceptual skills in pre-school children from Hong Kong were a significant predictor of reading ability a year later.

Conclusion

One important conclusion that emerges from the research reviewed in this chapter is that learning an alphabetic script (Pinyin in mainland China, and Zhu-Yin-Fu-Hao in Taiwan) appears to exert an enormous effect on the subsequent reading behaviour and phonological awareness skills of Chinese children. Phonological awareness of Taiwanese children improves immediately after they have learnt Zhu-Yin-Fu-Hao (Huang and Hanley, 1997), and children from Hong Kong, who have not learnt such a script, perform much worse on tests of rhyme detection and phoneme deletion (Huang and Hanley, 1995). Although it may also be related to the rote learning strategies that are generally used to teach new characters in Hong Kong, it is particularly striking that Hong Kong children seem less likely to use the phonetic components in compound characters when they read novel words (Chen and Yuen, 1991) than students familiar with Pinyin. When they come to read English, students from Hong Kong appear much less likely to take advantage of the alphabetic nature of the English writing system and read it instead by the use of visual strategies (Holm and Dodd, 1996).

Most important of all, however, there is now overwhelming evidence that phonological processing strategies play a crucially important role

in the way that children read Chinese, including those who have learnt
to read in Hong Kong (So and Siegel, 1997; Ho and Bryant, 1997a).
First, Chinese children seem to rapidly develop sensitivity to the phonetic component of compound characters when they are attempting to
read new words (Chen and Yuen, 1991; Tzeng *et al.*, 1995). Second,
children's ability to read Chinese characters appears to be correlated
with their ability to read Pinyin or Zhu-Yin-Fu-Hao (Ko and Lee,
1997a). Third, there is evidence that Chinese children with reading
problems perform badly on tests of phonological processing ability (Lee,
1997; So and Siegel, 1997).

Of course visual memory skills must be important also; as we pointed
out at the start of the paper, a child must learn to distinguish thousands
of different visual symbols if he or she is to become proficient in reading
Chinese. Because written words in Chinese are more visually distinct
than words written in an alphabetic script, it is conceivable that a child
who relied exclusively on visual rather than phonological strategies to
learn new words could more readily become a fluent reader of Chinese
than of English. However, it seems likely that the amount of visual
processing that is required to memorise new characters will be significantly reduced if a child is able to identify the phonetic component in
compound characters. If a child can also use the phonetic component,
or the representation of the word in Pinyin or Zhu-Yin-Fu-Hao, to
generate the pronunciation of a new character, then this is likely to
make it much easier for the child to learn to associate the new character
with its correct pronunciation (cf. Share, 1995). The importance of
phonological as well as visual processes in learning to read Chinese
indicates that the underlying cognitive skills and strategies involved in
learning Chinese and English are probably not as different as was once
imagined.

However, the phonological information that is contained in phonetic
compounds is much less reliable than that which is available even in a
deep alphabetic writing system such as English. In addition, the phonological information that the Chinese writing system provides is at the
syllabic level rather than at the level of the phoneme, and the use of
separate scripts such as Pinyin and Zhu-Yin-Fu-Hao in the teaching of
Chinese reading has no counterpart in the way in which literacy skills
are taught in Europe or the USA. This means that we should not
expect the reading of Chinese children to mirror precisely the stages of
reading development that have been observed in alphabetic orthographies
such as English. Studies of learning to read Chinese contribute to the
field by revealing its unique aspects in addition to those that it shares
with the acquisition of alphabetic writing systems.

REFERENCES

Campbell, R. and Butterworth, B. (1985). Phonological dyslexia and dysgraphia in a highly literate subject: a developmental case with associated deficits of phonemic awareness and processing. *Quarterly Journal of Experimental Psychology*, 37A, 435–75.

Castles, A. and Coltheart, M. (1993). Varieties of developmental dyslexia. *Cognition*, 47, 149–80.

Chan, L. and Nunes, T. (1998). Children's understanding of the formal and functional characteristics of written Chinese. *Applied Psycholinguistics*, 19, 115–31.

Chen, M. J. (1996). An overview of the characteristics of the Chinese writing system. *Asia Pacific Journal of Speech, Language and Hearing*, 1, 43–54.

Chen, M. J. and Yuen, J. C.-K. (1991). Effects of Pinyin and script type on verbal processing: comparisons of China, Taiwan and Hong Kong experience. *International Journal of Behavioral Development*, 14, 429–84.

Coltheart, M., Curtis, B., Atkins, P. and Haller, M. (1993). Models of reading aloud: dual-route and parallel-distributed processing approaches. *Psychological Review*, 100, 589–608.

Ellis, A. W. (1993). *Reading, Writing and Dyslexia*. Hove, UK: Lawrence Erlbaum Associates.

Fang, S. P., Hrong, R. Y. and Tzeng, O. (1986). Consistency effects in the Chinese character and pseudo-character naming tasks. In H. S. R. Kao and R. Hoosain (eds.), *Linguistics, Psychology, and the Chinese Language*. Hong Kong: University of Hong Kong Press.

Frith, U. (1985). Beneath the surface of developmental dyslexia. In K. Patterson, J. C. Marshall and M. Coltheart (eds.), *Surface Dyslexia*. London: Lawrence Erlbaum Associates.

Goswami, U. and Bryant, P. (1990). *Phonological Skills and Learning to Read*. Hove, UK: Lawrence Erlbaum Associates.

Hanley, J. R. and Gard, F. (1995). A dissociation between developmental surface and phonological dyslexia in two undergraduate students. *Neuropsychologia*, 33, 909–14.

Hanley, J. R. and Huang, H.-S. (1997). Phonological awareness in learning to read Chinese. In C. K. Leong and R. Malatesha Joshi (eds.), *Applied Research in Reading and Spelling in Different Languages*. Dordrecht, Netherlands: Kluwer.

Ho, C. S. and Bryant, P. (1997a). Learning to read Chinese beyond the logographic phase. *Reading Research Quarterly*, 32, 276–89.

(1997b). Phonological skills are important in learning to read Chinese. *Developmental Psychology*, 33, 946–51.

(1997c). Development of phonological awareness of Chinese children in Hong Kong. *Journal of Psycholinguistic Research*, 26, 109–26.

Holm, A. and Dodd, B. (1996). The effect of first written language on the acquisition of English literacy. *Cognition*, 59, 119–47.

Hoosain, R. (1991). *Psycholinguistic Implications for Linguistic Relativity: A Case Study of Chinese*. Hillsdale, NJ: Erlbaum.

Hu, C. F. and Catts, H. W. (1993). Phonological recoding as a universal process? Evidence from beginning reading. *Reading and Writing*, 5, 325–37.

Huang, H.-S. (1996). Early phonological awareness, visual skills and Chinese character recognition ability three years later. *International Journal of Psychology*, 31, 47.

Huang, H.-S. and Hanley, J. R. (1994). Phonological awareness, visual skills and Chinese reading acquisition in first graders: a longitudinal study in Taiwan. In H.-W. Chang, J.-T. Huang, C.-W. Hue and O. J. L. Tzeng (eds.), *Advances in the Study of Chinese Language Processing: Selected Writings from the Sixth International Symposium on Cognitive Aspects of the Chinese Language*. Taipei: National Taiwan University.

(1995). Phonological awareness and visual skills in learning to read Chinese and English. *Cognition*, 54, 73–98.

(1997). A longitudinal study of phonological awareness, visual skills and Chinese reading acquisition amongst first graders in Taiwan. *International Journal of Behavioral Development*, 20, 249–68.

Huang, H.-S. and Zhang, H. R. (1997). An investigation of phonemic awareness, word awareness and tone awareness among dyslexic children. *Bulletin of Special Education and Rehabilitation*, 5, 125–38.

Hung, D. L. and Tzeng, O. J. L. (1981). Orthographic variation and visual information processing. *Psychological Bulletin*, 90, 377–414.

Ko, H. (1992). Reading Chinese characters. *The World of Chinese Language*, 62, 121–31.

Ko, H. and Lee, J. R. (1997a). Chinese children's phonological awareness ability and later reading ability – a longitudinal study. *Journal of the National Chung-Cheng University*, 7, 49–66.

(1997b). Phonological awareness and learning to read in illiterate adults. *Journal of the National Chung-Cheng University*, 7, 29–47.

Lee, J. R. (1997). Phonological awareness and Chinese character acquisition in Taiwan dyslexic children: reading ability control design research. Paper presented at the International Symposium on Cognitive Processes of the Chinese Language. University of Hong Kong, September 1997.

Leong, C. K. (1997). Paradigmatic analysis of Chinese word reading: research findings and classroom practices. In C. K. Leong and R. Malatesha Joshi (eds.), *Applied Research in Reading and Spelling in Different Languages*. Dordrecht, Netherlands: Kluwer.

Li, H. T. (1977). *The History of Chinese Characters*. Taipei, Taiwan: Lian-Jian.

Lien, Y. W. (1985). *Consistency of the Phonetic Cues in the Chinese Phonograms and their Naming Latencies*. Taipei, Taiwan: National Taiwan University.

McBride-Chang, C. and Chang, L. (1995). Memory, print exposure and metacognition: components of reading in Chinese children. *International Journal of Psychology*, 30, 607–16.

Maclean, M., Bryant, P. and Bradley, L. (1987). Rhymes, nursery rhymes, and reading in early childhood. *Merrill Palmer Quarterly*, 33, 255–81.

Mann, V. A. (1986). Longitudinal prediction and prevention of early reading difficulty. *Annals of Dyslexia*, 24, 117–36.

Morais, J., Cluytens, M. and Alegria, J. (1984). Segmentation abilities of dyslexics and normal readers. *Perceptual and Motor Skills*, 58, 221–2.

Perfetti, C. A., Beck, I., Bell, L. C. and Hughes, C. (1987). Phonemic knowledge and learning to read are reciprocal: a longitudinal study of first grade children. Special issue: Children's reading and the development of phonological awareness. *Merrill Palmer Quarterly*, 33, 283–319.

Rack, J. P., Snowling, M. J. and Olson, R. K. (1992). The non-word reading deficit in dyslexia: a review. *Reading Research Quarterly*, 27, 29–53.

Read, C., Zhang, Y., Nie, H. and Ding, B. (1986). The ability to manipulate speech sounds depends on knowing alphabetic writing. *Cognition*. 24, 31–45.

Rozin, P., Poritsky, S. and Sotsky, R. (1971). American children with reading problems can easily learn to read English represented in Chinese characters. *Science*, 171, 1264–7.

Share, D. (1995). Phonological recoding and self-teaching. *Cognition*, 55, 151–218.

Snowling, M. J. (1995). Phonological processing and developmental dyslexia. *Journal of Research in Reading*, 18, 132–8.

So, D. and Siegel, L. S. (1997). Learning to read Chinese: semantic, syntactic, phonological and working memory skills in normally achieving and poor Chinese readers. *Reading and Writing*, 9, 1–21.

Stevenson, H. W., Stigler, J. W., Lucker, G. W., Lee, S., Hsu, C. and Kitamura, S. (1982). Reading disabilities: the case of Chinese, Japanese, and English. *Child Development*, 53, 1164–81.

Taraban, R. and McClelland, J. L. (1987). Conspiracy effect in word pronunciation. *Journal of Memory and Language*, 26, 608–31.

Treiman, R. (1985). Onsets and rimes as units of spoken syllables: evidence from children. *Journal of Experimental Child Psychology*, 39, 161–81.

Tunmer, W. E. and Nesdale, A. R. (1985). Phonemic segmentation skill and beginning reading. *Journal of Educational Psychology*, 77, 417–27.

Tzeng, O. J. L., Zhong, H. L., Hung, D. L. and Lee, W. L. (1995). Learning to be a conspirator: a tale of becoming a good Chinese reader. In B. de Gelder and J. Morais (eds.), *Speech and Reading: A Comparative Approach*. Hove, UK: Erlbaum.

Tzeng, O. J. L., Hung, D. L. and Wang, W. (1977). Speech recoding in reading Chinese characters. *Journal of Experimental Psychology: Human Learning and Memory*, 3, 621–30.

Wagner, R. K. and Torgesen, J. K. (1987). The nature of phonological processing and its causal role in the acquisition of reading skills. *Psychological Bulletin*, 101, 192–212.

Wang, W. S.-Y. (1973). The Chinese language. *Scientific American*, 228, 50–63.

Wimmer, H., Landerl, K., Linortner, R. and Hummer, P. (1991). The relationship of phonemic awareness to reading acquisition: more consequence than precondition but still important. *Cognition*, 40, 219–49.

Zhou, Y. G. (1978). To what extent are the 'phonetics' of present-day Chinese characters still phonetic. *Zhongguo Yuwen*, 146, 172–7.

11 Reading skill development in bilingual Singaporean children

Susan Rickard Liow

This chapter begins with a description of the main spoken and written languages used in Singapore. Local research on the reading skills in English of Mandarin-English- and Malay-English-speaking children is then reviewed with reference to stage theories and cognitive models for unilingual English-speaking children. Emphasis is given to writing script compatibility and L2 to L1 strategy transfer (see below), oral language foundations, phonological awareness, visual analytic strategies, and the nature of reading difficulties.

Spoken and written languages in Singapore

The ethnic composition of Singapore's three million population is 77 per cent Chinese, 15 per cent Malay, 6 per cent Indian and 2 per cent others, and over thirty different languages are in use (Pakir, 1988). Multi-lingualism is the norm for adults, but only four languages have official status. For historical reasons *Bahasa Melayu* remains the national language, *English* is now the main medium for instruction and commerce, *Mandarin* is the unifying script for the many different oral Chinese groups,[1] and *Tamil* is the most widely used Indian language. The Ministry of Education's bilingual policy now requires that all children from primary 1 (rising seven years) learn English as their first language (L1) and one of the other three official languages as a mother tongue or second language (L2) in school. Thus English has steadily become the most important language for children's literacy skills although it often remains their second or third language for oral communication.

Singapore children's skills in English have been compared to those of unilinguals in terms of overall levels of literacy (Moore, 1982), reading accuracy and comprehension (Ng, 1984), and developmental aspects of writing (Foley, 1991). However, the republic's linguistic diversity also provides an unusual opportunity to observe biscriptal children learning to read and write in English when their L2 scripts are maximally contrasted. This is the case for English-Mandarin- and English-Bahasa Melayu-speaking children, the two largest groups in Singapore primary schools.

English is a deep alphabetic script. Although much of the phonology can still be predicted from the orthography, there are no simple rules that can be applied infallibly. All Singaporean children, whatever their oral language background, start learning to read English from five years of age (or earlier), and they are mostly taught the look–say method. This involves pairing the word's meaning with its visual representation for reading, whilst for spelling letter name sequences are learned by rote. In predominantly unilingual English settings, such as the UK, the look–say method is rare; its popularity in Singapore seems to be a legacy of the traditional Chinese pedagogical methods originally designed for learning logographic scripts.

Mandarin is usually written in a deep, logographic script which is not very amenable to analytic decoding either in terms of phonemes or tones (see Hanley *et al.*, this volume; Rickard Liow, Tng and Lee, 1999). High-frequency Chinese characters are learned using a look–say method in kindergarten from the age of five years (or earlier), and in school they are taught in a prescribed order according to school level. This means that local age-of-acquisition norms for characters are easy to collate and tests to assess reading and spelling ages are reliable and easy to devise (e.g. Rickard Liow and Tng, 1992c). Hanyu Pinyin, the romanised version of Mandarin, is a very shallow alphabetic script with the four tones denoted by diacritics or Arabic numerals (1 to 4), e.g. shi(4). Although Hanyu Pinyin is a very shallow alphabetic script, many of the grapheme–phoneme correspondences are different from those in English, e.g. *q* corresponds to *ch* in *church*, and transcriptions are based on the standard Beijing pronunciation, not Singaporean Colloquial Mandarin (SCM). Perhaps for these reasons, Hanyu Pinyin is introduced into the Singapore curriculum later than in China or Taiwan, and its use is discouraged except for dictionary work. As a result, it seems that the Mandarin-English-speaking child's opportunity to develop better phonological awareness through exposure to Hanyu Pinyin (see Hanley *et al.*, this volume; Read, Zhang, Nie and Ding, 1986 on readers from China), may come too late to support alphabetic decoding skills in English in the way that exposure to Bahasa Melayu helps the Malay-English-speaking child.

Bahasa Melayu is used widely in neighbouring Malaysia and the informal version is understood by a large proportion of Singapore's adults. Like Hanyu Pinyin, but unlike Chinese characters, the orthography is alphabetic and very shallow. With the exception of 'x', all the graphemes of English are used, but their phoneme correspondences are not always the same; e.g. in Bahasa Melayu the 'ch' phoneme in the English word 'church' would be written 'c'. The letter 'e' is solely responsible for minor irregularities because it is the only grapheme in Bahasa Melayu that is pronounced in two different ways. Given the shallow nature of the script, it is not surprising that the regular grapheme–phoneme correspondences are explicitly taught as part of the Bahasa Melayu curriculum, and a phonic strategy is encouraged for reading and spelling.

Mandarin-English-speaking children learn to read and write in a deep alphabetic script (English) and a deep logographic script (Mandarin) well before they are exposed to a shallow alphabetic script (Hanyu Pinyin). In sharp contrast, the Malay-English-speaking children learn to read and write in a deep alphabetic script (English) alongside a shallow alphabetic script (Bahasa Melayu) which is usually a strong mother tongue. The contrasting nature of the Mandarin and Malay scripts and the different teaching practices for the respective L2 classes, have created a natural experiment in strategy transfer to the children's L1 (English).

Teachers in primary schools have long been aware of differences in literacy skills between Mandarin-English and Malay-English children, but until recently there has been relatively little empirical work to support their observations. To facilitate clinical assessment of children with reading and spelling difficulties, and to overcome some of the methodological problems common in bilingual research, Tng Siok Keng and I translated and re-normed some of the standardised UK tests before testing for qualitative and quantitative differences between the two subgroups. These tests included the British Picture Vocabulary Scale (BPVS), the Schonell Graded Word Reading and Spelling, and some sub-tests of the British Ability Scales (BAS), (see Rickard Liow, Hong and Tng, 1992; Rickard Liow and Tng, 1992a; Rickard Liow and Tng, 1992b respectively). We also collected self-report information on oral and written language skills; children as young as six years are able to rank-order their best language, next best language, etc. with adult help (see Rickard Liow and Poon, 1998, for sample questionnaire).

Fortunately, at least for research on L2 (Mandarin/Malay) to L1 (English) strategy transfer, the school curriculum is uniform across Singapore whatever language background a child belongs to. This uniformity means that the development of reading skills in English is probably a function of the relationship between the two scripts being taught to different sub-groups of children. Although the Bahasa Melayu script is more regular than English and the grapheme–phoneme correspondences are not identical, children learning Bahasa Melayu as their L2 in school would be more likely than the Mandarin L2 learners to develop the kind of alphabetic phonological awareness that is considered fundamental for English literacy acquisition. Much of what now follows is a summary of the research which has tested these predictions about L2 to L1 strategy transfer in different bilingual groups.

Using unilingual cognitive models of reading in English as a framework, I will first characterise English literacy acquisition by these two groups of bilingual biscriptal children. Cognitive models of the development of reading have evolved from theories of skilled reading, notably the dual route model,[2] e.g. Morton and Patterson (1987), Coltheart, Curtis, Atkins and Haller (1993). As its name suggests, the dual route model postulates two different mechanisms underlying the conversion of print to speech: direct visual access to lexical entries, and indirect phonological processing which can be carried out non-lexically. These models are concerned with reading an alphabetic script and so phonological awareness receives more attention than the kind of visual analytic skills that seem appropriate for logographic scripts.

Modelling the development of reading skills (as opposed to skilled reading) is complicated because quantitative and qualitative changes in processing must be accounted for. A popular way of conceptualising such changes is to invoke discrete stages in literacy acquisition with different emphases because the two routes develop separately. Frith (1985), for example, proposed a stage model of spelling and reading which is sequential and comprises (in order) a logographic stage, an alphabetic stage and an orthographic stage. At the logographic stage, the child reads and spells by pairing a visual representation of the word with its meaning. Spelling development lags behind reading development at the logographic stage, but during the alphabetic stage, the child learns the two-way relationship between graphemes and phonemes, and spelling skills then enhance reading skills. Frith's final phase of literacy development is called the orthographic stage when the child has learned higher-order spelling patterns, and (again) the literacy processes are not simply phonological.

Literacy development is known to be affected by phonological awareness and script exposure (Read et al., 1986; Morais, Cary, Alegria and Bertelson, 1979), so there are several reasons why the development of reading and spelling in English among Mandarin-English children might be different from that of unilingual uniscriptal English-speaking children and also from Malay-English bilingual children. First, the Mandarin-English children are bilingual and sometimes have weaker oral English proficiency than unilinguals. This alone could affect their ability to develop phonological awareness (Mann, 1986), but since the Malay-English-speaking children may also have weaker oral English, the most important difference between the two bilingual groups is likely to be the extent of their phonemic awareness. Note that knowledge of grapheme–phoneme rules can be explicitly taught or implicitly acquired through exposure to a shallow L2 script.

Like the pupils in Seymour and Elder's (1986) study, Mandarin-English-speaking children are not usually exposed to the phonic approach that is typical of 95 per cent of UK schools (HMI Report, 1990) and there is no reason to expect that maturation alone will sufficiently enhance phonological awareness in English (see Bentin, Hammer and Cahan, 1991). Instead, these children are exposed to the logographic script of their L2 in school. This would be more likely to enhance whole-word look–say strategies and direct route reading than non-lexical phono-logical processing, thereby prolonging (or favouring) Frith's logographic stage for English reading indefinitely. In fact, Holm and Dodd (1996) showed that Chinese-English-speaking undergraduates from Hong Kong have limited phonological awareness but their extensive logographic processing allows them to become relatively skilled readers of English words (but not non-words).

In contrast to the Mandarin-English children, the Malay-English children are exposed to the shallow Bahasa Melayu script and learning to read this L2 in school does involve explicit training in grapheme–phoneme correspondences. Although some of the correspondences are different, this is likely to enhance phonemic awareness in English and facilitate an early shift to non-lexical alphabetic processing, thus making the logographic stage either redundant or very short-lived (see Wimmer and Goswami's (1994) work comparing German and English-speaking children).

These differences in phonological awareness suggest that Frith's three-stage model may not account for reading skill development in many bilingual children. In Singapore, and elsewhere, Seymour's (1990) Dual Foundation theory of reading development seems better able to accom-modate the differences which arise as a result of children's varying language backgrounds. Although Seymour also distinguishes logographic, alphabetic and orthographic processes, his theory is not a single-stage, single-sequence account. Seymour and Evans (1994) claim that a logo-graphic processor and an alphabetic processor can emerge in parallel, but together they provide a foundation for the orthographic processor. So far, the research in Singapore (described below) seems to support a dual foundation model with different emphases between the two pro-cessors for our children: the Mandarin-English children seem to rely more heavily on the logographic processor, whereas the Malay-English children seem to rely more heavily on the phonological processor. The evidence supporting these two hypotheses comes from three main areas: the bilingual children's oral language foundations, their phonological awareness and their visual analytic skills.

Oral language foundations

Amongst young unilingual English-speaking children, the importance of metalinguistic awareness for literacy skill development has been widely recognised, e.g. Mann (1986), Mann and Brady (1988), Chaney (1992). Also, Hatcher, Hulme and Ellis (1995) showed that phonological skills need to be taught in the context of spoken language not just print exposure. Taken together these studies suggest that some Chinese-English-speaking children might find reading and spelling in an alphabetic script rather difficult given their limited exposure to Standard English and no explicit phonemic awareness training. They are likely to adopt visual (logographic) strategies for an extended period because such processing does not rely on a good auditory vocabulary, nor on an understanding of the relationship between spoken and written forms. Eventually, with an enhanced vocabulary in English, and more exposure to an alphabetic script, their metalinguistic (phonological) awareness in English might make an alphabetic stage more feasible.[3]

There are two lines of evidence suggesting that Chinese-English-speaking children find learning to read English difficult as a result of weak oral language foundations. First, Wong and Underwood (1996) compared English word list reading and prose reading of eleven-year-old Singaporean children classified as either English dominant or English non-dominant bilinguals. Their results showed that the cues in the prose passages were more important to the English non-dominant group, i.e. the less proficient readers, with more limited exposure to oral English, who relied more on context to compensate for weaker decoding skills.

Although Wong and Underwood report that the English non-dominant group were not poor readers of their other school language, they do not make a distinction between the different L2 sub-groups. Rickard Liow, Mok and Tng (1998), however, used structural equation modelling to look at lexical and non-lexical influences on Schonell reading and spelling performance for 284 pupils (aged six to nine years) from three different language backgrounds: English-Chinese ($N = 86$), Chinese-English ($N = 136$) and Malay-English ($N = 62$). The latent variable for lexical influences comprised school examination marks and BPVS raw scores in English, and for non-lexical influences we used the results of non-word reading and spelling tests. The fit indices for each sub-group were good (ranging from 0.97 to 0.99), but the coefficients for the

Malay-English children were rather different from the other two sub-groups. Non-lexical skills were relatively strong predictors of reading and spelling for the Chinese-English and English-Chinese children (who supposedly had poor phonological skills), but for the Malay-English-speaking children, whose phonological awareness was well developed, lexical influences seemed to enhance literacy skills. At first these results seem counter-intuitive but clearly a balance between the two strategies (visual and phonological processing) would optimise Schonell scores since the test is a mixture of regular and exception words.

The second line of evidence concerning the effect of weak oral language skills in some bilinguals comes from a recent evaluation study I conducted for the Dyslexia Association of Singapore (DAS) (Rickard Liow, 1997). Most of the DAS pupils are Chinese-English (some English-Chinese and a few Malay-English). The remedial programmes are conducted in English and the Neale Analysis of Reading Ability (NARA) (Neale, 1989) has been used as a test-retest measure because it has parallel forms, and provides a reading age for accuracy and comprehension.[4] If NARA comprehension does not improve as fast as NARA accuracy, this suggests the child has poor oral English skills (auditory comprehension of vocabulary and syntax) which limit progress in reading comprehension. About 80 per cent of the 85 pupils who had been tested and retested at an interval of six months or more, had made some progress for reading comprehension, but 93 per cent showed gains for reading accuracy. For example, after a year in a remedial programme, one Mandarin-English-speaking boy, aged 10;3, had made a gain of over two years (from 5;7 to 7;9) for reading accuracy but his reading comprehension score remained unchanged at 6;1. This kind of discrepancy may be common for a sub-set of unilingual as well as bilingual pupils exposed to phonic-based training but, as expected, limited oral language exposure may have made reading accuracy easier to improve than reading comprehension in English.

Phonological awareness

It seems, then, that there are several types of readers in the Singapore school population. Although children from predominantly English-speaking families might be similar to unilinguals in that they develop a balance of Seymour's visual and phonological processing skills, especially if they are given some form of phonemic awareness training in private tuition sessions, children from Mandarin- or Malay-speaking families might be more likely to correspond to Baron and Strawson's (1976) 'Chinese' and 'Phoenician' groups respectively. Mandarin-English-speaking children with limited exposure both to English vocabulary and alphabetic scripts, might be expected to adopt 'Chinese' word-specific (look–say) strategies of the kind they would be encouraged to use for logographs in their L2 lessons, whilst the Malay-English-speaking children would be more likely to adopt 'Phoenician' rule-based (phonic) strategies, irrespective of their oral vocabulary in English because they have been exposed to phonemic awareness training in their shallow L2 script.

Whether or not a sequence of stages is postulated, phonological aware-ness is considered an important factor for normal reading and spelling in alphabetic scripts (see Goswami, this volume; Wagner and Torgesen, 1987). An awareness of phonemes seems especially important for en-coding (in spelling) and decoding (in reading) new and unfamiliar words. Moreover, as Bradley and Bryant (1985) demonstrated, interventions involving phonemic awareness training are more likely to enhance read-ing skill development and have lasting effects. Despite this accumulat-ing literature on the advantages of phonemic awareness training, most children in Singapore are still taught to use a whole-word method for English so the role of phonological awareness in English reading varies according to the language background of the child. Private tuition, often using rather rigid phonic methods, is becoming more common, but many experienced teachers consider explicit grapheme–phoneme training is inappropriate for English literacy skills because the script is irregular and many bilingual children have weaker oral skills than their unilingual counterparts.

Ho (1993) examined the strategies of groups of young bilingual biscriptal readers in Singapore to test whether phonological awareness actually is less important for Singapore pupils. She looked at the per-formance of forty nine-year-old English-Mandarin-speaking children matched for non-verbal skills (BAS matrices) and vocabulary (multi-lingual BPVS), but divided into four groups using local norms for the BAS reading test: Good English/Good Chinese (GEGC), Good Eng-lish/Poor Chinese (GEPC), Poor English/Good Chinese (PEGC) and Poor English/Poor Chinese (PEPC). Ho's battery of tests, which were adapted to take account of the Singapore Colloquial English/Standard English differences, included reading and spelling of different types of words and non-words (Rickard Liow and Tng's (1992d) list of regular consistent, regular inconsistent and exception words with matched non-words), as well as phonological awareness tasks (Goswami and Bryant's (1990) alliteration and rhyme oddity, phoneme deletion, and phoneme detection tests). Ho's results showed that although most of the children had acquired basic levels of phonological awareness, all four groups were relying on visual strategies in reading. However, consistent with

Barron (1980), the good readers of English (GEGC, GEPC) were using a phonological approach significantly more often on the reading tests; the poorer readers could identify intra-syllabic units but were unable to isolate and manipulate single phonemes on the phonological awareness tasks.

Most of the literature on the importance of phonological awareness for literacy development has been concerned with alphabetic reading and spelling, but Rickard Liow and Poon (1998) compared skills in English and Mandarin across three groups of Singaporean children with different language backgrounds: English, Chinese (Mandarin/other Chinese languages), or Bahasa Indonesia. (Bahasa Indonesia is similar to Bahasa Melayu at the level of orthography and phonology though some lexical items are different.) The three groups were all studying English (as L1) and Mandarin (as L2) in the same school, so the influence of their script exposure could be seen in the absence of differences in teaching strategies. In English, the results of a homophone decision task (adapted from Kay, Lesser and Coltheart, 1992), and a lexicality spelling test comprising regular words, exception words and non-words (Rickard Liow and Tng, 1992d), showed that a relationship between script exposure and phonological awareness develops in line with orthographic depth: the Bahasa Indonesia group exhibited the highest levels of alphabetic phonological awareness, followed by the English group, and then the Chinese group. Hitherto tonal phonological awareness has been considered analogous to alphabetic phonological awareness (Chen and Yuen, 1991). However, on the Mandarin Hanyu Pinyin spelling test, the performance for tone transcription was equivalent across groups, suggesting that alphabetic and tonal phonological awareness develop independently. These findings extend Holm and Dodd's (1996) work on adult Cantonese-English readers, and support the view that language background can influence strategies for the subsequent acquisition of second (and third) written languages as a result of differences in phonological awareness.

If a lack of alphabetic phonological awareness negatively affects English literacy development in biscriptals, as it does in unilingual English-speaking children, a large number of Mandarin-English-speaking children in Singapore ought to be experiencing specific difficulties with reading and spelling in English. As far as local teachers and researchers can ascertain,[5] the incidence of dyslexia is within the international range of 3 per cent to 6 per cent, suggesting that 'Chinese' readers are either compensating by relying on enhanced (or different) visual analytic skills, or spending extra time acquiring basic levels of literacy by rote.

Visual analytic skills

Recent experimental evidence on orthographic neighbour effects and visual search strategies suggests that there might be differences in visual analytic skills across the different groups of biscriptal readers in Singapore. First, the orthographic neighbour effects. Rickard Liow and Masterson (1995) investigated the underlying cognitive processes which differentiate good from poor alphabetic-logographic biscriptal readers by looking at reading accuracy (in English) of forty English-Chinese bilingual children aged eleven years. Three variables were investigated: the subject's relative L1/L2 reading proficiency (Good English/Good Chinese, Good English/Poor Chinese, Poor English/Good Chinese, and Poor English/Poor Chinese); word type (regular consistent vs. exception); and word neighbourhood count (high neighbourhood count vs. low neighbourhood count). All main effects were significant, but low neighbourhood words were read more accurately by all four biscriptal groups. This finding contrasts sharply with previous accounts of neighbourhood effects (high neighbourhood > low neighbourhood) for unilingual English-speaking children, and suggests that a visual discriminability factor (i.e. few, rather than many, orthographic neighbours) is salient for biscriptal Chinese-English and English-Chinese children (even) when they are reading English.

The second kind of research on visual analytic skills uses the visual search paradigm to look at an early stage in processing. An upward-sloping M-shaped function (reaction time by target position) characterises the letter search strategy for skilled (unilingual) readers of English but a U-shaped function describes the search for non-alphabetic stimuli (Mason, 1982). Less skilled unilingual readers (young children) of English, and skilled readers of logographic scripts, do not show this difference across stimuli; they employ U-shaped strategies for all targets (Green, Hammond and Supramaniam, 1983; Green and Meara, 1987).

Taken together these results suggest that visual search functions reflect important aspects of reading skill acquisition that might differ across the Malay-English (bi-alphabetic) and Mandarin-English (logographic-alphabetic) readers. As children develop reading skills, any change of strategy is likely to reflect progress towards optimal search functions for particular kinds of writing scripts. For adult skilled readers, Rickard Liow, Green and Lokanathan (1995) showed that Chinese-English biscriptals, whose L1 is logographic, show search functions that are different from English-Chinese biscriptals, whose L1 is alphabetic, i.e. search functions depend on text experience. In a study of adolescents,

Rickard Liow, Green and Tam (in press) investigated strategy development in these two kinds of biscriptals. We predicted that limited exposure to an alphabetic script in English is related to reduced end-effect in readers' visual search functions, i.e. that the Malay-English pupils would show stronger M-shaped trends with letters than the Chinese-English pupils. This proved to be the case: for letter search, the clearest M-shaped trends emerged for the Malay-English pupils, suggesting that L1 to L2 transfer effects can occur at an early stage in script processing.

Chinese-English biscriptals eventually acquire the clear M-shape for letters and the U-shape for characters (Green, Rickard Liow, Tng and Zielinski, 1996), but there appear to be stages of development before the two strategies are clearly separable. The most important finding with respect to English proficiency is that it does appear to influence the letter search functions of the Chinese-English pupils much more than those of the Malay-English. This is in keeping with Brown and Haynes' (1985) suggestion that knowledge of script-specific processes could be important in second-language learning, and that the extent to which the scripts of a reader's first and second languages (L1 and L2) differ might have implications for reading progress in the L2. When the second script (L2) requires totally different component skills (e.g. Mandarin-English and English-Mandarin), the reader would have to learn these from first principles. The reading process would then be slowed down, and the child's ability to engage in higher-level activities involving word meaning and sentence comprehension would be adversely affected. Alternatively, the highly automated skills from the L1 could interfere with the acquisition of the new skills required by the L2, leading to non-optimal strategies. When the two languages are similar (Malay-English and English-Malay) L2 skills will facilitate reading accuracy (for regular words) in the L1, whilst reading comprehension will necessarily depend on the child's oral language foundation.

For *written word* recognition, the development of letter position effects towards an M-shaped search function is not addressed in current theories of skilled reading or reading skill development. For example, Coltheart *et al.* (1993) assume linear left-to-right processing for the non-lexical route of their Dual Route Cascaded (DRC) skilled reading model, and the alphabetic stage of Frith's (1985) model of reading skill development does not specify any end-advantage for the grapheme–phoneme translations typical of the alphabetic stage. By contrast, for *spoken word* recognition in English, Cole and Jakimik (1980) have argued that sounds at the beginnings and ends of words are more salient than those in other (central) syllables. The initial phonemes are thought to be used to access candidates from the lexicon (which are also constrained by context), whilst only the final phonemes will allow the hearer to eliminate, with confidence, all candidates but one.

The end-effect observed in letter visual search tasks suggests there may be parallels between written and spoken word recognition beyond the fact that the ends mark word boundaries and give information about length. The extent to which written word recognition depends on spoken word processes is unclear, but the relationship might be stronger, or perhaps it develops more readily, in speakers with experience of reading shallow scripts and/or those exposed to phonemic awareness training. Whatever the nature of the relationship between reading skill acquisition and visual search, it seems reasonable to expect that reader-specific differences are related to script exposure and oral language proficiency. Hence the various language sub-groups in Singapore might be relying on different processing strategies, rather than a balance between skills more typical of unilinguals (cf Seymour, 1990). Some strategies will prove non-optimal and may result in reading difficulties.

Reading difficulties in bilingual biscriptal children

In a systematic study of fifty-six unilingual children, Castles and Coltheart (1993) showed that two different varieties of developmental dyslexia are common. In terms of cognitive models, the children's difficulties were specific to either lexical (visual) processes or to non-lexical (phonological) processes. When reading and writing in English, problems with phonological processing manifest themselves as an inability to make use of the relationship between orthography and phonology. Children with such problems often resort to rote-learning strategies. Their reading of single unfamiliar words and simple non-words is thus poor, and their text processing relies heavily on context-informed guesses.

When reading and spelling in Chinese, a large amount of rote learning is obligatory because the relationship between orthography and phonology is less predictable. These contrasting orthographic demands led us (Rickard Liow and Tng, 1994) to investigate phonological problems in Singaporean bilingual biscriptals. Unlike Stevenson (1984), we were not interested in overall skill levels, except to demonstrate that LJY was experiencing severe difficulties with reading and spelling.

Case study of dyslexia: LJY

This case study illustrates how strategies appropriate for the logographic L1 script (Mandarin) transfer for L2 (English) processing in the absence of efficient (alphabetic) strategies.

LJY, a Chinese (Mandarin/Hokkien)-English-speaking boy, was twelve years ten months when we tested him in school at the request of the principal. His reading and writing of Chinese characters was average for his age, but he was identified as one of the poorest readers of English in his cohort: Schonell reading age of 8;6 (i.e. four years four months below his chronological age on UK norms). We ruled out the possibility of limited exposure to English for LJY's reading problems using the British Picture Vocabulary Scale: LJY's age-equivalent score was 11;10 (UK norms), and his intellectual functioning was well within the average range on the British Ability Scales (UK norms): verbal IQ = 98–106, visual IQ = 110–118. As expected, his lowest percentile score on the BAS was for word reading (fifth percentile).

We then assessed LJY on a series of diagnostic reading and spelling tests, which included regular and irregular words (similar to those used by Castles and Coltheart 1993), and simple non-words (such as 'hile', 'nain'). In reading aloud, LJY did not show the usual advantage for regular words and he found the non-words almost impossible; his errors were mostly real words. In spelling, he showed a slight advantage for irregular words, and could only produce sounds for 10/24 letters. Given that this pattern of performance was also apparent on Coltheart's (1980) tests of silent phonology, it seemed that LJY was reading, albeit poorly, without the benefit of phonological awareness.

The nature of his responses during oral reading tasks in English also suggested that he was depending heavily on a direct lexical-semantic route which would be more appropriate for Chinese characters. LJY read thirty-six out of a hundred Schonell words correctly and three words incorrectly. He refused to read aloud the remaining sixty-one words, but he was prepared to give brief definitions which often confirmed approximate semantic access. These definitions included words well above his measured reading level, e.g. *antique* → 'something don't have; it is very special', *choir* → 'group of people playing instruments', *genuine* → 'really things', *audience* → 'like someone watching a football match', *sabre* → 'like a sword'.

LJY's reading difficulty would be termed phonological dyslexia in unilingual English-speaking children (see Temple and Marshall, 1983). If a Chinese-English bilingual child is faced with learning two different scripts whose processing demands (optimal strategies) are different, certain kinds of reading problems may be more common. We reasoned that a kind of phonological dyslexia might be common amongst Chinese-English readers but without careful assessment their difficulties might not be obvious because enhanced (visual) logographic strategies could

compensate, albeit inefficiently, for failure to acquire alphabetic processing skills.

This case study draws attention to a number of issues relevant to
educational practice: how should a biscriptal child be taught two different scripts whose optimal strategies are so different? What negative (or
positive) transfer effects might accrue for either script? Do some biscriptal
children adopt inefficient strategies when they are learning to read? Do
reading problems in one script necessarily manifest themselves in the
other script? For LJY, some of the reading difficulties could well be
attributable to the incompatibility of the two writing scripts for skill
transfer from L1 to L2. His lack of phonological awareness seems to
have led him to apply a logographic strategy to an alphabetic script. In
Chinese, his reading skill remained average throughout primary school,
but by primary 6 his abilities in English proved inadequate.

Conclusion

In this chapter I have focused on the empirical work that has been
carried out on reading skill development in Singapore, but new work on
models of spelling skill development in bilinguals is showing comparable
results (Poon and Rickard Liow, 1998). Much of this research raises
more questions than it answers but resolving some of the theoretical
issues will have important implications for classroom practices. Although
the linguistic diversity of the country's school population raises a number
of methodological problems, the data gathered (so far) suggest that
stage models of alphabetic *unilingual reading*, based on English-speaking
children living in the UK, cannot account for reading skill development
in Singapore children. Models of *bilingual reading* development must
accommodate the importance of the child's pre-literate language proficiencies and their influence on subsequent written language processing, and models of *bilingual biscriptal reading* development must take
account of the relationship between the two scripts, and the likelihood
of strategy transfer.

NOTES

Much of the research reported in this chapter was funded by the National
University of Singapore and the Shaw Foundation. I am particularly indebted
to the pupils and teachers of Ghim Moh Primary School, and to Olivia Wee
May Ling for her help with the manuscript.

1 The term 'Chinese' is used for ethnicity and writing script, whereas 'Mandarin' refers to a particular spoken form of the Chinese language.

2 This is the modular approach but see Seidenberg and McClelland (1989) and Brown and Watson (1991) for connectionist accounts of normal and abnormal reading development.

3 For both groups of bilingual children, there are differences between the L1 (English) and the L2 (Mandarin/Bahasa Melayu) taught in school and that used at home. Singapore Colloquial English, rather than Standard English, is spoken widely by both groups; Mandarin-English-speaking children use Singapore Colloquial Mandarin, as well as other Chinese languages, such as Cantonese and Hokkien at home, whilst most Malay-English-speaking children use the informal version of Bahasa Melayu at home, not the formal version used in school. Thus for all three languages the relationship between the child's spoken and written versions is weakened.

4 Unfortunately the NARA has not yet been standardised and normed for local bilingual pupils, but given that the purpose of the evaluation was to look at relative change in reading age scores over a specified time period, rather than absolute scores, the data proved useful.

5 In unilingual populations consensus about dyslexia is hard to come by, and in bilingual populations oral language proficiencies further complicate the assessment procedure.

REFERENCES

Baron, J. and Strawson, C. (1976). Use of orthographic and word-specific knowledge in reading words aloud. *Journal of Experimental Psychology: Human Perception and Performance*, 2 (3), 386–93.

Barron, R. (1980). Visual and phonological strategies in reading and writing. In U. Frith (ed.), *Cognitive Processes in Spelling* (pp. 195–213). London: Academic Press.

Bentin, S., Hammer, R. and Cahan, S. (1991). The effects of ageing and first grade schooling on the development of phonological awareness. *Psychological Science*, 2, 271–4.

Bradley, L. and Bryant, P. (1985). *Rhyme and Reason in Reading and Spelling*. Ann Arbor: University of Michigan Press.

Brown, T. L. and Haynes, M. (1985). Literacy background and reading development in a second language. In T. H. Carr (ed.), *The Development of Reading Skills. New Directions for Child Development*, no. 27 (pp. 19–34). San Francisco: Jossey-Bass.

Brown, G. D. A. and Watson, F. L. (1991). Reading development in dyslexia: a connectionist approach. In M. J. Snowling and D. Thomson (eds.), *Dyslexia: Integrating Theory and Practice* (pp. 165–82). London: Whurr.

Castles, A. and Coltheart, M. (1993). Varieties of developmental dyslexia. *Cognition*, 47 (2), 149–80.

Chaney, C. (1992). Language development, metalinguistic skills, and print awareness in 3-year-old children. *Applied Psycholinguistics*, 13, 485–514.

Chen, M. J. and Yuen, J. C. K. (1991). Effects of Pinyin and script type on verbal processing: comparisons of China, Taiwan and Hong Kong experience. *International Journal of Behavioral Development*, 14, 429–48.

Cole, R. A. and Jakimik, J. (1980). A model of speech perception. In R. A. Cole (ed.), *Perception and Production of Fluent Speech* (pp. 133–63). Hillsdale, NJ: Lawrence Erlbaum Associates.

Coltheart, M. (1980). Analysing acquired disorders of reading. Unpublished manuscript, Birkbeck College, University of London.

Coltheart, M., Curtis, B., Atkins, P. and Haller, M. (1993). Models of reading aloud: dual-route and parallel-distributed processing approaches. *Psychological Review*, 100 (4), 589–608.

Foley, J. (1991). Developmental features of children's writing in Singapore. In A. Kwan-Terry (ed.), *Child Language Development in Singapore and Malaysia*. Singapore: Singapore University Press.

Frith, U. (1985). Beneath the surface of developmental dyslexia: are comparisons between developmental and acquired disorders meaningful? In K. Patterson, J. C. Marshall and M. Coltheart (eds.), *Surface Dyslexia: Cognitive and Neuro-Psychological Studies of Phonological Reading*. London: Lawrence Erlbaum Associates.

Goswami, U. (1988). Orthographic analogies and reading development. *Quarterly Journal of Experimental Psychology*, 40A (2), 239–68.

Goswami, U. and Bryant, P. E. (1990). *Phonological Skills and Learning to Read*. London: Lawrence Erlbaum.

Green, D. W. and Meara, P. (1987). The effects of script on visual search. *Second Language Research*, 3, 102–17.

Green, D. W., Hammond, E. J. and Supramaniam, S. (1983). Letters and shapes: developmental changes in search strategies. *British Journal of Psychology*, 74, 11–16.

Green, D. W., Rickard Liow, S. J., Tng, S. K. and Zielinski, S. (1996). Are visual search procedures adapted to the nature of the script? *British Journal of Psychology*, 87 (2), 311–26.

Hatcher, P. J., Hulme, C. and Ellis, A. W. (1995). Helping to overcome early reading failure by combining the teaching of reading and phonological skills. In E. Funnell and M. Stuart (eds.), *Learning to Read* (pp. 130–60). Oxford, UK: Blackwell Publishers Ltd.

HMI Report (1990). *The Teaching and Learning of Reading: Qualities and Standards*. HMSO, London: Department of Education and Science.

Ho, L.-K. P. (1993). Phonological awareness in English-Chinese bilingual children. Academic exercise, Department of Social Work and Psychology, National University of Singapore.

Holm, A. and Dodd, B. (1996). The effect of first written language on the acquisition of English literacy. *Cognition*, 59, 119–47.

Kay, J., Lesser, R. and Coltheart, M. (1992). Psycholinguistic assessment of language processing in aphasia (PALPA). Hove, UK: Lawrence Erlbaum.

Mann, V. A. (1986). Phonological awareness: the role of reading experience. *Cognition*, 24, 65–92.

Mann, V. A. and Brady, S. (1988). Reading disability: the role of language deficiencies. *Journal of Consulting and Clinical Psychology*, 56 (6), 811–16.

Mason, M. (1982). Recognition time for letters and non-letters: effects of serial position, array size and processing order. *Journal of Experimental Psychology: Human Perception and Performance*, 8, 724–38.

Moore, B. J. (1982). English reading skills of multilingual pupils in Singapore. *The Reading Teacher*, March, 696–701.

Morais, J., Cary, L., Alegria, J. and Bertelson, P. (1979). Does awareness of speech as a sequence of phones arise spontaneously? *Cognition*, 7 (4), 323–31.

Morton, J. and Patterson, K. (1987). A new attempt at an interpretation, or, an attempt at a new interpretation. In M. Coltheart, K. Patterson and J. C. Marshall (eds.), *Deep Dyslexia*, second edn (pp. 91–118). London: Routledge and Kegan Paul.

Neale, M. D. (1989). *Neale Analysis of Reading Ability*. Windsor: NFER-Nelson.

Ng, S. M. (1984). Reading acquisition in Singapore. *Singapore Journal of Education*, 6 (2), 15–20.

Pakir, A. (1988). *Education and Invisible Language Planning: The Case of English in Singapore*. Centre for Advanced Studies; Department of English Language and Literature, National University of Singapore.

Poon, K.-L. K. and Rickard Liow, S. J. (1998). Models of English spelling development for multilingual children. First International Workshop on Written Language Processing (IWWLP), University of New South Wales, Sydney, Australia (December).

Read, C., Zhang, Y. F., Nie, H. Y. and Ding, B. Q. (1986). The ability to manipulate speech sounds depends on knowing alphabetic writing. *Cognition*, 24 (1–2), 31–44.

Rickard Liow, S. J. (1997). Dyslexia Association of Singapore (DAS): preliminary report on DAS pupils' progress 1993–1996. Department of Social Work and Psychology, National University of Singapore.

Rickard Liow, S. J., Green, D. and Lokanathan, K. (1995). Visual search processes in bilinguals. Seventh International Conference on Cognitive Processing of Asian Languages. Hong Kong, December.

Rickard Liow, S. J., Green, D. and Tam, L.-J. M.-M. (in press). The development of visual search strategies in Malay-English and Chinese-English biscriptals. *International Journal of Bilingualism*.

Rickard Liow, S. J., Hong, E. L. and Tng, S. K. (1992). Singapore primary school norms for the multilingual British Picture Vocabulary Scale: English, Mandarin and Malay. Working paper no. 43, Department of Social Work and Pschology, National University of Singapore.

Rickard Liow, S. J. and Masterson, J. (1995). Reading strategies of English-Chinese bilingual children. Sixth American Psychological Society's Conference, New York, June.

Rickard Liow, S. J., Mok, L. W. and Tng, S. K. (1998). Lexical and non-lexical contributions to reading and spelling in two kinds of bilinguals. Workshop for Speech, Language and Hearing Association (Singapore), Special Interest Group meeting: Language in Focus. Singapore.

Rickard Liow, S. J. and Poon, K.-L. K. (1998). Phonological awareness in multilingual Chinese-speaking children. *Applied Psycholinguistics*, 19, 339–62.

Rickard Liow, S. J. and Tng, S. K. (1992a). Singapore primary school norms for the Schonell graded word reading and spelling tests. Working paper no. 45, Department of Social Work and Psychology, National University of Singapore.

Rickard Liow, S. J. and Tng, S. K. (1992b). Singapore primary school norms for the British Ability Scales subtests: word reading, spelling, matrices and basic number skills. Working paper No. 44, Department of Social Work and Psychology, National University of Singapore.

Rickard Liow, S. J. and Tng, S. K. (1992c). Chinese reading and spelling test battery: character age of acquisition, consistency, tone, strokes and non-character subtests. Working paper No. 47, Department of Social Work and Psychology, National University of Singapore.

Rickard Liow, S. J. and Tng, S. K. (1992d). English reading and spelling test battery: word familiarity, word consistency and nonword subtests. Working paper No. 46, Department of Social Work and Psychology, National University of Singapore.

Rickard Liow, S. J. and Tng, S. K. (1994). Phonological dyslexia in Chinese-English bilingual biscriptals. Paper presented at the Cognitive Processing of Asian Languages Workshop. Sydney, Australia, December.

Rickard Liow, S. J., Tng, S. K. and Lee, C. L. (1999). Chinese characters: semantic and phonetic regularity norms for China, Singapore and Taiwan. *Behaviour Research Methods, Instruments and Computers*, 31 (1).

Seidenberg, M. and McClelland, J. (1989). A distributed, developmental model of word recognition and naming. *Psychological Review*, 96 (4), 523–68.

Seymour, P. H. K. (1990). Developmental dyslexia. In M. W. Eysenck (ed.), *Cognitive Psychology: An International Review* (pp. 135–96). Chichester, England: John Wiley.

Seymour, P. H. K. and Elder, L. (1986). Beginning reading without phonology. *Cognitive Neuropsychology*, 3 (1), 1–36.

Seymour, P. H. K. and Evans, H. (1994). Levels of phonological awareness and learning to read. *Reading and Writing: An Interdisciplinary Journal*, 6, 221–50.

Stevenson, H. W. (1984). Orthography and reading disabilities. *Journal of Learning Disabilities*, 17 (5), 296–301.

Temple, C. M. and Marshall, J. C. (1983). A case study of developmental phonological dyslexia. *British Journal of Psychology*, 74 (4), 517–33.

Wagner, R. K. and Torgesen, J. K. (1987). The nature of phonological processing and its causal role in the acquisition of reading skills. *Psychological Bulletin*, 101 (2), 192–212.

Wimmer, H. and Goswami, U. (1994). The influence of orthographic consistency on reading development: word recognition in English and German children. *Cognition*, 51 (1), 91–103.

Wong, M. Y. and Underwood, G. (1996). Do bilingual children read words better in lists or in context? *Journal of Research in Reading*, 19 (1), 61–76.

12 Learning to read and write in Japanese

Kiyomi Akita and Giyoo Hatano

The process of literacy acquisition can be regarded as one of gaining expertise in specific cognitive skills. Children participate in literacy activities guided by adults. In such an environment, children can master reading and writing skills. In this chapter we discuss from both cognitive and socio-cultural perspectives the acquisition of literacy skills by young Japanese children. We deal with four topics: (1) the structure of Japanese orthographies; (2) the processes through which Japanese children learn to read kana letters; (3) the socio-cultural context in which children learn to read and write; and (4) the progress from reading kana letters to advanced literacy skills.

Characteristics of Japanese orthographies

Three kinds of letters – two types of kana syllabaries (hiragana and katakana) and Chinese characters (kanji) – are used in Japan. Standard Japanese sentences are written by using both Chinese characters and hiragana in combination. Nouns and verb and adjective stems are usually written in kanji. Function words and inflectional affixes are written in hiragana in most cases. Katakana is typically used for words of foreign origin and onomatopoeic expressions (see figure 12.1).

There is a one-to-one correspondence between the hiragana and katakana letters. They consist of seventy-one letters each that represent five vowels (V), sixty-five consonant-vowel combinations (CV), and the nasal coda (N). Of the sixty-five CV letters, twenty-five that represent voiced and semi-voiced consonant-vowel combinations are formed from the corresponding letters for unvoiced consonant-vowel combinations with the addition of a special mark for voicing or semi-voicing. For example, the voiced letter 'ga' corresponds to the unvoiced 'ka'. Therefore, there are only forty-six basic kana letters (representing five vowels, one nasal coda, and forty unvoiced CV combinations).

Most kana letters, when used as individual units, have a single, unique pronunciation, with the exception of two letters, 'ha' and 'he'. These

214

その子は、クレヨンで絵を描く。

The child draws a picture with crayon.

Figure 12.1   A Japanese sentence written in the standard Japanese orthography.
Note: three words, 'child, 'draw' and 'picture' are written in kanji; 'crayon' is written in katakana.

letters are pronounced differently when they represent case particles: 'ha' and 'he' are usually pronounced /ha/ and /he/, respectively, but when they are case particles, they are pronounced /wa/ and /e/.

The Japanese language has a mora-based rhythm; that is, it is segmented into morae or sub-syllabic rhythmic units. Kana letters represent morae, though they are called syllabaries. This discrepancy between the actual unit of representation and the label is not marked, because most Japanese syllables comprise single morae and are represented by single kana letters. This is due to two characteristics that the Japanese language possesses: (a) no consonants other than a nasal coda (N) and a geminate stop consonant (Q) come after a vowel, and (b) consonants seldom cluster before a vowel. Thus ordinary syllables have either the CV (consonant-vowel) or the V (vowel only) structure.

However, there are five kinds of syllables, generally called 'special' syllables, that contain two morae, or have a single mora but a phonological structure other than CV or V, and are represented by two or three kana letters: (1) those having a nasal coda (CVN or VN); (2) those having a geminate stop consonant (CVQ or VQ); (3) those having two preceding consonants (CCV), the second of which is usually a glide; (4) those having a long vowel, which has a length comparable to two morae (CV- or V-); and (5) various combinations of (1)–(4), most often the combination of (3) and (4). All cases have two morae except for (3), which has one mora. Cases (1)–(4) are represented by two kana letters, and case (5) by three (or more) letters. The nasal coda is represented by a single kana letter of the regular size and a geminate consonant, a small letter. A CCV syllable including a glide is expressed by using a letter indicating the combination of the first consonant and the vowel 'i' with another letter, smaller in size, for the combination between a glide and a vowel. Blending is thus needed to pronounce pairs of kana for CCV syllables correctly. For example, a pair of 'ki' and 'ya' of a small size notates /kya/, a sound similar to the onset of the English word, 'can'.

Table 12.1 *Comparison of syllables, morae and letters.*

Types of syllables		Example word	Number of syllables	Number of morae	Number of letters
(1) CV,V	ordinary syllables	うみ (umi: sea)	2	2	2
(2) CVN, VN	syllables including nasal coda	けんか (kenka: quarrel)	2	3	3
(3) CVQ, VQ	syllables including geminate stop consonants	きって (kitte: stamp)	2	3	3
(4) CCV	syllables comprising two preceding consonants	きゃく (kyaku: guest)	2	2	3
(5) CV-, V-	syllables including a long vowel	こおり (kori: ice)	2	3	3
(6) CCVC	(1)–(4) combinations	やきゅう (yakyu: baseball)	2	3	4

This notation is never pronounced /ki/ya/. Table 12.1 shows the syllable, morae and letter representations for various types of sample words.

Even though kana orthography is more complicated than is often assumed, it is not hard to master, as we will see below. However, because the Japanese language has a highly restricted phonological inventory, there are inevitably many more homonyms than in most other languages. For example, 'hashi' means three different things: a bridge, a pair of chopsticks, and an end as in edge. In speech, people can distinguish those meanings with the help of intonation and/or context. However, in written language, to resolve the homonymic ambiguity and understand the meaning quickly, kanji (Chinese characters) must be used. Kanji are sometimes called ideograms, but in fact possess unique pronunciations. Kanji have been preserved in the Japanese writing system for a variety of cognitive and cultural reasons, though every Japanese word can be written by using kana only (Hatano, 1986; 1995).

There are more than 2,000 kanji characters used in everyday life in Japan. Thus, children have to learn many more kanji than kana. Most kanji characters also consist of more strokes than kana. Because of their small number and simplicity of form, kana are easy to learn. Therefore, Japanese children are expected to learn kana, especially hiragana, earlier than kanji. In elementary school, the curriculum is designed to teach hiragana first. After that, kanji are taught. Beginning with eighty characters in the first grade and more in the higher grades, by the end of elementary school children have mastered 1,006 characters. In junior high school they master another 950. Thus, children master nearly 2,000 characters by the end of junior high school.

According to social expectations, sentences written for children change in their use of kanji with the development of reading ability. Sentences in picturebooks, magazines and letters addressed to young children are written entirely in hiragana and spaces are used between words or sentence segments. The use of kanji in sentences increases as children become older. More difficult books are written without a separation between word segments, and Chinese characters are used to represent the nouns and verbs previously written in hiragana.

Acquisition of hiragana orthography

Three phases of reading

As indicated in chapter 1, Frith (1985) proposes a three-phase theory of reading development in English, focusing on types of learning strategy: the logographic strategy phase in which children learn to recognise words on the basis of their overall appearance; the alphabetic strategy phase where they pay attention to individual letters; and the orthographic strategy phase, in which they break words down into orthographic units. Similar phases can be identified in the developmental processes of learning to read hiragana.

In the first phase, children read some specific words as global patterns, often with the help of context. Children cannot read the constituent individual letters of words, however. In the second phase children decode and read each letter. They have learned to read basic kana letters, but they cannot read special syllables. In the third and final phase children use more advanced strategies for reading special syllables. They have mastered the orthographic rules for combining kana letters to represent these syllables and assign different readings to the two letters, depending on their morphological status.

We will describe these three phases, especially the last two phases, in detail, after briefly discussing the pre-reading phase. Like English-speaking children, young Japanese children develop an awareness of the existence of letters and the distinction between letters and non-letters, numerals and kana letters, and kana letters and kanji, before they begin to read. In other words, in this pre-reading phase, children can differentiate kana letters from other symbols, without naming any of them.

Pre-reading phase: awareness of the literal world and pretend reading Japanese children's behaviour in this phase is very similar to that of children learning to read alphabetical languages. Research on emergent literacy has shown that young children are sensitive to the difference between writing and drawing and can find a word or a sequence of letters representing a particular meaning long before they can read each of the constituent letters (Adams, 1990; Landsmann and Karmiloff-Smith, 1992; Teal and Sultzy, 1986). Japanese children too may say, 'It's a letter', pointing to a hiragana letter in a picture book or 'I write letters', scribbling on a paper. They may pretend to be reading, and try to write letters and invent new letters. Shibasaki (1987) has argued that children become aware of the existence of the writing system at about two and a half to three years of age. At this stage they cannot read any letters, but can distinguish between writing and drawing. Moreover, they can distinguish between hiragana, katakana, kanji and Arabic numerals. However, his claims may be too strong. Inagaki (in preparation) has found that four-year-olds could recognise hiragana letters as letters even when they could read almost none of them. However, the children in her study mistook figures that had curvilinear lines for letters, though they were more accurate at rejecting those consisting of straight lines. She also found that, when young children were required to classify hiragana, katakana, kanji and alphabet letters into three categories (hiragana, kanji and neither), those who could read very few hiragana characters had great difficulty.

First phase: reading with use of a word's gestalt and context   In the first phase, children can often read their names and familiar words written in hiragana. Reading in this phase uses non-phonological procedures that are similar to the 'logographic' strategy (Frith, 1985). Muto *et al.* (1992) tested sixty three-year-olds (range: 39–46 months) and four-year-olds (range: 51–58 months) on reading their own names, friends' names and kana letters. They found that there were some children who could read their own names but could not read any of the constituent kana letters. They could read their family names, but could not read friends' first names. Some children gave their full names, when being shown only their first names; other children read their names as 'Masao-kun' or 'Masao-chan', adding a personal title '-kun' or '-chan' used in everyday life, when they were shown their given names only. This result suggests that children identify their own names as gestalts referring to themselves. In addition, pre-school children are often observed to read their own class name, written at the entrance, and pets' names, which are posted at the pen in the playground.

Muto *et al.* (1993) examined whether four-, five- and six-year-old children could read words with illustrations. Two types of cards were prepared. On one, the name of the object was written and on the other, a verb associated with the object was written. For example, a picture of a flower was accompanied by the words, 'flower' and 'bloom', respectively. Even children who could read fewer than twenty letters could read 'flower', with the aid of the illustration. This result shows that the second phase of reading overlaps with the first, which lasts until children are able to read more than half of the forty-six basic letters quickly.

Second phase: phonological awareness of morae and letter naming Children vary in the age at which they start reading individual letters, probably because reading hiragana depends on phonological awareness rather than on age or cognitive maturity. Amano (1970) showed that children's ability to segment a word into morae and to abstract the first mora of a word enables them to learn to read kana letters. To examine young children's ability in moraic segmentation, he used a picture with a row of squares below it. The experimenter asked children to put blocks in the squares corresponding to the pronunciation of the target word (figure 12.2). To examine their moraic abstraction ability, he

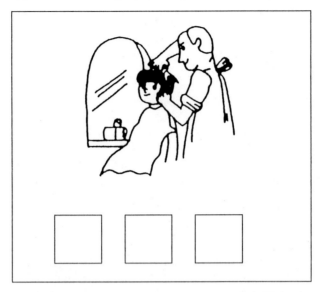

Figure 12.2   A picture used by Amano (1986). This picture depicts 'tokoya' /to/ko/ya/ (barber shop).

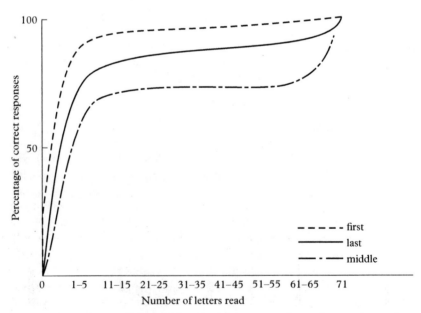

Figure 12.3   The relationship between numbers of correctly read kana letters and performance in moraic identification (Amano, 1986).

asked children what the first, middle and last mora was. As shown in figure 12.3, moraic identification was related to the numbers of letters correctly read. This relationship was also confirmed by Amano's intervention research on mildly retarded children. Based on these and related results, Amano (1986) proposes a five-stage development model of moraic abstraction. He suggests that children must reach the stage at which they can segment a word and abstract the initial mora to learn to read kana letters.

Dairoku (1995) traced this process in a longitudinal study that involved training a retarded child, who could name most kana letters but could not recognise a string of letters as a word, to segment words into morae and to identify each mora. This child was six years of age and his mental age was two years and two months. His training lasted eight months and was intended to raise his level of phonological awareness. Dairoku presents, based on his findings, an alternative hypothesis that phonological awareness is not necessary for learning the names of individual kana letters, but is required for grasping the meaning of words or identifying a series of letters as a word. Considering that Amano (1986) did not clarify the relationship between the grasp of a word's meaning and phonological awareness, the research by Dairoku (1995), though using only one subject, is illuminating. However, normal children at least tend to develop some phonological awareness long before they learn to read the great majority of individual letters. For example, Hatano and Inagaki (in preparation) asked four-year-olds, who could read only a few hiragana letters, to choose between the correct string of letters that comprised a word and an apparently similar string that had one letter more or less. The children could almost always choose the correct string, probably relying on the correspondence between the number of morae in the word and the number of kana letters. Further research is needed to clarify the relationship between phonological awareness and the development of understanding of written words and sentences.

The moraic awareness needed to learn kana syllabaries emerges earlier than the phonemic awareness needed for alphabetic orthographies. Most Japanese children acquire moraic awareness and thus begin to name kana letters as early as age four (Amano, 1986). A nationwide survey at the National Language Research Institute (NLRI) in 1967 tested over 2,200 five- and six-year-old children and reported that 34 per cent of five-year-olds (mean: sixty-one months) and 64 per cent of six-year-olds (mean: seventy-three months) could read sixty or more of the seventy-one kana letters. More recently, Shimamura and Mikami (1994) investigated 1,202 young children's reading ability in thirteen daycare centres and nineteen kindergartens. They reported that 16 per

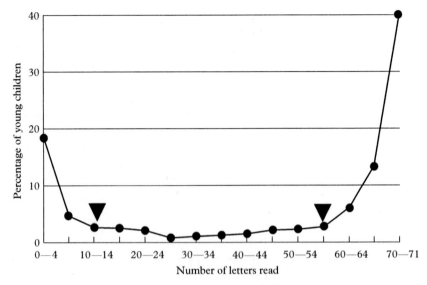

Figure 12.4   The distribution of the number of kana letters read by young children (Shimamura and Mikami, 1994).

cent of four-years-olds (mean: fifty months), 59 per cent of five-years-olds (mean: sixty-two months), and 89 per cent of six-years-olds (mean: seventy-four months) could read sixty or more of the seventy-one letters. Thus, most Japanese children learn to read hiragana before grade school.

Shimamura and Mikami also reported that by forty-nine months 25 per cent of children could read the forty-six basic letters and by seventy months, 90 per cent could do so. Once children begin to read a few letters, most of them will master all seventy kana letters within a year. Figure 12.4 shows the distribution of the number of kana letters read correctly by children. It is U-shaped: the percentage of children who could read 10–59 letters was low. This observation suggests that, although the speed of letter acquisition is slow at first, it accelerates after children have learned to read ten letters or so. This pattern of acquisition was also observed in the NLRI survey in 1967. Because kana letters represent morae, learning to read some of them enhances children's moraic awareness, which in turn facilitates learning to read other letters.

Third phase: morphological knowledge, advanced phonological awareness and reading special syllables   As mentioned in the first section, the kana orthography has five types of special syllables and two specially

Table 12.2 *Percentage of correct reading by kana types with age (Shimamura and Mikami, 1994).*

Types	Four-year-old	Five-year-old	Six-year-old
Unvoiced letters and nasal coda	30.4	75.4	95.2
Voiced letters	19.3	63.0	90.3
Semi-voiced letters	14.7	49.3	81.7
(1) two preceding consonants	6.4	30.5	65.7
(2) geminate stop consonant	8.7	36.2	72.9
(3) long vowel	7.3	25.8	55.4
(4) combination of (1) and (3)	6.6	28.2	60.1
(5) case particle 'ha'	9.1	33.8	65.6
case particle 'he'	7.9	30.8	65.5

pronounced case particles, which are much harder to read than other letters representing ordinary syllables or morae (except for the one representing the nasal coda, which is as easy as the other letters representing ordinary syllables). Table 12.2 shows that the percentages of children capable of correctly reading these more difficult syllables are broken down by age (Shimamura and Mikami, 1994). It is obvious that the seventy-one letters and these special syllables are not acquired simultaneously. The NLRI survey also reported the following order of acquisition. Children became able to read the forty-six basic unvoiced letters (including the one for the nasal coda) first, voiced and semi-voiced letters next, and these special syllables and case particles last. Because there are no consistent one letter–one mora (syllable) correspondences for the special syllables and case particles, children must acquire context-dependent pronunciation rules before they can read them. In an elementary school, teachers give lessons systematically about both reading and writing these special syllables in the first term of the first grade.

Among these special syllables and case particles, which ones are acquired relatively quickly? According to the NLRI survey, the case particles are learned earlier than the special syllables, but according to Shimamura and Mikami (1994), the special small letter representing the geminate consonant is learned first. What is common between the two surveys is that the hardest syllable to learn represents CCV letter sequences, in which the second consonant is the glide and the vowel may be extended.

Most children learn to read the special syllables and case particles perfectly during the first grade, that is, when they are taught systematically. But some children can infer the special rules by themselves before taking formal education. How can they acquire the rules? As the special syllables and the case particles require different knowledge, we will discuss them separately below.

The case particles   Morphological knowledge is needed to pronounce the case particles properly. The letters 'ha' and 'he' are pronounced /ha/ and /he/, respectively, except when being used as case particles. This means that children have to know that these letters have two pronunciations, and choose one of them, judging whether each letter is used as a case particle or as part of a word. Akita and Hatano (in preparation) asked five- (mean: sixty-one months) and six-year-old children (mean: seventy-four months) who read forty-six basic kana letters to read familiar and unfamiliar words and three types of short sentences involving the letters 'ha' or 'he'. In the word-reading task, the letter 'ha' or 'he' was placed at the beginning, middle and end of the letter sequence. In the sentence-reading task, the following variations were given. The first type of sentence contained 'ha' or 'he' embedded in a word, with the usual pronunciation, as in 'taroukun, hanashitene' (Taro, please tell me). The second type included 'ha' or 'he' as a case particle, with its other pronunciation /wa/ or /e/: 'taroukunha otonashii' (Taro is obedient). The third also included 'ha' or 'he' as a case particle, but this time followed by another, sentence-final particle, like 'taroukunhane, yasashiiyo' (Taro is kind). Since 'ha' or 'he' as a case particle usually comes at the end of a sentence segment consisting of a noun and particle(s), correctly pronouncing it /wa/ or /e/ should be harder in the third type of sentence, which was less familiar to children. In other words, some children would read the second sentence type correctly but fail with the third.

The results of this study by Akita and Hatano suggest four developmental stages for reading 'ha'. In the first stage children do not know its pronunciation as a case particle. They read 'ha' always as /ha/, without any hesitation. In the interview, a child at this stage said, 'I can read all sentences. They are very easy for me', even though his reading was not entirely correct.

Children at the second stage know that 'ha' or 'he' may be pronounced /wa/ or /e/, and overextend this pronunciation to the letter embedded in words. For example, they pronounce the word 'Yokohama' (a place name near Tokyo) /yokowama/. These errors occur especially often for unfamiliar words. They do not often overextend this pronunciation to highly familiar words such as 'hana' (flower), or 'ohayou' (good morning). At this stage, the special pronunciations as case particles have priority over the usual pronunciations, but the word meaning constrains the overextension in reading.

The third stage, which is not necessarily preceded by the second one, occurs when children pronounce 'ha' or 'he' properly as /wa/ or /e/, relying on its position and familiarity in a sentence segment. So, they can read the letter correctly in the familiar wording of the particle, 'tarou<u>ha</u>' (as in the second type of experimental sentence), but they fail to do so when given the unfamiliar wording of the particle, 'tarou<u>hane</u>' (as in the third type). This observation suggests that the children are not yet fully sensitive to the letter's morphemic status.

Children at the last stage can discriminate the letter's morphemic status and pronounce it correctly. The overextension to words is inhibited. The number of children at this stage is very small before the first grade and this developmental change does not occur simultaneously for both letters. Those children who reach this stage may have induced an implicit discrimination rule that they can apply to various situations, and their ability to do this may be reinforced by feedback from adults. Nunes *et al.* (1997) pointed out that morphology plays an important role in learning to spell in English (see also Bryant *et al.* in this volume). In Japanese kana orthography, morphological knowledge also plays an important role in reading and writing, at least for these two letters.

CCV syllables/morae Endo (1990) investigated the acquisition of reading CCV syllables/morae by testing thirty-seven children at age six (mean: seventy-two months) and then retesting them after a year. She asked the children to read the thirty-three CCV syllables and to make CCV syllables by combining letter cards. She found the distribution of numbers of CCV syllables read correctly was U-shaped. In other words, a majority of the children could read either almost all or almost none of the CCV syllables. She found that, whereas the typical reading error for children who could read fewer than twenty syllables was literal reading (e.g. mistaking /shi-ya/ for /sha/), for children who could read more than twenty syllables the most common error was to mistake one CCV for another CCV, for example, reading 'shu' as /sya/.

Endo (1990) also asked these children's mothers whether they had taught reading of these CCV syllables. Half of them answered that they had not given any instruction at all. Most of the remaining half answered that they had taught them when they read picture books and their children asked them how to read. None of the mothers reported that she had taught reading systematically. As the children could read about ten CCV syllables at the second testing, they must have found a way to read these syllables spontaneously. This process of 'discovery' may be as follows. At the beginning, children master the reading of a few CCV syllables independently. Then, they may rely on analogies for reading a new CCV syllable, basing their analogy on the known reading of a similar syllable. Goswami and Bryant (1990) suggest that children can make analogies to determine how to read new words. This seems especially true for special syllables. Finally, after the mastery of a certain number (probably ten to twenty) of the syllables, they abstract the spelling pattern-pronunciation rule(s) for CCV syllables by themselves. They then try to apply this rule to the reading of new CCV syllables.

Further, as Goswami and Mead (1992) pointed out, the onset-rime division should be related to the ability to make analogies between spelling patterns of a new word with old ones. Young Japanese children possess phonological awareness at the syllable or mora level, which at least helps them learn the kana letters for ordinary syllables. But to apply analogies to CCV syllables, children have to be aware of phonemes or be able to divide a CCV into the first consonant and the last CV (a glide + a vowel a, u or o). When children are able to divide a CCV into C and CV, they can readily recognise both the similarity and difference between two CCV syllables, for example, /kya/ and /rya/ or /kya/ and /kyu/.

Endo (1991) examined the relationship between this advanced phonological awareness and the number of CCV syllables read correctly. Six-year-old children were asked to select a card having the same onset (or last) phoneme as the target phoneme. The experimenter showed them three cards and said, 'We will play a sound-guessing game. Listen to me carefully and select the card that has the same first [or last] sound as the first one. Which has the same onset sound as /hyo/, /hya/ or /mya/?' The score on this detection task, especially the detection of the last phoneme, had a significant positive correlation with the number of CCV syllables read correctly (the detection of the last phoneme, $r = 0.41$; and the detection of first phoneme, $r = 0.30$). Endo (1991) claims that Japanese children also have phonological awareness at the phoneme level, and that this awareness is related to reading CCV syllables. Endo's findings clearly show that young Japanese children recognise the similarities and differences between words at the phonemic level when the task is very simple. Although Mann's (1986) comparative study showed that, on a phoneme manipulation task, Japanese first-graders had difficulty and were considerably behind Americans, she too concludes that children's phonological awareness develops with age, even if children are not exposed to any notational systems for phonemic phonologies.

Kana literacy acquisition and speech segmentation units   Japanese is 'mora-timed' in contrast to 'stress-timed' (e.g. English) and 'syllable-timed' (e.g. French) languages, as reported by Otake and his associates (1993;

Cutler and Otake, 1994). This raises the question of how and when Japanese children acquire an understanding of morae as the basic speech segmentation unit and whether their understanding changes with their ability to read kana.

Hatano and Inagaki (1992; Inagaki, Hatano and Oura, 1997) investigated this issue. They paid particular attention to special syllables that can differentiate mora- vs. syllable-based segmentation, using the vocal-motor word segmentation task (similar to Amano's task mentioned above) and a word game called 'shiritori'. In the shiritori game, one has to say a word beginning with the last unit of the preceding word. Inagaki and Hatano presented words that end with special syllables (e.g. those including a long vowel) to determine the basic segmentation unit used by children who varied in their mastery of kana. They concluded that children learn mora-based segmentation only after the acquisition of kana letters.

Takahashi (1996) also examined three-year-old (mean: forty-four months), four-year-old (mean: fifty-five months), and five-year-old (mean: sixty-four months) children's basic segmentation unit with another, though similar, task: 'phonological tapping'. This task required children to tap on a keyboard after listening to a word. Their performances were analysed in terms of reading levels: whereas syllable segmentation was dominant among the three- and four-year-olds, mora segmentation was dominant among the five-year-olds. This result suggests that segmentation is closely related to the number of kana letters and special syllables read correctly. Based on a sophisticated statistical analysis, Takahashi claims that the shift from syllable-based (or syllable-mora-mixed) to mora-based segmentation occurs after children learn to read special syllables, which is apparently inconsistent with Hatano and Inagaki (1992).

It is safe to conclude that Japanese children's speech segmentation changes from syllable-based (or syllable-mora-mixed) to mora-based, and that this change occurs because children are able to read kana letters, including those for special syllables. Rudimentary phonological awareness is a facilitating condition for learning to read kana letters. Then, in turn, the ability to read letters, especially special syllables, enhances children's phonological awareness at finer levels. Both processes interact and have mutual effects.

Social support for reading at home and at school

Japanese children are not generally formally instructed in hiragana in kindergarten or at home. But almost all children learn basic kana letters before the first grade. One reason is the ease of learning moraic letters.

Once children learn letter–sound correspondences, they can read kana letters in words and sentences. In addition to this characteristic of kana orthography, we think that the Japanese socio-cultural environment prompts children's acquisition of literacy skills. Japanese children participate in various activities relevant to literacy during early childhood.

Azuma (1995) investigated 1,259 young children's mothers' ideas about how their children learn to read letters. They asked the mothers to choose one of three ideas proposed. The first was that it is not necessary to teach young children directly how to read letters because children naturally come to read by themselves. The second was that parents should create rich environments for learning to read and they should actively respond to children's requests when they are interested in reading. The third was that parents should voluntarily teach kana letters as early as possible. One thousand and thirty-two mothers (82 per cent) chose the second one. The third one was selected by only thirteen (1 per cent). This tendency was consistent across children's ages. Thus, most Japanese mothers attempt not to teach letters directly but rather to set rich environments for learning to read.

According to the Survey of the Ministry of Education in 1986, only 10 per cent of kindergartens formally teach reading and writing. In kindergartens and daycare centres, very few teachers want to teach letters systematically, as is done in elementary schools. They believe in fostering children's interest in reading and writing through playing and creating rich learning environments during young childhood. For example, mothers and teachers in kindergartens might invite their children to participate in reading books.

Akita and Muto (1996) asked 293 middle-class mothers of young children living in Tokyo when they began to read picture books to their children. Two hundred and twenty mothers (72 per cent) answered that they began before their children were two years old. Even though at this age letters are meaningless to the children, they implicitly learn how books are read and the value of reading, through enjoying these activities with adults.

Also, there are various games for fostering phonological awareness and interest in letters. As mentioned above, a word game 'shiritori' ('cap verses') is one that is very popular in Japan, and most children play this game at home and in kindergarten. Two kinds of phonological processing abilities are needed to play shiritori without adults' help. One is to isolate the last segmental unit of a word and the other is to retrieve a word that begins with this specific unit. To be an able participant in shiritori one must have a rich vocabulary, but one also must be able to organise one's mental lexicon appropriately. Even children who have an insufficient command of these abilities can participate in the shiritori game with adults' help. Gradually they play it by themselves. This game helps young children to refine their phonological awareness.

Takahashi (1997) compared three help conditions and one control condition. In the first condition, the child was asked for the last syllable of a word and given instructions to say a word beginning with that syllable. In the second condition, the child was told the last syllable and asked to retrieve a word beginning with it. The third condition involved giving hints about a proper word by suggesting its superordinate category label and/or showing its picture to help elicit the target word. This type of help is most frequently used when shiritori is played in everyday situations. In the control condition children were given no help. Twenty-seven five-year-old children (mean: sixty-three months) and twenty-eight four-year-old children (mean: fifty-two months) were assigned to these four conditions. The highest performance was obtained using the third help condition, and the second highest with the second help condition. With the third help condition, even the four-year-old children played shiritori at the same level as the five-year-old participants.

In addition to these word games, there are some toys that are used to learn kana letters. One of them is a card game called 'karuta' ('carta'). This game consists of letter cards and sentence cards. One kana letter is written on the letter card with a picture of an associated object. An adult reads aloud a sentence card that is to be paired with the letter card. Children try to find as quickly as possible the letter card on which the first syllable (or mora) of the sentence read by the adult is written. Most Japanese families with young children play this game in winter, especially during the New Year's holidays. Through these games, children develop phonological awareness and learn to read kana letters.

Though Japanese mothers rarely teach letters systematically during young childhood, they never neglect their children's literacy acquisition. They have cultural beliefs that literacy is very important for mental development and as a basic learning skill. Historically, literacy education has been important since the seventeenth century, with practical training in reading, writing and arithmetic offered by formal and informal education systems (US Department of Education, 1987). In addition, various toys and games have been devised and transmitted from generation to generation.

Beyond reading kana letters

Japanese children learn to read each kana letter with ease. After that, three aspects of literacy development emerge. The first is that children learn to read not only individual letters but also words, sentences and texts. The second is that children become able to write kana letters. And the third one is that children learn to read (and write) kanji characters. We will briefly discuss each of these below.

As far as the first line of development is concerned, it is generally believed that children cannot comprehend the meaning of a sentence before reading words smoothly. Among others, Perfetti (1985) has asserted that the extent of efficiency and automatisation of word recognition has an effect on reading comprehension. Takahashi (1993) researched the relationship between reading ability and basic word-processing abilities among kindergarten, first- and third-grade children. A Stroop task, word-reading task, and a visual and auditory word-memory task were used to measure the speed and the degree to which they had automatised the processing of words. The result of path analysis in fact showed that the reading ability among the kindergarten children was explained by the speed and the degree of the automatisation of processing words. Likewise, Inagaki and Hatano (in preparation) have shown that the speed of reading a list of words aloud is a very good predictor of reading comprehension, and that the speed is dramatically increased when children shift from character-by-character reading to smooth reading. Kuhara-Kojima *et al.* (1986) indicated that, even in the fifth grade, there were differences in vocalisation latencies for words written in hiragana and kanji between skilled and less skilled readers, though the difference was greater for words in kanji than for words in kana.

How do children come to read beyond letters? For example, when do children begin to read a sentence for meaning? The survey by the NLRI (1972) indicated that children who could read more than twenty kana letters began to read sentences. They moved from the letter-by-letter reading to the smooth reading of, initially, words and then sentences. Inagaki and Hatano (in preparation) also observed that children became able to read words smoothly at approximately the same time as they began to read special syllables, and to comprehend what was described in a sentence more or less accurately a little later. Akita *et al.* (1995) asked children in kindergarten to read a short picture book. The children who could read more than twenty letters tried to read sentences. As they made the transition from reading sentences letter by letter to reading smoothly, their comprehension of the sentences became more accurate.

As for the second line of development, writing kana, Japanese children pretend to scribble and write before they can read each letter. Children participate in writing activities embedded in everyday contexts.

For example, three-year-old children write letters to teachers and to friends who are in kindergarten. Takahashi (1995) traced the developmental process of one child from one year of age when he began to scribble to age six when he was able to write correct letters. Takahashi pointed out that there are infant letters that can be distinguished from both scribbles and authentic kana letters, and that the authentic ones replace infant letters gradually.

The surveys of the NLRI (1972) and of Shimamura and Mikami (1994) indicate that few pre-school children can write all seventy-one kana letters (including both unvoiced and voiced ones), and that letters vary in terms of how difficult they are to write. Shimamura and Mikami reported that the mean numbers of kana letters children could write correctly were 3.7 at four years, 15.9 at five years, and 31.6 at six years of age. Children learn to write unvoiced letters and the nasal letter before voiced and semi-voiced letters. Children often make two types of errors. One type is of the letter form. Some children write wrong forms, for example, mirrored letters (i.e. left–right reversal), or omissions or additions of a stroke. Another type is an error of writing order. The order of writing strokes for each multi-stroke kana letter is fixed by convention. Children have to learn the correct order. Unlike reading, some intervention by adults seems necessary for children's mastery of writing.

Of course, most children voluntarily write kana letters and words, referring to printed letters as a model. Azuma (1995) reported that the frequency of reference to a model was highest at four years of age. Moreover, although at age three the frequency of reference was positively correlated with the score for correct writing, at four and five years of age it was negatively correlated.

The third line of development is the acquisition of skills for reading and writing kanji characters. As mentioned in the first part of this chapter, Japanese children have to learn kanji after entering school. Thus, the development of reading and writing abilities continues for several more years. The acquisition of kanji literacy skills cannot be discussed in this chapter because of limited space. Those who are interested might refer to the following sources: Taylor and Taylor (1995) review briefly the general developmental trends for kanji skills; the NLRI (1988) reports a detailed investigation of the acquisition of kanji by elementary and junior high school children; characteristics of kanji information processing is reviewed by Kaiho and Nomura (1983); and how Japanese culture enhances children's kanji learning is discussed by Hatano (1995).

Conclusions

The following three conclusions can be derived from the above discussion of the acquisition of reading and writing skills for kana letters.

Japanese kana orthography for children is basically mora-based. Because of this, Japanese children learn to read earlier than children using most alphabetical orthographies. In Japan, children learn to read kana letters before formal schooling commences.

There are, however, some exceptional reading/writing rules. In learning these rules, morphological knowledge, advanced phonological awareness, and analogical reasoning are involved. Before receiving formal education, children can sometimes discover some of these rules for themselves, but their complete acquisition usually requires formal instruction. The three phases of learning to read kana letters are very similar to and have many cognitive processes in common with those for learning the English alphabet.

These acquisition processes are supported by the socio-cultural environment. Specifically, Japanese parents actively guide children into participating in activities that promote literacy, including various word games and toys as cultural tools that help children acquire literacy. By participating in these activities and being mediated by these cultural tools, children are encouraged to become members of the community of readers and writers.

REFERENCES

Adams, M. (1990). *Beginning to Read: Thinking and Learning about Print*. Cambridge, MA: MIT Press.

Akita, K. and Hatano, G. (1998). Morphological knowledge in reading case particles in hiragana. Paper presented to the 40th Annual Meeting of the Japanese Association of Psychology.

Akita, K. and Muto, T. (1996). Why do mothers read picture-books to their children? Mothers' conceptions and their setting environment on reading. *Japanese Journal of Educational Psychology*, 44, 109–20 (in Japanese with English summary).

Akita, K., Muto, T., Fujioka, M. and Yasumi, K. (1995). The development of children's reading of story books: a longitudinal study of relations between the acquisition of kana-letters and book-reading. *Japanese Journal of Developmental Psychology*, 6 (1), 58–68 (in Japanese with English summary).

Amano, K. (1970). Formation of the act of analyzing phonemic structures of words and its relation to learning Japanese syllabic characters (Kanamoji). *Japanese Journal of Educational Psychology*, 18, 76–89 (in Japanese with English summary).

Amano, K. (1986). Acquisition of phonemic analysis and literacy in children. *Annual Report of Educational Psychology in Japan*, 27, 142–64 (in Japanese with English summary).

Azuma, H. (ed.) (1995). Research on the process of literacy acquisition in childhood and environmental factors on it. Reports of Grant-in-Aid for Scientific Research. Tokyo: Shirayuri Woman's College (in Japanese).

Cutler, A. and Otake, T. (1994). Mora or phoneme? Further evidence for language-specific listening. *Journal of Memory and Language*, 33, 824–44.

Dairoku, H. (1995). Is awareness of morae a requisite for acquisition of kana reading? *Japanese Journal of Psychology*, 66 (4), 253–60 (in Japanese with English summary).

Endo, M. E. (1990). How do young children learn to read and spell yoo-on (a small-seized kana character)? *Japanese Journal of Educational Psychology*, 38, 213–22 (in Japanese with English summary).

(1991). Phonological awareness of Japanese young children and learning to read and write yoo-on (a small-sized kana character). *Japanese Journal of Educational Psychology*, 39, 448–54 (in Japanese with English summary).

Frith, U. (1985). Beneath the surface of developmental dyslexia. In K. E. Patterson, J. C. Marshall and M. Coltheart (eds.), *Surface Dyslexia* (pp. 301–30). Hillsdale, NJ: Erlbaum.

Goswami, U. and Bryant, P. (1990). *Phonological Skills and Learning to Read.* Hillsdale, NJ: Erlbaum.

Goswami, U. and Mead, F. (1992). Onset and rime awareness and analogies in reading. *Reading Research Quarterly*, 27 (2), 152–62.

Hatano, G. (1986). How do Japanese children learn to read? Orthographic and eco-cultural variables. In B. Foorman and A. Siegel (eds.), *Acquisition of Reading Skills: Cultural Constraints and Cognitive Universals* (pp. 81–115). Hillsdale, NJ: Erlbaum.

(1995). The psychology of Japanese literacy: expanding 'the practice account'. In L. Martin, K. Nelson and E. Tobach (eds.), *Sociocultural Psychology: Theory and Practice of Doing and Knowing* (pp. 250–75). New York: Cambridge University Press.

Hatano, G. and Inagaki, K. (1992). Phonological awareness of young children (2); focus on playing shiritori. Paper presented at the 56th annual meeting of the Japanese Psychological Association (in Japanese).

(1998). Preliterate intuition for different scripts. Paper presented at the 62nd Annual Meeting of the Japanese Association of Psychology.

Inagaki, K. (1998). Accuracy of letter recognition by young children. Paper presented at the 62nd Annual Meeting of the Japanese Association of Psychology.

Inagaki, K. and Hatano, G. (in preparation). Letter-sound knowledge, word naming speed, and sentence comprehension among young children.

Inagaki, K., Hatano, G. and Oura, Y. (1997). The effect of the kana orthography on speech segmentation among Japanese young children. Paper presented at the European Conference on Developmental Psychology, Rennes, France.

Kaiho, H. and Nomura, Y. (1983). *The Psychology of Information Processing in Kanji.* Tokyo: Kyoiku Syuppan (in Japanese).

Kuhara-Kojima, K., Hatano, G., Saito, H. and Haebara, T. (1996). Vocalization latencies of skilled and less skilled comprehenders for words written in hiragana and kanji. *Reading Research Quarterly*, 31 (2), 158–71.

Landsmann, L. T. and Karmiloff-Smith, A. (1992). Children's understanding of notations as domains of knowledge versus referential-communicative tools. *Cognitive Development*, 7, 287–300.

Mann, V. (1986). Phonological awareness: the role of reading experience. *Cognition*, 24, 65–92.

Muto, T., Akita, K. and Fujioka, M. (1993). Relations between reading names and reading hiragana. Paper presented at the 34th annual meeting of the Japanese Association of Educational Psychology (in Japanese).

Muto, T., Endo, R. M., Sakata, R. and Takeshige, J. (1992). Acquisition of Japanese syllabary and ability to read names. *Japanese Journal of Developmental Psychology*, 3 (1), 33–42 (in Japanese with English summary).

National Language Research Institute (NLRI) (1972). *Reading and Writing Ability in Preschool Children*. Tokyo: Tokyo Shoseki.

National Language Research Institute (NLRI) (1988). *The Acquisition of Common Kanji by Elementary and Secondary School Children*. Tokyo: Tokyo Shoseki.

Nunes, T., Bryant, P. and Bindman, M. (1997). Morphological spelling strategies: developmental stages and processes. *Developmental Psychology*. 33 (4), 637–49.

Otake, T., Hatano, G., Cutler, A. and Mehler, J. (1993). Mora or syllable? Speech segmentation in Japanese. *Journal of Memory and Language*, 32, 258–78.

Perfetti, C. A. (1985). *Reading Ability*. New York: Oxford University Press.

Shibasaki, M. (1987). How do young children learn to read kana-letters? In J. Murai and S. Moriue (eds.), *Development: Science of Childhood Care and Education* (pp. 187–99). Kyoto: Mineruba Shobou (in Japanese).

Shimamura, N. and Mikami, H. (1994). Acquisition of hiragana letters by pre-school children: in comparison with the investigation of the National Language Research Institute. *Japanese Journal of Educational Psychology*, 42, 70–6 (in Japanese with English summary).

Stuart, M. and Coltheart, M. (1988). Does reading develop in a sequence of stages? *Cognition*, 30, 139–81.

Takahashi, N. (1993). Becoming skilful at reading in beginners. *Japanese Journal of Educational Psychology*, 41 (3), 264–74 (in Japanese with English summary).

(1996). Acquisition of children's reading skill. Doctoral dissertation, Kyoto University (in Japanese with English summary).

(1997). A developmental study of word play in preschool children: the Japanese game of 'shiritori'. *Japanese Journal of Developmental Psychology*, 8 (1), 42–52 (in Japanese with English summary).

Takahashi, T. (1995). Learning letters and the transformation of 'Infant Letters'. *Research on Early Childhood Care and Education in Japan*, 33 (2), 156–65 (in Japanese with English summary).

Taylor, I. and Taylor, M. (1995). *Writing and Literacy in Chinese, Korean and Japanese*. New York: John Benjamin.

Teale, W. H. and Sulzby, E. (1986). *Emergent Literacy: Writing and Reading*. Norwood, NJ: Ablex.

US Department of Education (1987). *Japanese Education Today*. Washington, DC: US Government Printing Office.

Index

Abaurre, B. 73, 74
accuracy of reading
  exceeds accuracy of writing 25–6, 30
  and speed of reading 15–17, 19
  word and non-word reading 27, 30
Adams, M. 218
adult reading
  Chinese via Pinyin 181–2
  'dual route' model of acquisition of
    orthographic lexicon 18
  role of morphemes in 113, 114, 131
adults
  cross-national comparisons of literacy
    169
  illiterate and phonemic awareness 137
  illiterate Taiwanese 182
  inability to read what they have written
    22
African societies 168–9
Agard, F. B. 11
age
  and development of phonological
    awareness 103, 137, 226
  and levels of writing competence 94–5,
    96
  of school start 157, 158, 161–4, 165
Aidinis, Athanasios 4–5, 64, 112–33
Akita, Kiyomi 8–9, 214–34
Albrow, K. H. 36
Alegria, J. 51, 103, 137, 183, 199
alphabetic principle 71, 72–3, 77, 178
alphabetic script
  effect of learning on phonological
    awareness of Chinese children 191
  importance of morphemes in reading
    113
  learning to read and spell 1–6, 71, 81
  transparency and spelling 4–5
alphabetic stage (Frith) 34, 85, 199,
    200–1, 206
alphabetic strategy for reading 52, 54, 56,
    63, 67, 218

alphabetic writing systems 173, 176
  of Chinese 178
  dyslexia in 189
Alvarenga, D. 73
Amano, K. 219–21, 227
American children
  compared with Italian pre-school 21
  reading ability compared with Japanese
    and Taiwanese children 189–90
  reading English written in Chinese
    characters 189
Amsterdamer, P. 91, 93, 94
analogy
  reading by 20, 187, 225–6
  see also lexical analogy models;
    morphological analogy task;
    orthographic analogies; sentence
    analogy; word analogy
Ancient Chinese 174
Anderson, M. 52
Anderson, R. C. 97
Arabic 166
  non-literates speaking 103
Argentina 72
assimilations 160–1, 170
Atkins, P. 199
auditory word memory task 230
Austria 143, 154, 161
Azuma, H. 228, 231

Bahasa Indonesia 204
Bahasa Melayu 196
  alphabetic shallow orthography
    197–8
Bahasa-Melayu-English-speaking children,
    in Singapore 197
Bargai, N. 90
Barnhart, J. 92
Baron, J. 20, 202–3
Barron, R. 204
Beck, I. 183
Beech, J. 57